INSTITUTIONAL CHANGE IN TRANSITION ECONOMIES

T0272003

Transition and Development

Series Editor: Professor Ken Morita
Faculty of Economics, Hiroshima University, Japan

The Transition and Development series aims to provide high quality research books that examine transition and development societies in a broad sense – including countries that have made a decisive break with central planning as well as those in which governments are introducing elements of a market approach to promote development. Books examining countries moving in the opposite direction will also be included. Titles in the series will encompass a range of social science disciplines. As a whole the series will add up to a truly global academic endeavour to grapple with the questions transition and development economies pose.

Forthcoming titles:

The Social Impact of Informal Economies in Eastern Europe
Edited by Rainer Neef and Manuela Stanculescu
ISBN 0 7546 1950 8

Small Firms and Economic Development in Developed
and Transition Economies: A Reader
Edited by Anna Watson and David A. Kirby
ISBN 0 7546 3060 9

Enhanced Transition Through Outward Internationalization
Outward FDI by Slovenian Firms
Andreja Jaklic and Marjan Svetlicic
ISBN 0 7546 3134 6

Institutional Change in Transition Economies

Edited by
MICHAEL CUDDY and RUVIN GEKKER
National University of Ireland, Galway

Routledge
Taylor & Francis Group

LONDON AND NEW YORK

First published 2002 by Ashgate Publishing

Reissued 2018 by Routledge
2 Park Square, Milton Park, Abingdon, Oxon, OX14 4RN
52 Vanderbilt Avenue, New York, NY 10017

Routledge is an imprint of the Taylor & Francis Group, an informa business

A Library of Congress record exists under LC control number: 2001099222

ISBN 13: 978-1-138-73017-5 (hbk)
ISBN 13: 978-1-138-73015-1 (pbk)
ISBN 13: 978-1-315-18828-7 (ebk)

Contents

List of Figures and Tables   *vii*
List of Contributors   *ix*
Acknowledgements   *xi*
Introduction   *xii*

PART I: INSTITUTIONAL CHANGES IN THE RUSSIAN ECONOMY

1   The Russian Economy: Market in Form but "Feudal" in Content?   3
     Richard E. Ericson

2   Corruption and Organized Crime in the Russian Transition   35
     Jim Leitzel

3   Strong Institutions are more Important than the Speed of Reforms   55
     Vladimir Popov

4   An Evolutionary Analysis of Russia's Virtual Economy   72
     Clifford Gaddy and Barry W. Ickes

5   Russia's Economic Policy at the Beginning of the New Phase   100
     Vladimir Mau

PART II: TAXATION IN TRANSITION ECONOMIES

6   The Tax System and the Peculiarities of the Russian Economy   121
     Michael V. Alexeev

7   Soft Budget Constraints and Tax Arrears in Transition Economies   137
     Ruvin Gekker

8   Effective versus Statutory Taxation: Measuring Effective Tax   145
     Administration in Transition Economies
     Mark E. Schaffer and Gerard Turley

**PART III: REGIONAL DEVELOPMENTS AND INSTITUTIONAL
REFORMS**

9   Regional Disparities and Transfer Policies in Russia: 179
       Theory and Evidence
       Era Dabla-Norris and Shlomo Weber

10   Regional Development Theory and Policy: an Example for Russia?   198
       Michael P. Cuddy and Sarah Callanan

Index   222

List of Figures and Tables

Figures

3.1	Liberalization and output change	57
3.2	Aggregate distortions in industrial structure and external trade before transition and GDP change during transition	59
3.3	Government expenditure, % of GDP	63
3.4	Indices of the rule of law and political rights (democracy), 0-10, higher value represent stronger rule of law and democracy	66
3.5	Ratio of the rule of law to democracy index and output change	67
4.1	R-D space diagram	80
4.2	Some evolutionary dynamics	87
5.1	Subsistence level appraised by public opinion polls respondents versus the official subsistence level	116
8.1	Effective tax administration and progress in transition	166
8.2	Effective tax administration and progress in transition	169
8.3	Effective tax administration and bribery	172
8.4	Effective tax administration and bribery	174
9.1	Russia's transfer system, 1992-1998	192
9.2	Bilateral arrangements	194
10.1	Institutional factors and regional economic development	204

Tables

2.1   Some potential economic consequences of corruption   46

3.1   Regression of change in GDP on non-policy and policy-   64
       related factors

3.2   Regression of change in GDP in 1989-96 on initial conditions,   68
       policy factors, and rule of law and democracy indices

7.1   Schaffer (1998) tax arrears in the Russian economy   138

7.2   Payoff table game 1   140

7.3   Payoff table game 2   142

8.1   Benchmark tax rates, gross and net equivalents rates defined   150
       by statute in bold

8.2   Statutory tax rates and tax/GDP ratios for 25 TEs, 1997   152

8.3   Statutory and effective taxation, 1997   153

8.4   Bribe tax and corruption for TEs   157

8.5   Data sources for the 25 TEs   164

9.1   Regional economic disparities, 1992-1997   182

9.2   Measures of regional fiscal disparities: per capita regional   183
       revenue collections, 1993-1998

9.3   Concentration of total revenue collections among oblast: 183
       share of total revenues collected by selected regions,
       1993-1998

9.4   Measures of horizontal fiscal imbalance: per capita regional   184
       expenditures, 1993-1998

9.5   Indicators of asymmetry in fiscal federalist relations   191

9.6   Disparity of per capita revenues across regions, 1999   193

10.1   Theories of regional development and associated policy   201
       measures

List of Contributors

Michael V. Alexeev, Department of Economics, Indiana University, Bloomington, Indiana, U.S.A.

Sarah Callanan, Department of Economics, National University of Ireland, Galway, Galway, Ireland.

Michael Cuddy, Department of Economics, National University of Ireland, Galway, Galway, Ireland.

Era Dabla-Norris, IMF Institute, International Monetary Fund, Washington DC, U.S.A.

Richard E. Ericson, Department of Economics and Harriman Institute, Columbia University, New York, New York, U.S.A.

Clifford Gaddy, Brookings Institute, Washington DC, U.S.A.

Ruvin Gekker, Department of Economics, National University of Ireland, Galway, Galway, Ireland.

Barry W. Ickes, Department of Economics, Pennsylvania State University, University Park, Pennsylvania, U.S.A.

Jim Leitzel, Public Policy Studies Program, University of Chicago, Chicago, Illinois, U.S.A.

Vladimir Mau, Working Centre for Economic Reform and the Institute for the Economy in Transition, Moscow, Russia.

Vladimir Popov, Graduate School of International Business, Academy of National Economy, Moscow, Russia.

Mark E. Schaffer, Centre for Economic Reform and Transformation and Department of Economics, School of Management, Heriot-Watt University, Edinburgh, U.K.

Gerard Turley, Department of Economics, National University of Ireland, Galway, Galway, Ireland.

Shlomo Weber, Department of Economics, Southern Methodist University, Dallas, Texas, U.S.A.

Acknowledgements

The book is based on the workshop "Institutions and their Change in Transition Economies" which was held at the National University of Ireland, Galway. We would like to thank all the participants in the workshop for very stimulating discussions that have helped to revise the conference papers. We also would like to thank Sarah Callanan, Elena Gekker, Imelda Howley and Claire Noone for their help in organizing the workshop and making it a success.

Aidan Kane and Claire Noone provided invaluable support on the final stage of preparation of the manuscript. Without their help we would not be able to cope with the deadlines.

Last, but not least, we would like to express our gratitude to the staff of Ashgate Publishing Company for their professionalism and efficiency in handling our manuscript. In particular, we would like to thank Adam Hickford, Commissioning Editor of the Development Studies and Transition for including our book in the Ashgate list. We also would like to thank Jacqueline Cox, Carolyn Court, Pauline Beavers, Ruth Peters and Louise Preston for their efforts in co-ordinating and expediting the publication of this book.

This publication was grant-aided by the Publication Fund of the National University of Ireland, Galway.

Introduction

By institutions the new institutional economics understands the rules of the game in a society (see D. North (1990, p.3)). These rules or mechanisms could be formal or informal. Economic transition from a centrally planned economy to a market economy involves a replacement of one set of institutions and mechanisms, namely such institutions of a command economy as Gosplan, Gossnab, Gosstroi etc with all allocative decisions made by planners, with another set of market institutions and mechanisms. Originally it seemed that such a replacement could be easily achieved by simply introducing the familiar market mechanisms such as price and trade liberalizations, currency convertibility, privatization etc. The implicit assumption was that the demise of a centrally planned economy would automatically wipe out all its institutions and rules. However, "although formal rules may change overnight as the result of political or judicial decisions, informal constraints embodied in customs, traditions and codes of conduct are much more impervious to deliberate policies" (D. North (1990, p. 6)). The new institutional economics emphasizes that these informal constraints and mechanisms have a tendency to survive a radical change or revolution precisely because they still help to resolve some basic exchange problems among the agents in the economy. This importance of informal mechanisms is crucial to understanding economic transition in Russia and other countries of Eastern Europe.

The present collection of papers is based on the workshop *Institutions and their Change in Transition Economies* which was held in July of 2000 at the National University of Ireland, Galway. The workshop attracted leading experts in transition economies from the United States, United Kingdom, Russia and Ireland. The participants focused their attention on institutional changes in transition economies, which have been occurring over the last decade. In particular, they concentrated on an ongoing tension between informal constraints and mechanisms and the new formal rules and mechanisms that have gradually evolved through the transition period. Experiences are drawn, primarily, from Russia. The papers are grouped into three sets. The first set, Part I, analyses, synthesises and provides some generalisations on the institutional adaptations, as a market economy slowly emerges in a fog of shifting rules and varying interpretations. The second set, Part II, analyses the behaviour of business and the taxation authorities as they try to minimise and maximise the taxation take, respectively. The third set, Part III, sets out the challenges facing the central and regional governments in delivering equitable public service levels across regions of vastly different economic levels, while, at the same time, trying to stimulate regional economic growth, so that each region might make its fair contribution to the national cake.

Part I: Institutional Changes in The Russian Economy opens with R.E. Ericson's paper "The Russian Economy: Market in Form, but 'Feudal' in Content". He emphasises the pivotal role of the institutions, in particular the political and legal environment in determining the evolution and performance of the market economy. The current institutions in all societies, normally, evolve over centuries. However, that evolution was abruptly and radically altered in Bolshevic Russia to support the autocratic and centrally planned system. A new direction was once again taken in the 1990s with a decision to move to a democratic market driven economy. Dismantling of the centrally planned system and effective removal of central control combined with price liberalisation and removal of state controlled bodies gave the semblance of a market system economy, but without the supporting institutions. What has emerged is ostensibly a market system but with exchange relationships and networks dominated by those of the old regime. They are controlled by local and regional elites, who have now usurped local powers in the absence of central control. In exchange for the maintenance of artificial borders to these local virtual fiefdoms and the right to participate in economic exchange, local enterprises must pay a seniorage to the local power brokers, the local authorities. These contributions are hidden in the intricacy of the issue of permits, licences and taxation concessions, which are exercised and controlled by the local authorities.

A market economy has certain characteristics, which include the voluntary participation of economic agents; the rights and freedom of actions enshrined in property rights; the existence of a 'real' money for exchange and interdependent holding of value; and an interdependent system of flexible, market responding prices. However the new laws and institutions are firmly rooted in content and implementation on the Soviet system, while many of the old industrial sub-hierarchy and the elites, which controlled them, remain effectively in place. Since legal norms are ambiguous and not enforceable in an objective fashion, local politicians and functionaries operate in this twilight zone to interpret, invent and police operational rules for those who are willing to pay the seniorage demanded. Accommodation is easily reached between old partners from the defunct system, the local political elites and the new economic elites.

Two interesting results emerge: (a) Enterprises survive which produce normally unmarketable products but which are exchangeable and usable within an integrated production system of obsolete technologies; and (b) Through this internal trade and mutual concessions between the local administration and enterprises, public services are maintained. Thus local employment and public services are maintained at the expense of economic and financial efficiency.

Ericson schematises this system into what he calls "industrial feudalism". The social, economic and political organisation of production is akin to that of medieval Europe, except that industrial rather than agricultural produce dominates and thus 'industrial feudalism' is the model which best describes current relationship between the local political and the local production elites. There are a number of core attributes. There is an absence of or weak central control, which has been usurped by local political elites. There are diffused property rights and a weak appeal system, which must defer to the local controlling power. There is a mixing of public and private roles of political elites, sustaining economic and social activity, while providing handsomely for themselves and theirs from the fruits of local value added.

Having created quasi dependence on the state at all levels, it is not surprising that the various socio-economic factors should continue to look to the state to resolve all problems. Having passed economic resources to enterprises, it is also not surprising that the government should look to enterprise for the financial resources for its political and social activities. So regional governments have set about managing their regions, protecting them from outside competition and extracting the price of operations from compliant enterprises. Local self sufficiency and controlled trading and investment relationships with outside entities have ensued. The disquieting aspect of this activity is the extent to which private gain is the objective of, or is extracted from, it.

There is a dichotomy of market structure in Russia today. First, there is a relatively flexible and unimpeded structure in new areas of economic activity or areas, which were not well developed under the soviet system, for example, new financial instruments, retailing of imported goods, food and final industrial products and for exported commodities. Second, there are the other economic sectors consisting mainly of intermediate inputs into the production process, which are predetermined by non-market forces. In this network of economic interactions, economic efficiency has little meaning. This second set exploits the dysfunctional capital market and low inter-enterprise labour mobility, while the transactions are carried out in a fog of unequal barter trading, hiding cross subsidisation and tax concessions and transfers between enterprises and public authorities.

The failure to expose vast parts of the Russian economy to market forces has left it with an industrial structure not too different from the Soviet period and certainly one that in a market economy would not be sustainable. It was not monetised or exposed to economic valuation or opportunity cost and was thus riddled with economic inefficiencies. In addition it incorporated many social services provided by way of income in kind to workers. Few of these enterprises, which remain relatively unchanged, would survive exposure to market competition. At present, there is an interlocking system of firms, liaising with the local authorities, where transactions are carried out using barter and deferred payments with each other and tax deferrals with the local authorities. Real prices reflecting real input/output relationships are obfuscated Costs are covered by non-market prices and subsidies through an opaque system of transfers from the more to the less efficient and lubricated/facilitated by the local authorities as intermediaries. The local development of the financial sector (under the patronage or franchise of the local authority), linking intricately to the local enterprise (local equity holder) has added to the flexibility and sustainability of the system and its enterprises.

Although Ericson postulates three possible future directions for the Russian economy, namely, a return to state authoritarianism, feudal conflicts and alliances leading to increased stability or an evolution towards a real market environment, President Putin has signaled a move toward the third option. He is moving carefully toward fulfilling at least some of the market requirements. He is re-establishing central control and insisting on the subservience of local authorities in the discharge of duties and responsibilities assigned to them. He is insisting on the uniform enforcement of federal legislation, including those governing property rights, throughout the Federation and the separation of political from economic interest and the public from the private interests of elected representatives. He is pushing for transparency in inter-enterprise and local authority dealings and the dissolution of non-viable enterprises, while securing definite access to the tax liabilities of the viable enterprises.

The future success of the Putin policy will hinge critically on the clarity of communication and the degree of "enforced" control in the descending power structure in the discharge of public responsibility. A call for patriotism where private interests are sacrificed for the public good, which was so well responded to in the past, is deeply needed at this time.

Corruption and organised crime, which normally arouses so much disdain in modern society and which now appears so endemic in Russian society in transition, at least according to the popular western media, is treated in robust and realistic terms by J. Leitzel in his paper "Corruption and Organized Crime in the Russian Transition". He sets a framework for discussing this topic. He also sets out a precise definition of corruption and its evolution over time, in particular the popular association of corruption with the transition economy, the possible advantages (as well as disadvantages, which are already quite well rehearsed) and possible approaches to dealing with the issue.

He confines the definition of corruption, in the present discussion, to the misuse of public office for private use. This may be linked to, or supported by, organised crime for mutual benefit. There is nothing especially new in this in modern industrialised societies. He interrogates the term transition and concludes that the objectives and process of transition are reasonably clear but that the starting point is far less obvious. He argues that certain costs, which have been identified with transition, are not new at all, but that covert activities in the Soviet period have been brought out into the open. Bribery and extortion were an intrinsic part of the Soviet economy. For example, since the managed demand and supply of goods was in disequilibrium, an active black economy was bridging the gap, to which the authorities turned a blind eye but which, inevitably, had to be paid for by bribes. Also, in getting access to the legally allocated inputs, which were decreed for enterprises in fulfilling quotas, bribes were a common means of lubricating the process.

He also suggests that some of the new costs identified with transition are indeed the results of partial or inadequate reforms. Legislation governing property rights is often ambiguous and left to the interpretation of local authorities. The latter also retain considerable discretion over the rules regarding the licence to operate locally, while effectively controlling local real estate markets. Hard budget constraints led to the destruction of social enterprises, while excessive taxation, extortion and protection rackets prevented the development of small enterprises. The liberalisation of international trade in natural resources led to various rent seeking activities linked to protection rackets.

Protection rackets are, generally, associated with poorly resourced policing. However, they are also linked to the demise of the communist party, which was the power base, which controlled illegal payments in the old system. The vacuum created was disputed territory for control of who to pay and for what. This vacuum has been filled by organised crime, which has thrived on old connections. The increased market activity has created additional targets from which to extract revenue.

Finally, Leitzel challenges whether changes during transition can be measured according to western criteria, in the context where the market is trying to break out, as against a context where the market has been evolving over a very long period. For example, in developed industrial society when we examine the impact of a monopoly the comparison is with a competitive situation; however in Russia, it makes little sense to compare it with a competitive situation, since such an environment does not and did not exist. In general, the norms, which are accepted in advanced industrial market economies, are not the current norms in Russia.

Leitzel argues that in addition to the negative aspects of corruption that there are also positive aspects, which should not be minimised and that instead of focussing on the elimination of corruption, policy should be one of harm limitation. Corruption facilitates greater flexibility in the system, thus lowering the existing level of inefficiency. It enables socio-economic actors to circumvent bad rules, in particular to evade inefficient taxes. It offers an incentive to officials to make the system work. It allows contact between socio-economic actors and government and provides feedback to policy makers to reshape alternatives to the existing inefficient rules.

Leitzel is optimistic about the future evolution of the market environment in Russia. To support his optimism, he cites the general desire to abandon the unpleasantness, particularly by those who have been successful (by fair or foul means). They wish new effective legislation/rules to be implemented. He also sees the present level of disorganisation of corruption and crime as analogous to that of the communist party before its demise. and so feels that it can be eventually eliminated. However, he cautions against a crackdown, since the outcome is too unpredictable, given the ambiguousness and ubiquity of corruption and associated crime. He sees corruption as being positively related to the concentration of power and the level of discretion associated with this power, and negatively related to accountability. Corruption may be reduced, therefore, by addressing the elements in this equation, namely, the limitation of the power of local authorities, restructuring the power and discretion of officials and increasing the accountability of both. The development of civil society through non-governmental organisations would greatly assist this evolution in demanding greater transparency in local government and its activities. The continuing liberalisation of society, more effective policing and enforcement of legislation and, above all, a commitment by politicians to the rule of law would create an environment more compatible with the market requirements.

V. Popov in his paper "Strong Institutions are more Important than the Speed of Reforms" challenges the debate on whether shock therapy or gradualism is more likely to be effective in bringing about reform. He argues that the debate is wrongly focussed and that it is the strength of institutions rather than the speed of reform, which is critical to the success of the transition process. His supporting evidence comes from an econometric study carried out on 28 transition economies in Europe, Asia and Africa. The key element in his analysis is the decoupling of production decline and production expansion during transition. Production decline comes primarily from an initial distortion in the production mix and international trade. Production in centrally planned economies is biased against consumer goods and so liberalisation in production and expenditure, combined with a reduction in state expenditure, leads to a drop in production. On the other hand, institutional flexibility, in facilitating the re-allocation of production factors to the expanding sectors *in transition, is key to* increased output and thus to the speed and success of reform. Increased supply depends on the ability of business to induce real assets and labour away from activities of declining demand, to be able to support this through access to the financial means and to have the legal and physical protection to ensure the integrity of the business activity.

It is well known that informal rules and mechanisms played a very important role in the Soviet system. The managers in a command economy developed a great variety of informal devices to cope with uncertainties and tautness of a planning process. In fact, during perestroika the role of these informal mechanisms was greatly enhanced due to the demise of some institutions that used to put some constraints on them. It is natural then that during transition many managers have continued to rely on the informal networks and mechanisms that they previously built. C. Gaddy and B.W. Ickes in their paper "An Evolutionary Analysis of Russia's Virtual Economy" show that this reliance on informal networks or mechanisms was a natural adaptive strategy for many enterprises to survive a so called shock therapy. Shock therapy was supposed to introduce hard budget constraints. Hence those enterprises that utilized such survival strategies as barter, tax offsets or tax arrears, could be less affected by the shock. Naturally other enterprises could also imitate behavior that they would perceive as being successful adaptation to the shock. Therefore, these adaptive or 'virtual' strategies will rapidly spread in the system. In fact, by utilizing a simple evolutionary model, Gaddy and Ickes show that such a virtual economy where all enterprises choose virtual strategies can be evolutionary stable. In this simple model all enterprises can choose among three strategies: M (Market), V (Virtual) and S (Soviet). Let $\pi(i,j)$ be the payoff to an enterprise choosing strategy i when all other enterprises choose strategy j (i,j = M,V,S). Gaddy and Ickes assume that the payoff to being a market enterprise is the greatest when other enterprises also choose M, and it is lowest when other enterprises choose S. They also assume that an economy fully populated by Soviet-type enterprises is least efficient, while the market economy is most efficient.

Hence we have:

$$\pi(M,M) > \pi(V,V) > \pi(S,S)$$

and also:

$$\pi(M,M) > \pi(M,V) > \pi(M,S)$$
$$\pi(V,V) > \pi(V,S) > \pi(V,M)$$
$$\pi(S,S) > \pi(S,V) > \pi(S,M).$$

The following payoff matrix is consistent with the authors' assumptions above:

	M	S	V
M	5	0	3
S	0	3	1
V	2	3	4

where the numbers are payoffs to a row strategy against a population of column strategies. Therefore, $\pi(V,V) = 4$, $\pi(M,M) = 5$, $\pi(S,S) = 3$, $\pi(M,V) = 3$, etc.

Gaddy and Ickes argue that $\pi(V,V) > \pi(M,V)$ due to the fact that when a market enterprise operates in an economy dominated by virtual enterprises it is under threat because of the fiscal pressure from the government. Notice also that while the authors treat the payoffs from (M,S) and (S,M) symmetrically (that is, $\pi(M,S) = \pi(S,M)$), they do not treat symmetrically the payoffs from (V,S) and(S,V) (that is, $\pi(V,S) \neq \pi(S,V)$). However, it is easy to check that if we will use the alternative payoff matrix:

	M	S	V
M	5	0	3
S	0	3	1
V	2	1	4

Then we still will have three pure strategy equilibria in the game: (M,M), (V,V) and (S,S). Hence the behavior will remain similar since we still have two basins of attraction (for an illustration see Figure 2 of the paper). One is the market economy (M,M) and the other is the virtual economy (V,V). In fact, given the replicator dynamics in their paper, the authors' result is robust with regard to various permutations in the payoff matrix. Hence when most enterprises are M, then being a market enterprise will dominate being a virtual one. However, if there is a sufficient mass of non-market enterprises, then it will pay to be virtual. It should be pointed out that if we assume that virtual enterprises are more likely to interact with other virtual enterprises, then the virtual trap could be more easily achieved compared to the case of random interactions.

The informal rules and mechanisms were present in all transition economies. The important difference between Russian economy and some successful Central European Economies (CEE), according to Gaddy and Ickes, is this. In the case of Russia, the energy and resource sectors made it possible for a large share of enterprises in the industry to survive through adaptation of informal rules and mechanisms. In the case of successful CEE, the cut off of the Soviet supplied cheap energy made it more difficult for the enterprises there to adopt informal rules. Hence the new formal rules and mechanisms could take root there but not in Russia.

V. Mau in his paper "Russia's Economic Policy at the Beginning of the New Phase" analyses the development of the Russian economy as enunciated in different planning documents under the reign of the new president, Putin. He is optimistic that the various weaknesses identified in the economy à la Ericson and Leitzel and the policy implications emerging in Popov's paper are central to the new policy direction.

Under Putin, political stability, which is the precondition for economic stability and growth is being realised. He has reasserted the supremacy of the central authority; there is harmony between the government and parliament; a clear understanding between the centre and the regions is being established, where the power and responsibility of the latter is clearly recognised. Regional access to central funds, which previously was based on political strength is being replaced by equal access to all regions.

There are however a number of weaknesses, which are critical to the efficient workings of the economic system. Although the Central Bank has played an important role in maintaining the internal and external stability of the rouble, there has been a general failure of the banking system, particularly in it role of inter-mediation between savers and investors. There is, also, a bureaucratic jungle to be negotiated by business in setting up and operating enterprise. This, allied to poor policing and law enforcement, makes it very difficult for enterprise, particularly small and medium size enterprise, to emerge and grow. This is evidenced by the fact that despite the boost to import substitution and exports of 1998 financial collapse, the industrial sector has failed to respond. There had been little increase in investment and minimal foreign direct investment.

New economic policy proposed in the Greff report and the short and medium term policy response from Putin has two principal components, namely, the strengthening and expansion of social policy to underpin the long-term development of the economy and creating the environment for market development. The state will, basically, leave the development of the industrial and commercial services sectors to the private sector and, according to Mau, "comparative advantage" will be established through competition. This is a rather strong assumption of neo-classical economics for which there seems to be no compelling evidence in international economic development. In addition, according to Mau, it is proposed that the development of certain public services, like transport and energy, be left to the private sector. This seems a rather foolhardy suggestion, given the recent experiences in the UK with transport and in California with energy, where the private sector has failed to deliver essential public services in a manner acceptable to the demands of the economy. These experiences are in countries where the private sector is at a rather mature state, in contrast to Russia where it is still in its infancy.

There is, thus, a very strong emphasis on social policy and creating the market environment for enterprise to develop but there is insufficient emphasis on how the value added is going to be generated to finance these policies. The industrial plan is weak or non-existent and there is no attempt at preparing an industrial operational programme. Industrial sectors are not prioritised. The role of the state in key industrial sectors is not elaborated. However, the role of the state, in transition Russia, must continue to be large. Private enterprise will have extreme difficulty in providing the necessary investment in the absence of developing financial and stock markets. Even if these markets were developed, some privileged incentives would be necessary to move investment in the desired direction. The private banking sector will not, however, be able to finance business investment in the short to medium term, so the state must have a significant role in the whole inter-mediation process.

The creation of competitive advantage must be assisted by public policy – government must draw up an indicative plan, however rudimentary, identifying those sectors which are essential to the future development of the economy, and support private research, development, technology and trade in these sectors. The state must also be significantly involved in investment to finance economic growth. This policy has been successfully implemented by the newly developed economies and was central to the success of the longer established developed economies. Active economic development policy is called for where the institutional environment is essential – here the emphasis on legal enforcement and decrease in bureaucracy as enunciated by Putin is a welcome direction – but for now it is insufficient to launch the economy onto the path of economic development.

Part II: Taxation in Transition Economies consists of three papers. R. Gekker in his paper "Soft Budget Constraints and Tax Arrears in Transition Economies", utilizes Kornai's concept of soft budget constraints (SBC) to provide an analytical explanation of tax arrears in Russia. According to Kornai, a paternalistic state is the cause of the SBC. The paper introduces some simple dynamic models that account for the existence of the SBC in transition economies. The author uses the definition of SBC as ex-post tax subsidies paid by the state to loss-making enterprises in transition economies.

It should be pointed out that big Russian firms simply reproduce a hierarchical system of bargaining with the state that was typical for the Soviet type economy. The bargaining occurs after firms have already accumulated their tax debts. Quite often the firms might also accumulate wage and interenterprise arrears. Many of these enterprises should be declared bankrupt. However, the implementation of bankruptcy law was neglected in Russia. As a result, the manager of the firm who typically is not its owner, is able to transfer valuable assets from the firm to his privately owned affiliates. Tax arrears, tax offsets, barter and wage arrears make firm's accounting non-transparent and facilitate the transfers of financial assets and valuable inputs.

A simple sequential game describes a bargaining between the government and the firm. The author assumes that the government maximizes both its tax revenues and the private benefits of the firm, that is, that the government is paternalistic. On the other hand, firms maximize only their private benefits. A soft budget constraint exists if tax arrears are tolerated by the government. Proposition 1 then establishes the existence of the SBC under certain parameters in the model.

It should be pointed out that the existence result of Propositions 1 applies only to firms that are in financial distress. R. Gekker then examines another sequential game where the managerial effort supplied could successfully restructure the firm. Without such effort, however, the firm will remain unrestructured and will continue to produce old goods. Proposition 2 establishes the existence of the SBC in this model and it also answers the question under what parameters in the model the firm will choose to restructure.

In his paper "The Tax System and the Peculiarities of the Russian Economy" M. Alexeev examines how tax evasion, corruption of tax administrative officials and widespread use of non-monetary means of payments and payment arrears affect the functioning of the Russian tax system. The author emphasizes the effects of the tax system's response to the above peculiarities on the economy at large.

In Section 3, Alexeev sketches an argument that shows the problem with a possible misperception on the part of the government about the extent of the tax evasion in the economy. For example, the problem with the overestimation of the degree of tax evasion is that there is no reliable feed back to correct the misperception leading to suboptimal outcomes.

Suppose there are two groups of taxpayers: one group consists of intrinsically honest taxpayers ($e_i(k) \equiv 0$ for all k for $i \in H$, where H is a set of honest tax-payers, and $e_f(k)$ is the amount of effort used by a risk neutral taxpayer to evade tax given the intensity of anti-evasion requirement k). The other group of taxpayers is characterized by $e_i(k) = e(k) > 0$ for all relevant k, i $\notin$ H. Also assume that the honest taxpayers represent certain proportion v of all taxpayers in the economy. Then the socially optimal value of k could be found by solving:

$$Min_k \{(1-v)\ e(k) + C(k)\},$$

where $C(k)$ represents the purely administrative compliance cost that anti-evasion requirements impose on the taxpayers.

The first–order conditions for this minimization problem are:

$$\partial C/\partial k = -(1-v)e'.$$

Differentiating the above expression with respect to v and solving for $\partial k/\partial v$, we have:

$$\partial k/\partial v = e'/(C'' + (1-v)e'') < 0,$$

that is, the optimal value of k is inversely related to v. Hence, if the government underestimates the proportion of honest taxpayers in the economy, it would set the intensity of anti-evasion requirement k higher that it is socially optimal. It should be pointed out that the increase in k may reduce the number of honest taxpayers in an open economy, because k may raise the honest taxpayers' costs above the world market price of the good. In that case then the government's initial misperception that everybody in the economy evades may become a self-fulfilling prophecy.

Alexeev believes that the Russian tax policy makers view virtually all entrepreneurs as tax evaders given the slightest opportunity for evasion. However, if this view is not correct, then the intensity of the anti-evasion measures in the Russian tax law and administration could be greater than it is socially optimal.

In section 4 and 5 the author outlines various measures to fight corruption in tax administration and also the spread of payment arrears (PA) as well as non-monetary means of payment (NMMP) in the Russian economy. For example, he argues that the reduction of statutory tax burden by itself could be too risky to fight corruption in Russia. It should, then, be accompanied by an increase in collection rate, as well as an increase in the tax inspectors' salaries, in order to prevent a drastic decline in the effective tax burden. The author also suggests the introduction of a system of specialized tax courts that should speed up the tax appeal process. If it is introduced, the system could make corruption more difficult and may create a possibility to improve tax inspectors' incentives by linking their bonuses with the taxes collected.

According to Alexeev a planned switch to the accrual method of accounting may help to combat a spread of NMMP and PA in the Russian economy. He claims that an introduction of accrual accounting will put some additional pressure on the sellers to obtain timely payments for their output and will facilitate the auditing of taxpayers.

He notes that the arguments against the accrual accounting are ironically the widespread use of NMMP and the frequency of PA. The opponents of accrual accounting argue that the introduction of the accrual method would create a cash flow problem and also impose an additional burden on the taxpayers precisely because of the current crisis in PA and the use of NMMP. Alexeev provides a spirited defense of the accrual method although he admits that a set of transition rules might be necessary to spread the shifted forward tax liability over some period of time (say 6–12 months). Another concession is to allow small businesses to continue with the cash method as it is typically done in industrialized countries.

M.E. Schaffer and G. Turley in their paper "Effective versus Statutory Taxation: Measuring Effective Tax Administration in Transition Economies" attempt to measure the effectiveness of tax administration in transition economies (TEs) by comparing statutory tax rates with effective tax yields.

Tax deferrals, arrears, write-offs and exemptions in TEs to a certain degree represent a politicization of the tax system. It is extremely difficult to measure the extent of these government concessions. The authors utilize methodology that allows them to obtain aggregate measures of the degree of effectiveness of tax collection in TEs. The methodology is based on one previously used for measuring fiscal or revenue capacity in federal states. With appropriate modifications, Schaffer and Turley apply this methodology to transition countries rather than to states within a federal system.

To measure the effectiveness of tax administration, the authors introduce two indicators. The first indicator represents the ratio of effective tax to statutory tax. Effective tax rates are the realized average tax rates. Statutory tax rates are the rates that taxpayers are required to pay by law. Let Y be the gross tax base and T be actual tax payments. Denote by t the statutory tax rate applied to gross income. Then the effective tax rate e could be calculated by dividing T by Y. The effective/statutory (E/S) ratio is defined as:

$$E/S \text{ ratio} \equiv e/t \equiv T/tY.$$

This indicator measures the extent to which the statutory tax rate diverges from the effective tax rate. For example, a ratio below 1 indicates that the effective tax yield is falling short of what application of the statutory tax rate would yield.

The authors use national accounts measures of income: for VAT, total national income; for social security tax (SST), income from labor; and for corporate income tax (CIT), income from capital. Of course, these measures provide only rough approximations of the actual statutory tax bases. It also should be pointed out that the national accounts statistics of TEs are not particularly reliable. However, these national accounts statistics are both readily available and comparable across countries.

The second indicator attempts to avoid some possible problems with national accounts statistics. The normal tax yield (NTY) relates tax payments adjusted for cross-country differences in statutory rates to GDP, and is defined as follows:

$$NTY \equiv T/GDP \ b/t,$$

where t is the statutory tax rate and b is a benchmark rate. Hence, the NTY simply tells us what the tax yield would be for a specific country if the statutory tax rate were the same for all countries.

Schaffer and Turley utilize data for 25 ex-socialist countries (10 of them are CEE countries, the rest are the countries of the former Soviet Union (FSU)). They use the mean of the EU-15 countries as a benchmark. By calculating E/S ratio and NTY for VAT, SST and CIT, the authors then compare the rates for 25 TEs countries with the EU-15 means. The results confirm that the 25 TEs on average are not as effective in tax administration, collection or enforcement compared to the average for EU countries. The research also underlines that TEs have relatively low tax effectiveness rates in addition to having a low tax capacity.

The authors then investigate various factors that are related to effective tax administration in TEs. They start by examining the relationship between the effectiveness of tax collection and progress in transition. Using the EBRD transition indicators for 1997, they have discovered that in cases of VAT and SST the relationship between progress in transition and effectiveness of tax administration comes out rather clearly. For example, in the case of VAT, all leading reformers (Poland, Hungary, Czech and Slovak Republics, the Baltic States) have E/S ratios that are close to the EU benchmark. The slow reformers, on the other hand, have E/S ratios below the EU benchmark. Notice, however, that a small number of slow reformers (Belarus, Moldova, Ukraine) have rather high E/S ratios. These high ratios could be accounted for by the observation that these TEs have maintained a functioning state.

Schaffer and Turley then examine another possible factor that contributes to the ineffectiveness of tax administration, namely corruption. They use for comparison Transparency International's Corruption Perception Index (CPI) as well as the measure constructed from the Business Environment and Enterprise Performance Survey (BEEPS). Perhaps not surprisingly, countries with effective tax administration (such as Estonia, Poland) have a relatively low average bribe tax. On the other hand, countries with ineffective tax administration (such as Armenia, Georgia) have a relatively high average bribe tax.

In the future, the authors hope to extend their data to a larger set of countries including non-EU OECD countries as well as developing countries. This extension may provide an alternative and possibly more suitable benchmark than the current benchmark of the EU-15. They also would like to explore some other factors contributing to the ineffectiveness of tax administration such as the size of shadow economy, tax evasion, the political constraints and the distribution of power among others.

Part III: Regional Developments and Institutional Reforms opens with the paper by E. Dabla-Norris and S. Weber "Regional Disparities and Transfer Policies in Russia: Theory and Evidence". The authors explore the uneveness of regional development in Russia, which derives from historical evolution, the natural resources base of the regions and the application of economic policies during and since the Soviet period. They explore the natural divergence of revenue and expenditure in these different regions and how the deficit, in particular, has been bridged. It is clear that attempts to use rational approaches to redistribution have been tempered by political expediency. Although, a policy of partial equalisation is being implemented at present, huge divergences exist in regional revenues and service provision, while differential growth rates are putting even greater pressure on the divergences. This has powerful implications for factor flows between regions, in particular labour flows.

The divergence in regional development across Russia has its origins in historic and political aspects over centuries, the occurrence of natural resources, including climatic factors and mainly political decisions relating to regional development during the Soviet and post Soviet periods. The Soviet period was characterised by extensive development, partly related to political control and security issues, following the Second World War, and partly due to the exploitation of natural resources. This extensive development was marked by limited infrastructure and local service development and consequently lacked long-term sustainability. The period since the break up of the USSR has been marked by the absence of regional development policy, except in so far as attempts were made by the Federal government to provide minimum levels of social services at the regional level.

According to Delors (1989) as quoted in MacKay (2001), "Compensation [regional transfer] is both a product of and a source of the sense of national solidarity, which all relevant economic and monetary unions share." Since there is a high level of regional divergence in Russia in the level of economic development and thus in GDP per capita, there is a divergence in regional tax revenues and regional need. If equity of access to public goods and services is to be maintained, the local deficit in the poorer regions must be made up by an inter-regional transfer, which is administered by the central government. Dabla-Norris and Weber present different formula and derive balanced budget conditions and values of transfer shares in achieving a level of inter-regional equity. However, they argue for a partial equalisation, based on the hypothesis that otherwise the deficit regions will not have an incentive to further their own economic development and that the surplus regions will not be encouraged to generate surpluses in the future. They also argue for "ranking invariance", that is the regions' rank order of revenue should be the same after transfers as before transfers. Against the backdrop of this "ideal" transfer system, they evaluate what has been happening in inter-regional transfers in Russia throughout the 1990s.

Since the break-up of the Soviet Union, there were two phases in addressing the equalisation policy. The first phase up to the mid-1990s was dominated by ad hoc agreements on tax concessions and intergovernmental transfers, arrived at through negotiation, the result of which depended on the political strength of the regions. The Federal government had attempted to push expenditure responsibility to the regions without providing means. This led to a call for political independence by a number of regions, which in turn led to negotiated agreements, which worsened the equalisation possibilities. The Federal government was eventually forced to continue to fund the provision of goods and services to the poorer regions. However, in the latter half of the 1990s, the Federal government has adopted a more formal approach to regional transfers based on formulae of 'partial equalisation', where exceptions are less likely to be tolerated.

There are conflicting views on the outcome of the revenue equalisation process. By 1994, the regional revenue inequality was exacerbated, when Federal Budget transfers to regions was 3.86 per cent of GDP or 22 per cent of regional revenue. Although transfers fell to 2.0 per cent of GDP or 14 per cent of regional revenue in 1998, the partial equalisation principal was re-established. This was due to a more focussed approach, targeting, in particular the poorer regions. For 20 of the least development regions federal transfers amounted to 50-60 per cent of revenue in 1999, while 30 regions were net contributors by 1996-98. Also, the ratio of maximum to minimum per capita regional revenue was reduced from a factor of 90 before to 20 after transfers were applied.

Clearly, however, there remains an enormous discrepancy in service provision between regions. The ever-growing divergence in economic growth rates between regions combined with this large divergence in service provision has powerful implications for inter-regional labour flows in the absence of more effective regional policy. This leads to the second objective of regional policy, namely, the mobilisation of regional resources into value-added creating activity. Unless this second strand of development policy is vigorously pursued, then the future looks bleak for the regions in relative and absolute decline.

Regional development theories and associated policies as pursued in advanced industrial economies and their appropriateness for current day Russia are explored by M. Cuddy and S. Callanan in their paper "Regional Development Theory and Policy: an example for Russia?" Regions across a national territory are normally at different stages of development and the quest is for theories to explain these divergences and from which to derive policies, which can bring about convergence. The focus is on theories and policies relating to increasing regional value-added and thus national value-added, rather than on issues of regional equity and transfers and national integrity. They summarise the competing theories of regional development and elucidate the different policy initiatives, which flow from these theories. They then ask how relevant these policies are to the development and the bringing about of convergence of Russian regions. They conclude that regional development theory does provide a framework for regional economic development analysis and the identification of policy measures, which have varying degrees of relevance to the Russian regions today. However, as a precondition to the success of these policies the more fundamental basis for the operation of a market economy, in particular the institutional environment, must be assured.

The neo-classical growth model has dominated the understanding of national economic growth and therefore it is not surprising that it has become the conventional model for explaining regional growth. Policy measures to enhance regional economic performance have their rationale in the in neo-classical growth theory. Regional output is determined by the principal production factors, land, labour and capital, and by the level of technology. The model assumes that there is full factor mobility and, consequently, markets clear with efficient use of the production factors. It postulates that in the long run regional convergence automatically occurs, as a result of market forces, and therefore regional disparities do not persist. Comparative advantage is an integral part of the theory. It explains regional specialisation and trade, based on different endowments of production factors and natural resources. Thus according to the model, specialisation occurs in regions according to their comparative advantage and in the long run markets clear and regions converge.

Non-intervention in the market is the clear implication of the neo-classical model as the explanatory model of regional growth. However, experience shows that certain assumptions of the theory do not hold in reality. Markets do not clear due to problems of factor mobility ("market failure") or clear in an inefficient manner due to the divergence of private and social costs associated with externalities. Decisions are taken by the individual economic actors in the demand and supply of factors of production, which collectively fail to clear the regional or national factor markets. This leads to an under or inefficient use of resources and sub-optimal output and economic welfare. Consequently, intervention measures are required to move the economy towards the optimum output. Market failure and intervention measures are normally in the factor markets, labour and capital and technology.

Regional characteristics, which differentiate regions, their differing levels of economic development and economic growth rates, are at the heart of the alternative theories of regional development. Policies to enhance the positive factors or to mitigate the negative factors flow from these theories. Location theory focuses on the preferential location of a particular place, with regard to its access to factor and product markets and the consequential effect on production costs and revenue. The principal policy recommendations emerging addresses those factors which influence the cost of distance from markets: reducing transport and communication cost, supporting the production of low transport cost goods, removing barriers to trade.

Agglomeration factors and the associated process of cumulative causation suggest that regions have initial conditions or attributes, which place them in a positive or negative competitive position vis-à-vis other regions. Those in a positive position will expand and move to higher and higher levels of advantage in a cumulative self-propelling fashion, while the opposite is the case with locations, which find themselves in the negative position. Policy recommendations focus on creating the external economies normally associated with concentration, and thus emphasise the creation of growth centres, growth corridors or grouping smaller centres together in order to capture these externalities.

Finally, indigenous development theory relates to a collection of ideas, emphasising local factors, which have been identified with creating local value added and thus contributing to economic growth. The factors identified under this rubric are predominantly institutional in nature, both formal and informal. Policy initiatives to strengthen these various factors are now part of the artillery of most regional authorities in the developed industrialised countries.

The formulation of regional development strategy and policy is now an integral part of the economic planning process in most western economies. Regional plans and programmes fit into a national plan framework. They are primarily of an indicative nature but are intended to steer socioeconomic actors along a certain development track using various incentives and disincentives. Regional development agencies or authorities, which are normally semi-autonomous entities, have come to play quite a significant role in regional planning and programming. Inter alia, they co-ordinate policy measures and implementing agencies of national ministries and promote the region nationally and internationally, for trade and investment purposes.

The major problems faced by the Russian regions are primarily associated with the transition process from an autocratic, centrally planned economy to a democratic, market-led economy. The question posed is to what extent regional development policies of the developed industrialised countries are relevant to the

Russian regions today. Since the creation of value added through market activity is at the core of regional development, the first priority must be to ensure that private business activity can operate within a stable political and economic environment where risk is minimised. This is a national rather than a regional issue.

The policy recommendations emerging from the neo-classical model are particularly relevant in the Russia of today, in the context of regional development. It is not just a question of "market failure" in the sense of the developed market system, but "market emergence", where markets did not previously exist. There are three areas where intervention is required, in the labour and capital markets and in technology. In the labour market, the supply of labour must adapt to the newly emerging areas and their corresponding skills requirement, while removing the barriers to enterprise creation and expansion will enhance labour demand. The supply of capital funds, especially to small and medium enterprises, is practically non-existent. Banks are not providing the inter-mediation between savers and investors, which is their normal role in market economies. The repressed demand for capital funds is magnified by the widespread obsolescence of technology. The state must play a critical role in ameliorating these restrictions and rigidities in the labour and financial markets.

Location theory emphasises the cost of distance, while policy initiatives address the reduction of these costs. The basic transport infrastructure in Russia in road, rail and air is strong, although requiring considerable in vestment to upgrade and modernise. However, the emergence of markets, particularly in air traffic, is problematic. The telecommunication system, while having a basic infrastructure, requires considerable upgrading, in particular to meet the requirements of the digital age.

Agglomeration factors theory focuses on the external economies deriving from centres of concentration and the "thickness" of the market. Associated policies try to strengthen these attributes in existing centres of concentration and try to overcome them in areas of weak concentration or dispersed population. Russia's geographic space is characterised by basically a two tier urban structure, large cities and towns, on the one hand and villages, on the other. The challenge for large cities and towns is to generate competitive production and support services will follow, thus strengthening competitive advantage and reinforcing growth. The principal challenge to Russian regional policy makers is in areas of dispersed population, extensive rural areas with little external economies; how to cluster small towns and villages in order to create a threshold concentration for the generation of external economies.

Theories explaining local development, which emphasise bottom-up policy initiatives, are predicated on a fairly evolved institutional structure and in particular its capacity to respond to local need and adapt to changing circumstances. They emphasise, in particular, the facilitation of local development led by the emergence of local entrepreneurs to create value added. This demands, in the first instance, an environment, which is favourable to business development, starting with an ethos among all the local institutions, which favour private business development. These local institutions, both formal and informal, are extremely weak in Russia and it will take much time and effort to reach the levels already achieved in most western industrial societies.

Despite the resistance to planning in Russia, because of the association which the word has with the central planning of the past, it is an essential part of the development process. Establishing a co-ordinating body, which can take the form of a regional development agency, which can carry this and other regional development responsibilities, has much to recommend itself as part of the regional government apparatus.

Regional development theory creates frameworks of regional analysis and policy measures to address regional development objectives. However, regional analysis, policy measures and their implementation put heavy demands on regional government in establishing the necessary institutional structures, providing the technical expertise and, above all, finding the financial resources.

Transition has presented three major problems from the regional perspective. First, there are the basic requirements of a market economy, a stable, hospitable and supportive environment for entrepreneurial activity. Second, there is the need to provide equitable social services to all regions. Third, there is the challenge to engage the regional resources in the most efficient fashion, in order to contribute to the local and national economy. The first and second problems have been formally recognised and are being addressed in present day Russia with less than glowing success. However, the third issue has yet to be seriously entertained.

The formal institutional structures in which the centrally planned system was imbedded was totally different to those demanded by a functioning market system. The same people who functioned in the former system have also to function in the new one where different behavior and norms are demanded. The enterprises, which operated in simple fashion under central command are now anchorless in market space and forced to be multi-functional to meet the exigencies of a market economy. Public administrations, which were provided with the necessary funding under the former system to deliver the necessary public services, are now obliged to deliver those same services under different rules and far less secure financial resources. The regions which were stitched into a seamless federal system, having equal access to financial resources are now obliged to rely, to a large extent, on their own resources. They now have a responsibility to generate much of their own finances which can only come from the local creation of value added and thus the need for regional development. The papers in this volume make a valuable contribution toward interpreting the realities of the transition process and appreciating the difficulties faced by all the political, social and economic actors in meeting the challenges together. However, it is clear that the role of the state and its democratically elected governments is paramount; it must create the vision for the future of the Russian society and the economy in particular; it must charter the future course for the economy; and it must play a very active direct and indirect role in reconstructing the productive sectors of the economy. But above all it has the central role to play in developing, weaving and adapting the institutions, which are the basis of and essential to the construction of a modern market led economy.

References

Delors, J. (1989), 'Regional Implications of Economic and Monetary Integration', in Committee for the Study of Economic and Monetary Union, *Report on Economic and Monetary Union in the European Community*, Office for the Official Publication of the European Community, Luxembourg.

MacKay, R. (2001), 'Regional Taxing and Spending: the Search for Balance', *Reg. Studies*, vol. 35, no. 6, pp. 561-74.

North, D. C. (1990), *Institutions, Institutional Change and Economic Performance*, Cambridge University Press, Cambridge.

PART I
INSTITUTIONAL CHANGES IN THE RUSSIAN ECONOMY

Chapter 1

The Russian Economy: Market in Form but "Feudal" in Content?

Introduction

One of the generally recognized lessons of the transition experience of east central Europe and the former Soviet Union has been about the absolutely critical role of the legal, political, social and economic institutions in determining the performance of modern market economies.[1] These institutions comprise a complete, coherent interactive system which allows for much variation in detail and superficial structure, but which can become severely dysfunctional if certain critical institutions or institutional functions are absent or deviate sufficiently from a common core. These institutions have evolved over centuries, some with roots in classical antiquity and Roman law, others in medieval faith and practice, in their reformation and in renaissance rebellions, and still others in the co-evolution of the modern state with science and technology. While each society and culture has developed its own variations, there is arguably a core of common functional characteristics which make all recognizable as functioning market economies.

This evolution of institutions consistent with and supportive of the proper functioning of a market economic system was also occurring in eastern Europe and the Russian Empire as the 20th century dawned, although the development was uneven and increasingly sporadic at greater distances from the core areas of Western civilization. Yet it seemed to be accelerating everywhere prior to the upheavals of World War I and the ensuing Bolshevik Revolution that destroyed the Russian Empire and sealed Russia and the other Soviet Republics off from the social, political and economic development of the rest of the world. At that point Russia explicitly and consciously departed from the evolutionary path of market economy development, and set about systematically destroying each and every one of the fundamental institutions on and around which coherent market behavior and interaction are based.[2] The resulting configuration of institutions, sustaining the survival and growth of the Soviet regime, formed the basis of the command economy and totalitarian (in aspiration if not, ultimately, achievement) polity that survived until the end of 1991 as the Soviet Union. These economic and political institutions were diametrically opposed, and inherently inimical, to the functioning of a democratic market economic system, yet provided a complete, coherent alternative for the organization and development of social, political and economic life on the basis of completely different principles and incentives.[3]

Beginning in 1989, that coherent system of socio-economic organization began to disintegrate as Gorbachev's well-intentioned, but economically irrational, "reforms" proceeded to dismantle, piece by piece, the essential institutional underpinnings of the command economy. Accelerated by centrifugal political pressures and newly released high powered economic incentives unmoderated by constraining market institutions, this disintegration culminated in the collapse of the Soviet Union into 15 newly independent states (NIS), among which Russia remained the key successor to Soviet statehood and its surviving institutions. In the face of a broad and expanding collapse of economic activity in the fall of 1991, the newly elected President of the Russian Republic, Boris Yeltsin, chose the path of radical "marketizing" reform and a core group of young, politically inexperienced, economists to guide post-Soviet Russia along that path. Driven by a sense of urgency, an aura of impending doom, they undertook truly radical measures to try to implant the seeds of a market economy into the inhospitable post-Soviet institutional soil.[4]

The story of the fate of this "big bang" reform has been often and well told.[5]   Price and enterprise liberalization, and the removal of controlling state bodies, were necessary to allow markets to form and develop; monetary stabilization and fiscal restraint were necessary if prices were to convey meaningful information for market-oriented decisions; and privatization was to provide high powered incentives to exercise new freedoms and respond to those market incentives in a manner that would maximize social economic wealth. And indeed, new markets arose, many new enterprises formed and appeared to operate, and new concentrations of private wealth appeared. Further, new regulatory organizations and institutions developed, often with substantial assistance from Western advisors, creating some of the regulatory and intermediating infrastructure on which well functioning market economies rely.

Yet underneath this flurry of change, much of the Russian economy, indeed most of its economic agents, remained in patterns of activity and interaction that they had inherited from the Soviet economic system, striving to merely survive in an environment of institutional chaos and economic collapse. The old, highly centralized order had broken down, and new, localized orders arose, focussed on maintaining familiar activities and relations to the extent possible, with leaders seizing "as much autonomy" and indeed sovereignty, as they could.

The empire had fallen, the center disintegrated, and effective sovereignty was rapidly parcelled out among those willing to seize it, particularly strong regional and local leaders. Local political structures stepped into directive economic roles abandoned by the central political and economic authorities, protecting their economic constituents, supporters and friends, and shutting out others who might pose a threat to their position and well being.[6] Old economic ties were explicitly resurrected and maintained, while new activities and arrangements, unless by a trusted insider, were resisted and blocked where possible. A defensive contraction, a reliance on personal political and business ties, a striving for autarky in essentials, and a focus on accumulating mobile (fungible) rather than fixed, productive wealth seems to characterize the economic activity and policy across many of these regions and "autonomies".

Thus, despite substantial and real change, the Russian economic system is one that is neither 'command' nor fully 'market'. For all the amazing changes, the 'liberalizations', 'stabilizations', and 'privatizations' that comprise the Russian process of 'marketization', substantial legacies of the Soviet period live on, melding with and mutating the new policies and institutions of 'transition Russia' to the point where the currently functioning economic institutions and structures often bear little resemblance to those of a modern market economy. The result seems to be a highly politicized hybrid of market- and administered-economy structures, of centralized pretense and decentralized power, of virtual production and actual decay, behind a commonly accepted pretext of "transition to a modern market economy".

In this essay I would like to explore the nature of this hybrid economic system and the question of whether it is best considered a variant of a market economic system. I begin in the next section with a summary of what I see to be the core, unifying characteristics of a market economic system, and outline how the Russian economy seems to deviate in essential ways. In Section III I propose a "feudal" paradigm for understanding the structure of economic interaction in Russia, and discuss its 'fit' to what we know about the Russian economy. Finally, I conclude with a discussion of how the "feudal" paradigm frames the discussion of potential paths of future development of the Russian economy, and how the apparent policies of Vladimir Vladimirovich Putin are apt to influence that development.

The Objective: A Modern Market Economy

Despite numerous variations in institutional structure and organizational form, all tolerably functioning modern market economies are essentially identical in their core institutions and operating principles - the essential general characteristics that identify them as true "market economies". At the heart of a market economy is a vast, continually adjusting and changing, complex set of interdependent markets.[7] These markets provide not only fora for interaction, but also the foci for economic decision making and behavior as the primary sources of both critical information and incentives. Despite varying degrees of political intervention and social constraint on their operation, these markets, and the agents who operate on them and respond to their signals, are substantially autonomous and not subject to direction or dictate by social or political 'superiors'. Rather, they comprise complex, flexible and continually changing networks of horizontal interaction in the pursuit of economic advantage and/or loss avoidance, reflected in flexible and continually changing patterns of business and industrial organization through entry, exit, mergers, acquisitions, divestitures, and bankruptcies.[8] Thus a market system is built around a thoroughly decentralized, non-hierarchical structure of interaction of independent economic agents.

The proper functioning of the complex interactive system that comprises a market economy requires the effective realization of a number of core "principles of the market". The first and foremost of these is "voluntary exchange" and voluntary participation in the system; agents cannot be compelled to participate in an activity or exchange, or be arbitrarily excluded when they agree to mutually acceptable terms of participation. This implies a general freedom of entry, exit, entrepreneurship and activity, the ability to experiment, and the freedom to succeed or fail in economic terms only. In a modern market economy, these rights and freedoms are enshrined in well-defined, uniformly, impartially and effectively enforced (predominately private) property rights, including the sanctity, protection and enforcement of (legal) private economic arrangements and contracts. For markets to operate effectively, political and social constraints on economic activity must be impersonal, transparent and universally applied, providing a stable, impartial framework for economic calculation and activity. Thus effective property and contract rights rely on uniform, transparent, and impartially enforced laws and legal norms.

A third core characteristic of a complex, modern market system is the existence of an effective, universal, depersonalized "value-equivalent" - a real money. This allows for effective economic calculation in the face of complexity, the minimization of transaction and coordination costs of complex exchange arrangements, and the effective implementation of complex intertemporal exchange and transfer of economic value. It also allows for effective, but non-disruptive of markets, social and/or political intervention/direction of market activity through monetary allocations and budgets, and similarly for internal budgetary coordination and control of complex economic organizations. Finally, it provides the foundation for a further essential characteristic of properly functioning markets: an elaborate, interdependent system of flexible prices, responsive to market pressures. Such prices, and more particularly their continual changes, aggregate the vast, changing and disparate information of all the participants in the market system, providing critical informational signals for the coordination and development of economic activity. It is the self-interested response of economic agents, both to these signals and to social and private information about alternative dangers and opportunities, that drives market outcomes and the continual change that characterizes a properly functioning market system.

The resulting dynamic has no overall direction or goals, but arises largely spontaneously from the continual experimentation and probing of opportunity, the both anticipated and unanticipated gains and losses, and the continual creation and destruction that comprise the essence of market economic activity. Hence, at a high level of generality, we might characterize a market economy as one with uncertain fates and outcomes, but certain institutions and procedures.

How "Market" is the Russian Economy?

The hallmark of the Soviet economic system was a near complete hierarchical structuring of control over economic activity, with a pretense of ultimate central control over all that was, or was not, done. This was facilitated by hierarchically structured centralized planning, and direct administration of economic activity and interaction in an essentially demonetized environment without property rights, where 'law' was the discretion of political and/or administrative superiors.[9] "Markets" and "contracts" were administratively controlled tools of plan implementation, agent autonomy was restricted to the (relatively fine) details of implementation, and 'money' (outside of personal transactions) could only legitimately be used in amounts and for purposes specifically authorized by superior organs. This system embodied in most respects the antithesis of a market economy, and it was that antithesis that was attacked by the reform triple of "liberalization", monetary "stabilization", and "corporatization / privatization".

The result has been a phenomenal change in the economic system. There is no longer any attempt at ex-ante central coordination (planning) or centralized administration of the economy. Most Soviet hierarchical structures controlling economic activity have been eliminated and control over economic activity has devolved to formerly implementing agents. Substantial "destatization" and privatization of both economic and political activities, decentralization of economic authority and control, and initial monetization of most economic activity and interaction, have taken place, and many new economic actors and activities have appeared. Thus there has been a substantial liberalization of economic activity and interaction, coupled with a dramatic political decentralization in the introduction of more pluralistic, democratic forms of political legitimation and governance. In the collapse of Soviet institutions, most assets, both economic and political, were "privatized" reuniting operational control and cash flow rights.[10] As a result there was an apparent flowering of new economic entities and activities, many however only nominally different from a Soviet predecessor, and a continuing diminution of levels of activity in entities, particularly industrial, inherited from the Soviet period. Among the new entities is a small but growing set of successfully restructured and new business operations, supporting a new middle class of business and technical professionals.[11]

This has dramatically reduced the ability of central authorities to influence economic activity and outcomes. Perhaps the most significant remaining central economic instruments are monetary and fiscal policy, made relevant by the 'monetization' of the economy, unifying the ruble and its exchange rates. A new constitution and civil code are in place, with many new market-tolerant laws and regulatory institutions established.[12] And a new set of laws and presidential decrees, including new criminal and civil codes have been promulgated to provide the legal framework for a more decentralized, substantially privately owned and operated, and hopefully market-based, economy.[13]

As a result many real markets have developed, including those for new financial, wholesale and retail activities, and commerce and trading are ubiquitous.

Now, in most spheres, money truly matters! Indeed, 'marketization' seems to have moved beyond economic goods and services and into the political and judicial spheres: almost anything can be bought and/or sold. Thus the Russian economy has, on the surface, all of the trappings and institutions of a market system, and is accepted as such by most observers.

This new Russian economic system was not, however built on a *tabula rasa*. While new laws and institutions have been created, they have been built on, and have derived much of their substantive content, from prior Soviet institutions, traditions, and understandings. Indeed, their roots in many cases go back further to Russian traditional and Imperial understandings.[14] More than the vestiges of the command economy have survived in the form of the industrial and political elites, patterns of behavior and interaction, and even in renamed organizations and activities.

Many of the old subhierarchies of the Soviet administrative economic structure remain in place, if often with new organizational names. For example, *Gazprom, UES, Transneft, Roskhleb,* and *Roskontrakt* merely replaced Ministerial organs with similar functions, most of the larger banks are successors to, or spin-offs from, the five Soviet *Spetsbanki,* and most intermediate product and wholesale trade remains monopolized by the offshoots of Soviet internal trade organs. The major industrial producers such as *AlRosa, Uralmash, Magnitka, Severostal', Norilsk Nikel, Novolipetsk Metallurgical,* etc., remain in place as all-encompassing socio-political and economic structures dominating their regions. And where industrial groupings were broken up with the dissolution of the Soviet Ministry, there have been trends toward mergers and amalgamations recreating structures similar to that of the previous Ministry.[15] Further, regional and local administrations have seized powers of regulation and control no longer exercised by central organs in the attempt to maintain inherited economic operations and "protect" the local population, and themselves in particular, from economic change.

Among the inherited structural legacies are vertically integrated industrial networks, monopolized intermediation in wholesale trade, transportation, and banking, and regional and local dependence on single enterprises and/or industries. These are clearly reflected in the so-called "natural monopolies", informal and formal FIG's (Financial-Industrial Groups), and the cities and enterprises of the military-industrial complex.[16] This has preserved both the lower administrative and economic structures of the hierarchical Soviet system, and the power and influence of those who manage them. Thus the old political elites, and enterprise and farm managements, have largely succeeded in entrenching themselves in both "new" and surviving economic and political organizations, albeit with substantial turnover toward younger cadre. They have been joined by a small group of new elite that was able to seize wealth and control of assets in the early 'wild' period of 1989-1993.[17]

But the primary legacies have been in behavioral patterns, in attitudes and understandings of the economic environment. Together with the old elites, old Soviet patterns of interaction have survived. In the struggle for survival, industrial enterprises rely on traditional partners and trade in customary products through networks that have also survived from the Soviet era. Much of this trade is in "soft goods", unsalable in open markets at a price above cost, yet usable by the obsolete technologies built into these Soviet enterprises. Hence this trade is to a growing extent in barter and non-monetary terms, returning to largely demonetized Soviet interaction.[18] Soviet behaviors survive in the paternalistic, control oriented, and self-serving attitude of the industrial elite; prestige, power and social obligation motivate enterprise management, rather than the pursuit of the creation of economic value (profit).[19] This includes the maintenance of status, the fulfillment of 'social obligation to workers', and resistance to uncontrolled "new", and hence disruptive, initiative and economic activity, unless initiated by one of "ones own".

We see regional governors arrogating to themselves the well understood powers of a Party First Secretary, and a continual striving (fetish) by members of the elite for regulation and control of all activity in one's 'domain', be it an administrative region, a branch of the economy or a group of enterprises. We see this also in the attitudes of local and regional governments toward new initiatives, inherently disruptive of existing order, and toward "unauthorized" activities. Licensing and regulatory restrictions stifle new business initiatives, unless initiated by an elite 'insider', and existing small and medium business is looked on as a source of continuing "rents" to be extracted through micro-regulation of activity, multiple fees, and creative taxation by local and regional elites.[20] Finally, there is the all-too-Soviet attitude that "everything is allowed" to sufficiently important people, and if you are not "important" then anything can be done to you (*bespredel'!*).

Further, a whole series of institutions and institutional arrangements inimical to the proper functioning of markets have survived from the Soviet period or grown on the rubble of destroyed Soviet institutions. Thus we see an absence of uniform, transparent, enforceable legal norms, and a lack of effective juridical institutions to enforce them, rendering contracts and their enforcement questionable. Property rights are diffuse, ill-defined, and often unenforceable (except by private means) against numerous stakeholders.[21] This is reflective of a general collapse of essential state functions, in particular the regular provision of social services and public goods, in part from their "privatization".

The provision of order, the enforcement of law and contract, and the provision of general public goods have been made subject to the discretion of agents who primarily pursue their private interests through the exercise of state functions and powers. Thus these functions, as well as the interpretation and enforcement of judicial norms and processes and the exercise of police power and use of force, have been arrogated by surviving subhierarchies and new "extra-legal" formations, sometimes collectively called the "mafia's".[22] Taxation is used more as a means of control and surplus extraction than as a source of public finance, and corruption is ubiquitous at all levels of the political hierarchy.[23] Further, resources and funds are allocated and spent largely at the discretion of industrial, agricultural, and local/regional bosses. These bosses typically exhibit behavioral patterns, mentioned above, that are destructive of the private property-based "equivalence of value in exchange" so essential to the proper functioning of markets. Finally, we see the norm of "non-payment" practiced by both large firms and governments at all levels; money is power, is scarce, and is only to be given up when there is no alternative. Only those without power must always pay, as only they can be deprived, or punished, for not paying.

There is a further critical attitudinal legacy that cripples the functioning of markets: the general belief in the irrelevance of finance for real economic activity. An important or desired activity must be carried out regardless of the availability of financing.[24] Payment reflects a personal or political obligation, rather than a legal or economic necessity. While sufficient money can buy anything, the lack of ability to pay, to generate revenue, is no reason to stop or avoid an activity. Hence economic relations remain substantially "personalized", relying on connections and influence rather than the opportunity for the creation of economic value, making 'who you are' more important than 'what you can do'. Money, in sufficiently large quantities, is sufficient to get outcomes, yet it is often not necessary, indicating a serious incompleteness in the monetization of the economy. Instead, traditional patterns of interindustry trade and industrial employment are maintained, activities are performed in support (at the request) of local and regional governments, and social services and public works provided, all without necessary payment.

It is worth noting that many these anti-market legacies have been recognized as such by the Putin economic team, and some vigorous measures have been instituted to alter them. As discussed below, the central state is vigorously reasserting its political and judicial authority in many areas, rebuilding social service and public good provision, meeting its financial obligations and demanding that others do the same, and attacking excessive bureaucratization at all levels.[25] Coupled with the new opportunities resources opened by the revival of economic activity in 1999-2001, these policies may indicate the beginning of the end to anti-market legacies of the command economy.

"Industrial Feudalism" as a Model

The ways in which the Russian economy has deviated from a market model appear to go far beyond variations between, for example, "East Asian" and "Anglo-Saxon" capitalism, touching on the very foundations of a market system. Indeed, despite the presence and operation of many markets, the structure, institutions (broadly conceived), and functioning of the Russian economy at the end of the 1990s seem to more closely resemble those of pre-modern social organization. Despite massive prior (indeed, hyper-) industrialization, the social, political and economic structures and institutions appear as, if not more, closely related to those of medieval Europe, to a form of "feudal" economic organization. Because of vast differences in technologies, and the social predominance of industrial rather than agricultural economic activity, I will call the new form of economic structures and organization an "industrial feudalism".

The traditional feudal economic system might be characterized as follows:[26]

- it arises as the result of decentralized self-organization in the wake of the collapse of a comprehensive social and political order;
- it has a hierarchical social and moral order, legitimizing rule by the elite; that legitimacy is traditional/inherited, based on social role and service, giving control/authority over a personal domain;
- there are multiple decentralized, hierarchical structures of information and authority, including juridical (the interpretation and enforcement of laws) - the "parcelization of sovereignty";[27]
- there is a weak center, with strong local authorities, each exercising authority over limited domains;
- personalized authority and discretion are dominant, limited only by power of superiors and traditional constraints;
- there is a lack of differentiation of economic, social, and political roles, and no separation of public and private roles and incomes;
- interaction is based on traditional patterns of coordination and control through overlapping networks of fealty and obligation;
- there is an absence of factor markets, with product markets at the "margins", regulated and/or monopolized where possible by the local authorities;
- property and contract rights are diffuse and traditionally circumscribed; every "property" has multiple "stakeholders" with traditional rights and privileges, with enforcement depending on the power of the stakeholder;
- non-economic motivations predominate, even in ostensibly economic activities: wealth is acquired, largely through transfer and seizure rather than investment and growth, for the power it gives over people;
- power is based on legitimacy, the strength of personal networks, and the ability to mobilize a surplus of both wealth and manpower from ones domain; control over the primary capital asset (land) as the material source of power and wealth.

These characteristics, after adjusting for the different technological and ideological/moral bases of society, comprise the structural foundation of any economic and social order that one might call "feudal". Most of these characteristics stand in substantial opposition to essential aspects of a properly functioning modern market economic system characterized above.

Although substantially decentralized and self-organizing, a market system is non-hierarchical and functions within an established political and legal framework providing "rules of the game" constraining behavior regardless of the political or social position of the agent. In a market economy, "sovereignty" resides in an autonomous state outside, and in some respects - above, the market system, rather than being "parcelized" among various political and economic actors. There is a clear separation of political and economic roles, of the public and private spheres, with rules and limits applicable equally to all regardless of rank or status. Similarly, property and contractual rights in a market system are clearly defined and socially protected, regardless of the status of the agent.

Interaction and networks are thus primarily based on the perception of opportunity and mutual benefit from cooperation and/or exchange, and are perpetually changing in pursuit of new opportunity and/or cost avoidance. Ties are contractual, specific, and subject to voluntary renegotiation and third-party enforcement, rather than traditional, general, and based of moral commitment and obligation. And incentives derive from the rewards to meeting the needs and desires of other market participants, to creating new products, services and wealth. Hence, investment in the pursuit of opportunity and of the wealth to develop further opportunities is a primary reflection of market economic motivation. In a market economy, economic power is clearly differentiated from political power and/or political/moral authority, and is based on success on markets rather than social or political legitimacy and power.

Thus the "modern" characteristics of a market system stand in sharp contrast to those of a "feudal" system. They lie behind the growth of active, complex systems of factor, product, service, and financial markets, operating independently of direct political/social controls, that are at the heart of a market economic system and provide the basis for investment and economic growth. In Russia, however, we see neither the deep structural characteristics of a modern market economy, nor the functioning of an integrated system of complex markets fostering investment and growth. Rather, "feudal" characteristics seem to be developing, without the foundation in agriculture and the restraining influence of a Church and its moral code, in the post-Soviet Russian industrial economy. Despite dramatic differences in technologies and capabilities for communication, for information processing, and for control of economic activity, a feudal "parcelization of sovereignty", a devolution of economic activity to quasi-autarchic networks, a fragmentation of markets, and a personalization of rule and interregional interaction seem to have taken hold, although it may now be challenged by the new regime of Vladimir Putin.

The Russian Economic System in the Late 1990s

When looking at the Russian economic system over the last decade, four general systemic characteristics stand out: (1) the primacy of political agents in economic decision making; (2) the dis-integration of the state; (3) a fragmentary market structure; and, (4) widespread market non-viability of economic organizations and institutions. These characteristics comprise a large part of the basis for characterizing the system as "feudal".

1. Conflation of Politics and Economics

A primary observation on the first characteristic is that we see far less separation between political and economic agents in Russia than in a typical market economy, where relations are intermediated by law and law-structured markets. The leading institutions of the Russian economic system are largely political, although social, political and economic roles and functions are not clearly separated/distinguished in practice.[28] There is a tendency at all levels to look to governments, with their ability to command resource flows, for direction, support and the solution of economic problems. And there is a tendency for governments to look to business (industrial, commercial and financial) organizations for direct access to the resources needed to maintain their power and control.

Decentralization has left a strong symbiosis between major businesses and local and regional governments, reflecting a continuation of the Soviet ties between political organs (LPO's) and the economic units on their territory.[29] This symbiosis is particularly facilitated by the fact that many of the same people who had been more junior in the same Soviet structures (*nomenklatura*) have now moved up to controlling positions while maintaining their old contacts. Thus the leaders of 'business' operations play a substantial role in the political life of their regions/cities, while mayors and governors strive to 'manage' their local economies and business activities, particularly in the face of the radical uncertainties of this transition period.[30]

This has created political-economic networks with a loose hierarchical structure subordinate to the most important leader involved, be he politician or businessman.[31] Increasingly, local and regional governments take actions to "manage" the economy of their region, protecting enterprises from outside (and new inside) competition and supporting them directly so that they might continue to supply valuable social services and jobs for the population, and political favors and support to the elite of the region. This has involved control of much of the "privatization" process of industrial, agricultural and commercial enterprises, and in particular, control over the use and privatization of land and other real estate.[32] It is this control over real estate that provides the source of much of the wealth and power of local and regional governments.[33]

Further, we see the creative use and acceptance of payment and wage arrears, local script, *vekseli,* and tax offsets in order to maintain some semblance of operation of enterprises and public/social services, and to maintain political leverage over businesses.[34] A growing number of regional and municipal governments have been actively pursuing local "renationalizations" of major industrial operations on their territories, using tax arrears to seize equity through offsets or the threat of bankruptcy. They have taken formal ownership of struggling enterprises, subsidizing them in return for equity and the appearance of "doing something" to maintain standards of living, and hence political support.[35] Many have imposed restrictions and licensing requirements on trade (movement of goods) across local/regional political boundaries, particularly in the wake of the financial crisis of August 1998.[36]

And many regions have initiated their own credit, money and foreign economic policies, including efforts to attract foreign credit and investment and barter deals with other regions of the Russian Federation, although the Putin government is taking steps to put an end to this.[37]

This politicization of economic decision making and the weakness of the state are reflected in the lack of clear separation between the public and private spheres. Corruption, defined as the use of public position and resources for private gain, is pervasive and ubiquitous, with official position exploited for immediate reward. Activities which generate a net positive cash flow or other surplus are treated as contributing to the private account, while those generating losses are treated as public, deserving of social support and subsidization. This is all the more the case when economic managers become political leaders, and politicians and governments become shareholders in businesses.

Further, in this environment non-economic objectives come to lie behind most economic decisions, as industrial firm and agricultural collective managements strive to maintain personal power, control, and prestige together with traditional social services and jobs, whatever the economic costs. Firms and farms thus remain self-contained social and political, as well as economic, organisms, much like the medieval manor. This situation is reinforced by the lack of effective property rights, undercutting any attempt to establish effective corporate governance or outside ownership. Property is viewed as power, prestige and guaranteed jobs, to be jealously guarded, rather than a tradeable source of wealth creation.[38] This attitude is reinforced by the rapacious, rent extracting, behavior of government agents at all levels, leading to non-transparent and extra-legal acquisition and use of property, and the resort to extra-legal enforcement and adjudication mechanisms. Such behaviors seem sufficiently common to be considered a defining characteristic of the Russian economic system.

2. Dis-Integration of the State

Among the consequences of this politicization of economic decision making have been serious conflicts over economic policy, which is far more tightly tied to issues of political power and even survival than it would be in a properly functioning market economy.[39] We saw this in the continuing conflict between the legislative and executive branches of the central government, and between the central executive organs and the regions, over issues of macroeconomic policy and of institutional/structural reform/change. Tax policy, revenue allocation, budgetary priorities, and even monetary policy have been disrupted by conflict among various governmental bodies. This has resulted in a plethora of conflicting laws, decrees and administrative rulings, and numerous frequently ignored judicial interventions, as each governmental body exercises what influence it can over those domains where it can.[40] Thus Federal law can be flouted even at the very center, where Moscow, for example, is 'illegally' maintaining passport restrictions on movement and residence. Local leaders can and do pick and choose what central laws to enforce and which to ignore, and impose their own legal and administrative frameworks, often borrowing from their Soviet past.[41] Thus there have arisen in every arena particularist zones of jurisdiction with overlapping boundaries and no universal center of competence or appeal, a true "parcelization of sovereignty" among political-economic units. This characteristic is now under serious attack by the Putin regime, one of whose first acts was a comprehensive administrative reform weakening the regional leaders and tightening Federal control over administrative and tax bodies in the regions.

These conflicts pointed to a substantial dis-integration of the state, with its attendant loss of legitimacy and power, albeit without dissolution of the political union, the Russian Federation. Regional and local governments, and even large production organizations, have effectively arrogated to themselves many of the functions of the state. The provision of law, order and justice, the police function of the state, had become and to some extent remains particular to regions, cities or even smaller collective entities, and has also to some extent been "privatized" to non-governmental (e.g. security firms) and/or criminal (e.g. *"vory v zakone"*) organizations. Thus, as Shlapentokh (1996) argues, every organization and activity, from the Federal level to street sellers, has to find a *"Krysha"* - a protective cover. Property is protected, and order maintained, more by organizational and private security forces than by the police, at least in their official capacity.[42] The amounts of revenue collected, public and private goods provided, and incomes generated in a region depend more on deals cut between local/regional business and political elites, than on any formal laws or market activity. And prior to the boom of 2000-1, these arrangements also appeared to be decisive for the revenue that the central government can collect through taxation.[43] The current economic expansion and its associated improvement in the liquidity position of most economic agents, together with recent tax reforms, have dramatically improved tax collections, reducing the influence of special deals and providing the appearance on normal state functioning. However, a question remains as to whether this will survive a deterioration in the economic situation.

Only with respect to monetary policy, financial market regulation, and the maintenance of strategic and elite military forces did the central government seem to be effective in this period. It, however, had ambitions that went far beyond this in pretending to support education, research, health, numerous social services, a large military establishment, and a large industrial manufacturing sector with substantial investment needs. Yet it's tax system and economic base were unable to support these ambitions, leading both to the use of extraordinary measures to capture surplus, and to growing tax evasion and 'demonetization' of any produced surpluses, and the devolution of responsibilities and objectives to lower governmental levels and to large production organizations.[44] This only strengthened the social and political autonomy of these entities, further dividing sovereignty and weakening the state. Regional and local governments regularly use assigned Federal funds, when they arrive, for purposes that they find more important than those for which the Federal government assigned them. Thus pension and social sector wage arrears payments apparently have been often diverted to support "important" local industry or to pay for inputs such as electric energy and/or oil for the region.[45]

3. Fragmentary Market Structure

These characteristics complement a further defining characteristic of the Russian economic system - a fragmentary market structure, reflecting more inherited ("traditional") relations than economic opportunity. Much, perhaps most, economic interaction remains traditionally structured, with markets appearing to work most and best in those areas where either Soviet market forms (consumer retailing and labor hiring), or no prior Soviet institutions (non-bank finance), operated. There are generally normally functioning markets for new financial instruments,[46] for simple products and commodities in retailing to final consumers, and for dealing with 'strong' outsiders, such as Western firms and trading organizations. Among the most highly developed are those for Western imported consumers' goods, food, and industrial final products, and for exported commodities such as raw materials, basic metals and chemicals, and energy products/carriers. But for most other economic interactions market forms are a superficial add-on to relations otherwise determined.

Most intermediate product and interindustry transactions in this period involved traditional, non-market exchange relations within networks that were largely inherited from the Soviet past. This is particularly true of "markets" for critical inputs, such as domestic energy and transportation, and for important assets where "privatization" generally involved predetermined transfers to "friends" and "insiders" with only a fig leaf of an auction or market sale.[47] Transfers of "property" are negotiated with important agents, reflecting more the correlation of political power than any market forces, and are arbitrarily imposed, by force if necessary, in the "unimportant" and on "weak" outsiders. This is reflected in the high degree of corruption and of involvement of criminal organizations in economic activity. The wholesaling and retailing of food products in particular is subject to extortion and monopolization by mafias and local political organs.[48]

Another related salient characteristic in this period was the "re-demonetization" of economic activity and interaction outside of retailing, finance, and foreign trade.[49] This involved a general "flight from the ruble" in both savings ("dollarization") and intermediation (barter), and in tax payments ("offsets"), particularly in the large enterprise sector.[50] It derived from a high degree of uncertainty with respect to both economic and political policy, the lack of legal protections ("rule of law") and property rights, the weaknesses and inefficiency of the banking system, and the rapacious nature of taxation, involving arbitrary and unpredictable confiscations unless the "right relations" are established with many different levels of authorities, both public and private.[51] Demonetization was particularly driven by the governments' Soviet-like use of banks as tax collectors and enforcers, giving economic agents a strong incentive to avoid the use of banks and money whenever possible. It also facilitated the maintenance of traditional (Soviet) networks and relations, as transactions can be arbitrarily and differently valued by different parties in the absence of a uniform currency measuring stick; it avoids the need for strict market "equivalence of value" in exchanges.

The Russian economic system is further characterized by the absence of effective factor markets. There is virtually no market for land or productive real estate, despite a constitutional right to such, as enabling legislation is locked up in political struggle.[52] While apartments and buildings can be bought and sold, and some land comes with the purchase of industrial plant, the purchase of land, and the conversion of non-industrial structures, as an input into new productive activity is generally not possible.

The capital market is also, although to a lesser extent, undeveloped. In the 1990s, investment capital was generally unavailable, as the budget was bankrupt, firms were unwilling to give up significant equity and control for outside investment, and the banking system was largely a mechanism for financing the state deficit through tax collection and the placement of government debt.[53] The banking system still generally fails to provide real intermediation, and provides investment funding only in limited amounts, for very limited periods, and only to those firms with fungible collateral or in which the bank has acquired a substantial ownership stake. The stock market is also largely a facade, allowing exchange of potential revenue shares but generating no new real investment or change in real ownership control. The need to finance a large budget deficit while preventing massive inflation, together with political and economic uncertainties, the lack of property and other legal protections, and the possibilities for harboring savings and wealth in dollars and/or abroad led to staggeringly high interest rates that would have cut off investment even if capital market structures were in place. Together with the absence of such structures, these factors insured that there was no real capital market. Finally, there is very little FDI due to uncertainties surrounding property rights, contract enforcement, and the legal and tax environment, as well as the negative impact of the August devaluation and default.[54]

Labor markets are similarly degenerate. While local labor markets are extremely free and flexible, the inherited Soviet industrial structure (see below) insures that local opportunities for labor redeployment are rather limited. Labor, while formally free to move, is tied to its (inherited) place of work by social services, including housing and medical care, provided by the enterprise, locally enforced residency and registration requirements, and growing wage arrears.[55] This tie is reinforced by the lack of any other, generalized social support mechanisms. Thus the labor market is localized, revolving around second jobs ("fiddling"), self-employment, and criminal activity.

The weakness of these critical factor markets is one of the primary reasons, together with the predatory behavior of political and criminal (mafia) authorities, for the lack of new entrepreneurship and small business growth in Russia. New enterprise is either controlled, or fought, by such "authorities".[56] Only if one has the right connections, is politically tied in, can one engage in new enterprise, in the "recombination of factors". Where pre-existing and politically powerful institutions/enterprises operate, it is extremely difficult to enter unless one has the political clout to take control of those institutions. Thus we see most successful new enterprise in areas where there were no, or only seriously underdeveloped, Soviet institutions - banking, finance, trade and services. And even here, control is rapidly asserted by local or regional "authorities", either official or criminal.

18 *Institutional Change in Transition Economies*

4. Wide-spread Market Non-Viability

As a consequence of these systemic characteristics, the Russian economy has preserved a large part the distorted structure of capital, production, and interaction that it inherited from the Soviet economic system. This is true despite substantial shifts in relative sectoral price and output levels; manufacturing and processing industries, agriculture and construction have shrunk, while extractive industries, communications, trade, and services - in particular financial - have expanded, with parallel movements in prices exaggerating the changes. Indeed, much of the apparent change in the structure of industry was due solely to price changes; the relative shares of the energy and raw material industries in 1995 were little different from their share Soviet shares in 1990, when those are measured in world market (rather than Soviet internal) prices.[57] These structural changes were largely completed by the end of 1995, at which point the features of this Russian economic system began to solidify. The result has been a structure of enterprises, capacities, and interactions that would not be viable in a market economic system; prior to devaluation and the dramatic increase in energy and resource prices, it was only sustainable as a "virtual economy" through the networks and behaviors discussed above.

The industrial base and network of interactions underlying the Russian economy was built over a period of more than 60 years in order to provide a specified bundle of goods and services deemed desirable by central planners and their subordinates in the industrial administrative hierarchy. While much effort was expended to maintain input-output consistency and balance in providing and expanding this configuration of outputs, there was virtually no consideration of economic valuation, opportunity cost or scarcity rents in determining the structure and level of economic activity. Prices were largely only accounting conveniences, allowing aggregation for incentive, measurement and control purposes, and were not supposed to have an independent influence on economic decisions in the state sector.[58] Prices/valuations were further distorted by ideology and arbitrary priorities; land and capital were virtually free, labor remunerated according to administrative priority categories generally independent of value produced, and inputs were priced to be low, often below even planned 'cost', for priority sectors and users, and high for use in consumers' goods industries and other final uses. Economic activity and interaction took place by virtue of commands from superior organs, independent of any costs or benefits to the parties involved; losses measured in monetary terms were fully subsidized while gains/profits were confiscated into the budget.

Thus economic interaction in the state sector was effectively demonetized, and there was no need for any equivalence in exchange. Cost was not allowed to interfere with priorities and arbitrary costs could be recovered from arbitrary pricing to users, particularly those not enjoying a special priority. This led to hypertrophic development of the priority sectors of heavy, resource and military industry, and inevitable endemic waste and inefficiency in these industries. That inefficiency, the non-viability of most of these industrial structures, was inherited by Russian firms and became obvious in the wake of the liberalization of prices and trade in the early 1990s. Few of these firms have the technology or the organizational and administrative capability to survive in a competitive market environment, as few can produce output at a cost, now determined by market pricing of material inputs and factors, below what the market will pay for their product.

These enterprises have also inherited a social structure far different from that of a modern market-oriented enterprise. Soviet enterprises were complete, and relatively closed, social entities, encompassing the political, economic and social life of all employees. Large industrial enterprises provided virtually all social services and activities, including housing, education and medical services, recreational and leisure activities, a job and access to consumer goods and services, and political life through the Union and primary Party organization at the place of work.[59] As with most other administration in the Soviet Union, management was personalized, with higher management dealing with superior structures outside the firm and passing down objectives and generalized assignments, while "masters" among the workers organized and controlled the flow of production and other economic activity in the firm. The result was a tradition-bound, rather rigid and inflexible structure, capable of responding to planning priorities and changes in overall physical targets of its traditional activities and/or products, but not to new requirements of technology and inputs, or to changes in sources of inputs or users' requirements of its output. This vastly increased the difficulties that enterprises faced when the planning and control superstructure of the Soviet economy collapsed; they were largely incapable of dealing with the new, rapidly changing and radically uncertain economic environment.

These structural characteristics indicate that Russian enterprises, in order to become viable firms in a market economy, must undergo a radical restructuring, a massive change in technologies, capital base, market interactions, administrative structure and social relations within the firm. But precisely what changes are needed to make the firm viable cannot be known in advance, particularly as the entire economic system is undergoing massive transformation. Hence these changes must take place in the face of unprecedented uncertainty and the real risk of catastrophic failure, providing Russian enterprises with strong incentives to look for other ways to survive.

One of the predominant survival techniques has been the escape to the "virtual economy" discussed in Gaddy and Ickes (1998, 1999). This has allowed Russian enterprises to avoid most wrenching changes in internal structure, their interactions with other economic and political agents, and the nature of the economic activity pursued by the firm. The firm can survive, like the medieval manor, as the center of life for its remaining employees, trading "soft goods" without the necessity of strict "equivalence of value", for the inputs necessary to maintain some semblance of productive activity, while absorbing subsidies in the form of tax offsets, the use of *vekseli*, and growing payments arrears.[60] The labor force that remains is tied to the enterprise by services still provided, by the ability to use unpaid wages to offset "overpriced" purchases in enterprise shops, by the hope of eventually recovering wages in arrears, and by the lack of better alternatives outside the enterprise. Thus there has developed a hierarchical network of strong mutual dependence - among firms in the "virtual economy"; between firms and the local/regional governmental organs that allow arrears and offsets to be used; and between firms and their dependent employees.

Russia as a "Feudal" System

The characteristics that we have indicated as central to the 1990s Russian economic system cast doubt on the claim that it was (or now is) a *market system*. For markets, market motivations, financial constraints, and the ability to cover costs and produce value at market prices are the essence of any *system* that can claim to be market based and driven. Rather we seem to see an economy whose characteristics have a number of striking parallels in the medieval feudal economy, outlined above, even if the identification is far from exact.

At the base of this system are industrial, agricultural and construction enterprises, whether privatized or not, regional and local governments, and some of the more important, as they are politically connected, new commercial and financial structures (FIG's). Most of these organizations are legitimated by tradition, having been derived from Soviet economic/political entities or built on connections from that period, and many of the new commercial and financial structures have acquired the status of the industrial enterprises over which they have taken control.[61] In addition, new forms of legitimation have arisen through elections and the mass media, but these are tightly controlled by an elite derived largely from the Soviet *nomenklatura*. Like the blessing of the medieval church, elections seem increasing a legitimizing formalism, as manipulation by the leadership, together with its control of the media, remove the possibility of any change in power.[62]

As we have argued, the Russian economic system in the 1990s was characterized by weak central authority, with strong regional, local and industrial/financial leaderships, each exercising authority over particular, limited domains, although those domains are less territorially, and more functionally, defined.[63] As with the European feudal economies, there seemed to be multiple, decentralized hierarchical structures exercising political, economic and juridical authority over their own domains. Personalized power was exercised through overlapping networks of personal ties and obligations, replicating to a large extent Soviet/traditional patterns of coordination and control.

Markets and market relations, even if more important than in medieval Europe, seem predominant only in dealing with strong outsiders, e.g. foreign firms and markets, and in areas outside the core interests of the major institutions surviving from the Soviet era; even there, markets are locally regulated or monopolized where possible, often by informal, extralegal organizations. And, as under feudalism, property and contract rights were diffuse, circumscribed by Soviet "tradition", and encumbered by conflicting claims of multiple stakeholders, rendering them unenforceable through regular legal channels. Hence there was, as in medieval Europe, very little investment beyond that required to maintain current, reduced levels of activity.[64] Finally, the sources of political and economic power were localized and relational, unencumbered by moral or overarching institutional constraint.

In this light, Yeltsin's Presidency appears as a weak crown, surrounded by courtiers whose power and influence depended on their relation to the President and connections to, and/or control over, powerful other institutions. The upper house of the legislature, the Federation Council, appears as a chamber of regional "lords" interested in protecting their domains more than the integrity of the Russian state. The *Duma,* ineffective as a working legislature, was quite effective in representing its members' outside collective corporate and private interests in areas where the state still had influence, and in prying favors out of the government as well as blocking changes ("reforms") that might adversely affect those interests.

At the core of this economic system are agricultural districts with their large "collective" farm structures, some medium and large cities, and major enterprises (or FIG's) that appear as the "manors" and "estates" on which the feudal economy is built. These largely self-contained socio-political production entities maintain themselves in the virtual economy through barter and network exchange. They further depend on primitive production of food and primary goods and services by individuals (on private plots and in their homes) in small-scale economic activity, necessary to survival yet too unimportant to be controlled or shut down. This is a survival mode, capable of simple reproduction at current levels of activity, yet unable to invest or generate economic expansion.

Finally, there are some major companies, and regions with "reformist" policies, that fill the role of medieval towns in intermediating both among these entities and with the rest of the world, rather than the plethora of small flexible firms that one would expect in a market economy. Despite their substantial market activities and roles, these intermediaries must still fit into the economic and political networks of the Russian Federation as corporate entities, with personalized ties to the "lords and nobles" of the system.

Thus, the structure and functioning of this Russian economy seem to be inconsistent with a market system, despite the fact that, as Åslund (1995) demonstrates, the command economy has been destroyed. Despite radical decentralization, the lack of ex-ante planning and coordination, and the absence of vertical integration and control of information, markets cannot play the role that they must in a true market economy. Essential institutions for the proper functioning of markets and market relations are lacking, including: transparent, uniformly enforced laws, rules and regulations; enforcement of property rights; and contractual commitment with third party enforcement.

There is virtually no "complex market intermediation", but rather networks based on personal connections and mutual dependence. The domain of impersonal, horizontal relations, characterizing much market interaction, is severely restricted, and there is a lack of "equivalence in exchange" that is reflected in the non-uniformity and "personalization" of prices. depending on the status of, and relationship between, the agents. Factor markets are degenerate to nonexistent, and full market relations predominate only when dealing with foreigners and/or advanced/luxury products. Economic behavior is not oriented toward the creation of wealth and minimization of opportunity cost, but rather toward the redistribution of property, and the seizure of wealth for consumption and political power. Survival and autarchy have become primary objectives. Incentives beyond personal derive largely from your "network" or "clan", and stimulate supporting its organizations and leadership, not creating market value.

Future Path of Systemic Development?

These "feudal" characteristics, this configuration of institutions and behaviors, appeared at the end of the Yeltsin regime to be rather stable. Those with the ability, the power, to act appear to have incentives to maintain the current structures of wealth, influence and interaction, and to repress serious opposition to the system as it has developed. Both these "winners" in the post-Soviet transformation of Russia and the relatively powerless losers and "masses" face tremendous uncertainties, unknowns, in any further changes and have reasons to fear the consequences of further change.[65] In the absence of clearly articulated, compelling alternatives, the current "industrial feudalism" stage in the "transition to the market" might seem to provide a stable base for the future development of the economic system. Its characteristics frame future possibilities much as the nature of the Soviet system framed the initial stages of this great transformation.

Just as European feudalism provided the basis for the development of modern market economies, the current systemic configuration in Russia may just be a passing stage in the market-system transition process. Anderson (1974) has argued that feudalism provided fertile soil for the development of the authoritarian monarchies of the early modern period, which in turn provided the basis for the evolution of market-based constitutional monarchies and democracies. While that process took centuries during which appropriate market institutions and forms arose and evolved, a Russian institutional evolution could arguably occur much more quickly. For much of the experimentation and discovery that was needed the first time around need not be repeated; only experimentation to properly adjust the basic principles and necessary institutions to Russian historical and cultural circumstances needs to occur.

For this kind of experimentation and development, itself a market-like process, to occur, Russia must get beyond or around its current institutions that are inimical to markets. The kinds of changes required are precisely those determining the "feudal" nature of the present system, and thus will take time; their achievement will undoubtedly be an evolutionary process.

Perhaps most fundamental is the need to separate realms of activity and being in ways appropriate to market interaction. The symbiosis of political and economic, of public and private, roles and spheres must be broken, allowing a defragmentation of the market structure. New terms of interaction, separate in the political, economic and social spheres, need to arise. This will create space for independent legal structures to develop between agents and spheres, allowing the clear social definition, assignment and impartial protection of the rights of property and private contract and agreement. The rule of law, separate from the interests of rulers, governments, businesses or any specific individuals, is needed, not a dictatorship (of law or otherwise) enforced by an all-powerful state.

A single sovereign, outside and above spheres of ordinary economic, political and social interaction needs to arise as the sole legitimate protector of order and stability, helping to maintain the institutions and structures of market intermediation. And the society and polity need to come to accept both the necessity and the consequences of economic change, of unpredictable and uncontrollable success and, especially, failure of economic agents and activities. In particular, in view of the still strong legacies of the Soviet Union, the Russian state and society will have to allow the disappearance and replacement of much of the current economic structure, i.e. of economically non-viable organizations and firms.

Despite the size and difficulty of the task, there exist natural economic incentives pushing political and economic agents in this marketizing direction, and the Putin regime appears to be responding to these. These largely arise from competitive pressures both within Russia and from the outside world. The global economy and its agents can not be completely shut out or only given controlled contact and access. They will present both opportunities and challenges that are best dealt with, exploited, through market institutions and behaviors. There is also natural experimentation occurring across regions, introducing a competition in which the more market friendly and liberal should enjoy greater economic success: This will provide opportunities for useful learning, as well as attacking regional autarchy, as local agents find it easier to evade restrictions and take advantage of the opportunities in other regions and cities. Hence this will erode the ability, essential to the maintenance of the feudal structure, to ignore the economic "bottom line". Further, without a strong ideological foundation, the special treatment and privileges of the elite is apt to generate growing resistance, and to erode with the passing and replacement of its current membership, both from natural causes and the turnover associated with increasing true marketization. Finally, the generally recognized need for investment will add to these pressures, bringing changes in economic institutions and behaviors in order to provide better incentives for the attraction of needed capital. And the resulting changes should also help stimulate the development of active factor markets to facilitate the needed changes in the physical structure of production.

Of course, this optimistic scenario of the evolution of a market system from a feudal foundation is not inevitable. There are at least two other possibilities: the authoritarian mobilization state, and a stagnation or freeze in the evolution from the current system. The first requires a substantial strengthening of central control, the elimination of regional and local autonomy, and the tight regulation of all significant economic activity. It relies on a model of directive control which is instinctively understood and appreciated by the Russian elite, and indeed may turn out to be the approach being pursued by the Putin regime.[66] Markets and private property would be harnessed through tight political direction and control, making it a directed, developmental economy hoping to emulate the Prussian/German (19/20th Century) or Japanese and South Korean (mid-/late-20th Century) experiences. It would not attempt "re-Sovietization", eschewing Soviet totalitarian methods and allowing private activity and markets. But it would face the danger that the lingering Soviet mindset, to which it is so congenial, may obstruct the necessary development of sufficiently free and flexible markets for strong developmental growth to take place. And it would still face the nearly overwhelming task of replacing most of the existing structures of capital and production.

An equally plausible alternative to the evolution toward true modern market development, however, is that of the solidification and medium term survival of this "industrial feudalism". This is a scenario of stagnation in institutional evolution and development. It would involve a reaffirmation of the legitimacy of the hierarchical structure and subdivision of political and economic authority. It would be characterized by continuing regionalization, local control, and political mediation of economic activity, and a political compromise over sovereignty. Business activities, in particular the wealth generating "natural monopolies", would be (even if only implicitly) allocated to personal 'domains', including the federal ("crown") demense, and regulated in the "social interest". And democratic process is apt to devolve to a rather empty ritual, a pseudo-democracy, empty of surprise, that legitimizes the rule of an increasingly hereditary elite. Thus real decisions would be made in, and negotiated between 'lords' and 'clans' with separate, if sometimes overlapping, political and economic power bases. The masses would remain divided among, and dependent on, one or more of these "financial-industrial-political" groups. Hence factor markets would remain restricted and controlled, and access to the outside would occur through a hierarchical cascade from the top of one of the political-economic structures. In short, such an institutional freezing of the transformational processes in Russia might produce a stable industrial to post-industrial "feudalism" with relatively decentralized, politically directed investment and development. It is apt to grow relatively slowly, if surely, emphasizing security and order over economic growth. Such an institutionalized industrial feudalism might even prove as enduring as its Soviet predecessor, although history would still predict its eventual demise under economic pressure from both within and without.

At this juncture we now see a new, highly active President, Vladimir Vladimirovich Putin, moving to take control of this industrial feudal structure. First and foremost he has moved to reassert control over Federal structures at all levels of the hierarchy through streamlining and reorganization. In a 13 May 2000 decree, he established seven super regions each headed by a presidential representative ("Governor-General"), and then forced legislation through the Duma that gives him an enhanced right to dismiss elected governors for malfeasance. He has demanded that all courts be solely financed by the center, and has begun challenging the laws, decrees, and constitutions of the "subjects" of the Federation that conflict with Federal law or the Russian Federation Constitution.[67] In doing so, he is strongly reasserting the "executive vertical" control in the hierarchy.

These moves have been so far limited, only recently beginning to challenge, for example, Tatarstan whose laws most flagrantly violate the Constitution, but have gone to the heart of the problem of "parcelization of sovereignty". Putin has particularly attacked local and regional laws that impinge on the power of the center to control the regional/local offices of its administrations and agencies, to appoint or approve those bureaucrats, or to finance their operations. His moves have also been aimed at cutting direct foreign ties of subordinate entities, and their (self-proclaimed) powers to maintain foreign relations independent of the Federation. And he has reasserted the right of the Russian Supreme Court to rule on the constitutionality or illegality of regional constitutions and laws. But in all these reassertions of Federal sovereignty, Putin has gone out of his way to avoid alienating regional leaders and elites through bargaining and dialogue, eschewing populistic forms of mobilization and anti-elite rhetoric. Thus he has avoided, so far, outright opposition, although the regional response has been footdragging and some obstructionism.[68]

In these actions (and in his handling of the media), Putin is clearly showing his authoritarian lineage. He is streamling the hierarchical structure, but in ways that look as much feudal rather as "federal". He has accepted the fealty/homage of the regional "lords", but seems to be moving to eliminate those members of the elite, such as Gusinsky, who oppose him. He is enforcing central laws, challenging the sovereignty of the regions, but only, so far, in rather restricted ways - to maintain the "royal fisc", to control interaction with foreigners, and to enhance the power of his administrative and political controls over subordinates. Thus the strengthening center is still allowing arbitrary local/regional discretion and control over non-federal economic entities and (non-tax) activities on their territory. The "crown" is clearly strengthening, but it is unclear whether this is lessening the feudal nature of economic interaction and decision making. However, economic performance has improved dramatically, markets appear to be operating with growing influence and confidence, and investment has experienced a sharp revival, albeit still largely based on the retained earnings of the resource and energy sectors and not financial market intermediation.

Thus the future of the system is wide open. The generally liberal, market friendly, tax and spending plans that have been announced and passed so far, and the intention to strengthen the law and make its application uniform, seem to promise a further effort to move toward a modern market economy. But inherited "feudal" structures and obstacles still loom large. There is a need not only for a reassertion of central sovereignty, but also for a "Magna Carta" limiting the "crown" and asserting the basic economic and democratic rights on which a market system relies for its proper functioning. And these rights need to be further enforced against the very same lords and elites that win them from the crown. This indeed may be the direction in which the Putin regime is groping in its search for economic recovery and the revival of the Russian state. Yet it is also possible that the revival of the state and the reassertion of central control will become the overwhelming imperative, crowding out real efforts to open the economy to modern market evolution. Building on the existing "feudal" nature of economic relations and processes and on favorable world prices for Russian exports, that reassertion of the central state could lead to the reappearance of the post-feudal absolutist state, mercantilist in aspiration and *dirigiste* in operation, that Anderson (1974) studies. It would certainly, given available technologies, be industrial, make use of markets, and engage in the world economy, but would exercise substantial control over property, markets, investment, employment, and economic intermediation in the pursuit of the security of the state and regime. And it would only much more slowly evolve in the direction of a modern market economy, as did the absolutist states of early modern Europe.

Notes

[1] This has been a key theme in the critique of the so-called "Washington consensus", particularly by Joseph Stiglitz and some of his former colleagues at the World Bank. See Stiglitz and Ellerman (2000) and Stiglitz (1999). It is now a core assertion of the so-called "post-Washington consensus".

[2] For a clear and convincing discussion of the aims and motivations of the founding Bolsheviks, see Peter Boettke (1990).

[3] The critical economic characteristics, distinguishing the Soviet economic system from a market system, are outlined in Ericson (1991). A broader political and economic analysis of the nature and principles of operation of the Soviet-type system, emphasizing its totalitarian political roots, is J. Kornai (1992).

[4] The situation as perceived by the core decision makers, and their intentions, are best described in Gaidar's (1996) memoirs, the collection of analytic papers edited by Gaidar (1998), and the recent paper by Mau (2000).

[5] Among others see Åslund (1995), Lavigne (1999), etc.

[6] A nice discussion, particularly with respect to monetary policies, can be found in Woodruff (1999).

[7] I take the concept of a specific "market" as a primitive in this discussion, one whose meaning is intuitively clear to all.

[8] This tremendous flux and change in the American economy is described and analyzed in Davis and Haltiwanger (1996).

[9] See Kornai (1992) and Ericson (1991) for analysis of the Soviet-type economic system.

[10] These achievements are chronicled in many places, including Åslund (1995), Boycko, Shleifer and Vishny (1995), OECD (1995), and Blasi, Kroumova and Kruse (1997). Shlapentokh (1996) emphasizes the negative aspects of all-encompassing "privatization", including the public sphere and governmental functions.

[11] The many "business success stories" are at the heart of the optimism of economists like Peter Boone and Simon Johnson (1999) and political scientists like Thane Gustafson (1999). See Harley Balzer (1998) for an analysis of the new Russian bourgeoisie.

[12] Among these new regulatory bodies were a new Securities and Exchange Commission, a Commission for Real Estate Validation, a State Anti-Monopoly Committee, and a State Committee for the Development and Support of Small Business. See OECD (1997), Annex IV, pp. 200-23.

[13] These institutions are outlined in Gregory and Stuart (1998) and in OECD (1997). It is worth noting that new Land and Tax Codes, both critical to defining the powers of, and limitations on, governmental and administrative organs, were only enacted in 2001,

with much of the critical content of the Land Code left to the discretion of the regions. They indeed remain the subject of deep political struggle between the executive and legislative branches at the center and between regions and the center.

[14]   This is a point make strongly by, among others, Hedlund (1999).

[15]   In early 2000, Berezovsky and Abramovich cut a deal with Deripaska to unite almost all aluminum processing capacity in a single firm, *Rossiiskii Alyuminii,* that essentially recreates the core on the Soviet Ministry of Non-Ferric Metals *(Minsvetmet).* There have also been moves, although not as comprehensive, toward consolidating the oil industry, and calls for the renationalization and consolidation of all natural resource and energy based corporations. See, for example, A. Privalov, "O 'Russkom aliuminii' i rossiiskom pravosudii", *Ekspert,* #29, 13 August 2001; P. Starobin, C. Belton, "Russia's Big Get Bigger", *Business Week* (International Edition), 16 July 2001; S. Tavernise, "Quietly, a Russian Oil Producer Tries to Consolidate Its Holdings", *New York Times,* 18 May 2001.

[16]   The legacies of the military-industrial complex are nicely discussed in Gaddy (1996) and Zisk (1997). They can also be seen in the analyses of *ZATO's* (closed administrative-territorial formations), for example in Brock (1998, 2000).

[17]   These include the infamous "oligarchs", such as Berezovsky, Potanin and Gusinsky, with their new financial/media structures. See Aleksandrov (1996), Kryshtanovskaya (1997), Goldman (1998), and Aikman (1998) and for partial listings and discussion. For some recent updates, see G. Winestock, L. Bershidsky, "The Oligarchs: Who's Up, Who's Down", *Moscow Times,* 12 January 1999; E. Kraus, "The Autumn of the Oligarch - Lunch with Putin", *Moscow Times,* 3 August 2000; and "Putin's Secret Friends", *Moskovskii komsomolets,* 4 April 2001. The new elite arose from academic, criminal and Party circles by boldly taking advantage of opportunities, not always legal, that arose in the chaos created by *Perestroika* and the collapse of central authority and then of the Soviet Empire. These were largely opportunities for asset stripping and rent extraction through arbitrage against the irrational price system and the exploitation of special favors/licenses and subsidies from the marcescing state. Among the many sources telling these stories are Bunin (1994), Åslund (1995), Kranz (1997), Solnik (1998), and Khlebnikov (2000).

[18]   This is the foundation of the "virtual economy" indicated in the Karpov (1997) Report of the State Interdepartmental Balance Commission, and discussed in Gaddy and Ickes (1998, 1999). For an earlier analysis of this situation, see IET (1997).

[19]   This point is made in Blasi, et. al. (1997), and is also clear from the enterprise survey work of Linz and Krueger (1998), Linz (1997), Hendley (1998), Hendley, et. al. (1997), Ickes, Murrell, and Ryterman (1996), and Ryterman and Weber (1996).

[20]   See Frye and Shleifer (1997), Shleifer (1997), and Åslund (1997).

[21]   This is illustrated in most of the articles in Sachs and Pistor (1997).

[22]   This point is made in both Verdery (1996) and Shlapentokh (1996), and is again reflected in Sachs and Pistor (1997).

[23]   The prevalence of corruption has been widely discussed in the wake of the "Fimaco", "Mabetex" and "Bank of NY" money-laundering scandals of mid 1999. Articles discussing the state of Swiss, U.S. and / or Russian investigations can be found in virtually every issue of *The New York Times* and the *Wall Street Journal* from 10 to 24 September 1999. This is considered by most Russians to be just the "tip of the iceberg". For a recent clear statement of the problem, see L. Barinov, "More than just a crime", *Nezavisimaia gazeta,* 7 September 2001.

[24]   This applies, for example, to the work of public sector employees, the provision of

transportation services and energy, and the supply of military bases, all often without (sometimes even partial) payment.

25 For a clear statement of intentions, see Putin's 'State of the Nation' address to the Duma, 3 April 2001, available from the Russian press, 4 April 2001.

26 This list is a distillation of the essential characteristics of the European, and in particular English, feudal economy, derived from my reading of the literature, in particular Andersen (1974), Angressano (1996) chapter 4, Postan (1973, 1975), Pryor (1980), and Rader (1971).

27 This felicitous phrase is due to Anderson (1974).

28 This characteristic does not seem substantially affected by the new Putin regime.

29 The classic analysis of the economic roles of local Party organs (LPO's) in the Soviet Union is Hough (1969).

30 Åslund (1998), p. 319, has called this "… a negotiated economy with ample privilege for large and powerful enterprises regardless of their economic efficiency".

31 Many of these are loosely called Financial-Industrial Groups (FIG's), consisting of a network of related enterprises and their controlling or subordinate "pocket" bank(s). They include the financial empires of the so-called "oligarchs" [note 17 above]. For a clear discussion of the origin and varieties of FIG, see Johnson (1997).

32 Moscow, in a singular defeat for Chubias and the State Privatization Program, was able to take control over Federal as well as regional and local privatization within the city, with the explicit support of President Yeltsin for his friend, political supporter, and successor as mayor of Moscow, Yuri Luzhkov.

33 This point is well noted in Shleifer (1997).

34 The ability of governments to grant or withhold access to use of such instruments as a means of controlling business behavior, income and wealth is stressed by Latynina (1999).

35 Among other examples, Belgorod has taken over its iron ore combine, Sverdlovsk has taken a stake in Alkar Aluminum, Krasnoyarsk has bought into the Krasnoyarsky Metallurgichesky Zavod, Kursk has taken equity in Mikhailovsky Iron Works, the Moscow city government is buying into the local automobile firm, Tataria has bought into KamAz and Tatneft Oil, and Samara into AvtoVaz. See *Izvestiia,* 17 October 1997. More recently, the *Moscow Times* has reported the St. Petersburg and Sverdlovsk, among other regions, are taking controlling interests in their leading regional banks, and Sverdlovsk is planning to take a 25 per cent share in Nizhnii Tagil Metal in exchange for restructuring the company's tax and wage arrears (*RFE/RL Newsline,* 4 November 1998). The *EWI Regional Report,* vol. 4, has noted further takeovers in 1999 in Ul'ianovsk (#3), Krasnoyarsk (#4), Voronezh (#10), Moscow (#11, #14), Primorye (#13), Sverdlovsk (#14), and Chel'iabinsk (#15).

36 In December 1998, Krasnoyarsk and Kemerova regions joined Tatarstan, Altai and the Volgograd region in introducing new restrictions on food trade and grain transportation (*Moscow Times,* 12/12/98). On earlier actions see S. Krayukhin, T. Zil'ber, "Regiony v bor'be s krizisom", *Izvestiia,* 09/12/98.

37 Moscow has been particularly active in wooing foreign investors, and cutting deals with other regions for the exchange of food or energy for manufactures. Other leaders have been Veliki Novgorod, Samara, the 'autonomous' Republics, such as Tatarstan and Sakha (Yakutia), and the industrialized regions of the Urals and western Siberia. Over a half dozen regions had issued Eurobonds, and another four had central permission to do so, when the August financial crisis struck. Among the earliest and largest borrowers was Tatarstan, which defaulted in November on $100 million of debt;

see J. Ingram, "Projects Halted in Tatar Republic", *AP*, 10 January 1999. Both Moscow and Nizhny-Novgorod are, in early 1999, also in technical default and renegotiation with creditors. See *EWI Regional Report*, vol. 4, #13 and #17.

[38]   This is reflected in prevailing attitudes and behavior during privatization, discussed in Clarke, et. al. (1994), Blasi, et. al. (1997), and Hendley (1998).

[39]   Well functioning markets have a "separation property" which tends to localize the consequences of decisions, unentangling the fates of different economic agents.

[40]   Evidence appeared at least weekly in the Russian press, 1996 through 1999. See, for example, *RFE/RL Newsline*, 4 and 7 September; 18 November; 9, 11 and 14 December, 1998. Indeed, the tax system is most reminiscent of medieval "tax farming", as noted in Åslund (1998), p. 321.

[41]   As 1999 began, several "Subjects of the Federation" announced that they were abandoning jury trials to return to the administratively cheaper Soviet procedure (lay assessors). See the *RFE/RL Newsline* for 4 January 1999 on the *Riazin* announcement.

[42]   The extent to which the use of force in business has become institutionalized is emphasized in Radaiev (1998).

[43]   This point is clearly made in Ickes, Murrell and Ryterman (1997).

[44]   Note here the Chubais "Extraordinary Commission" ["*Cheka*"] for tax collection in 1997-8, the Karpov (1997) Report, and A. Lebed's assertion, shortly after being elected governor of Krasnoyarsk in 1998, the he was ready to take over the financing of military ground forces in his province. In 1997, Governor Ishaev of Khabarovsk had already taken border and military units "on his balance" (NIC, 1999, p. 54).

[45]   The central government regularly releases lists of "naughty" regions; a recent list is in an *ITAR-TASS* report of 8 December 1998 (*RFE/RL Newsline*, 9 December 1998).

[46]   Westerners were impressed by the speed of development and apparent sophistication of new Russian financial markets and financiers in 1994-7. See, for example, C. Jones, "Russian Eyes are Smiling", *The Banker*, September 1995, pp. 18-27. Some of the shine came off with the collapse of late 1998.

[47]   This nature of the privatization is discussed in Blasi, et. al. (1997), Åslund (1995), Boicko, et. al. (1995), and Sutela (1998). It is much criticised in Russia, particularly by those who were "left out", and is noted as a defining systemic characteristic by Sutela.

[48]   This involves efforts to "protect" local markets by blocking outside supply and by forbidding export by local producers. See the sources referenced in notes 35 and 36 above.

[49]   Enterprise transactions in the Soviet Union were essentially demonetized, and that is again becomming the case in much of basic Russian industry. See Ickes, Murrell and Ryterman (1997), Aukutsionek (1998), and Åslund (1998).

[50]   This is the primary subject of the Karpov (1997) report.

[51]   There has been a slow but steady **remonetization** of economic activity during the current recovery. See any of the monthly reports of *Russian Economic Trends* (London: Blackwell, 2001). Whether this reflects a systemic change, or is merely an artifact of temporary favorable conditions remains to be seen.

[52]   The Duma again twice rejected a land code with presidential revisions on 23 December 1998, leaving Russia without enabling legislation for a land market. RFE/RL *Newsline*, 23 December 1998. A number of regions are attempting to impose their own "land codes" without enabling legislation from the center, e.g. Samara (*EWI Regional Report*, Vol 4 #13) and Perm (*EWI Regional Report*, vol. 4, #11). A compromise version of the code, leaving much to the discretion of the regions, passed two readings in late spring 2001, virtually assuring passage in the fall. See "Recent Developments in the Russian

Economy", *Russian Economic Trends* (London: Blackwell, 2001), 6 July 2001.

53 See, for example, the discussion of the banking system in RECEP's *Russian Economic Trends,* 11 November 1998, or Sycheva and Mikhailov (1998).

54 In particular, there was limited investment in the critical energy due to the failure of the Duma to approve a reasonable production sharing agreement, and pass enabling legislation, before mid-1999. See the discussion of FDI in RECEP's *Russian Economic Trends,* 11 March 1999. This situation is however turning around due to 2 years of strong recovery, political stability, and proposed reforms strengthening investor and outside owners' rights.

55 See the work of Friebel and Guriev (2000) for an analysis of some barriers to labor mobility.

56 The best recent discussion of new small business in Russia is Åslund (1997). For evidence on the political problems of small business in Ul'ianovsk see the *IEW Regional Report,* vol. 4, #3 and #10.

57 The changes in industry are investigated in detail in Kuboniwa and Gavrilenkov (1997) Chapter 4, while general sectoral and price changes are discussed in OECD (1995) Chapter 1, which also makes the point about the lack of significant change when Soviet structure is measured in world prices.

58 Grossman (1963) is the classic statement of the nature of planning and valuation in a command economy. The argument is further developed in Ericson (1991) and (1997).

59 See the case study of the Saratov Aviation Plant's struggle to survive in Hendley (1998), the work of British sociologist Simon Clarke and his collective, e.g. in Clarke, et. al. (1994), and the study of the fate of Soviet military industry by Gaddy (1996).

60 This behavior is analyzed in the Gaddy-Ickes discussion paper (February, 1998).

61 As Åslund (1998) notes, *Menatep* evolved from a bank to an industrial holding company, *Rosprom*, to an energy company based on *Yukos*. Similarly, *Bank Rossiiskii Kredit* has become a holding company in the metallurgical industry, and *Oneximbank* has combined *Noril'sk Nikel* with *Sidanko* oil.

62 Regional and city bosses are beginning to move to reduce or eliminate the authority of elected "inconvenient" subordinates in Nizhny-Novgorod, Rostov, Saratov, Voronezh, and Ul'ianovsk. See *EWI Regional Report,* vol 4, ##12 and 14-16. More recently, we have seen moves by the Presidential Administration and "family" to cement control over the major industrial fiefdoms of *Gazprom, UES, Transneft,* and the railroads, in preparation for the 1999 Duma and 2000 Presidential elections; see Peresvet (1999). And those elections themselves were manipulated to insure Putin's first-round victory; see *Moscow Times Special Report,* "Election 2000", and the articles by Elena Borisova, "And the Winner Is?" Parts I, II, and III, 9 September 2000, available on the web site: www.themoscowtimes.com.

63 Thus *Gazprom, UES,* or *Lukoil* might be considered single feudal domains, extraordinarily large "manors", integrating the political, social and economic life of their members. With recent appointments, they seem to be moving onto the Presidential 'demense' (Peresvet, 1999).

64 Investment has increased substantially following the devaluation of August 1998 and resource proce increases in 1999 and 2000. See recent issues of the monthly report of *Russian Economic Trends* (London: Blackwell, 2001). Yet the extent to which this investment is directed toward fundamental restructuring, *rather than reviving Soviet* capacities, remains unclear.

65 One frequently hears the refrain that "Russia is tired of change" and craves "stability and order". This indeed is a common explanation of Putin's first round victory in the

March 2000 presidential elections. Also see Joel Hellman's (1998) analysis of 'winners' blocking further progress.

[66] Putin has encouraged the development of a *dirigiste* development program, the so-called Ishaev Program, as a possible alternative to the liberal marketizing Gref Program that so far seems to be driving policy. He has spoken approvingly of "combining" these incompatible approaches. See J. Tennenbaum, "The Ishayev Report: An Economic Mobilization Plan for Russia", *Economic Intelligence Review*, vol. 28, #9, 2 March 2001.

[67] In early May 2000, a number of laws and decrees in Ingushetia, Amur, Tver, Smolensk, Bashkortostan, and Adygeya were nullified by Presidential decree, and all regions, in particular Bashkortostan, were given several weeks to bring their constitutions in line with the the Federal Constitution. See IEWS Russian Regional Report, vol. 5, ##16-22, 2000.

[68] Some regions are avoiding holding meetings to discuss their constitutions, and Bashkortistan has made a revision that falls far short of Putin's demands. See IEWS Russian Regional Report ##20--22.

References

Aikman, D. (1998), 'The Men Who Run Russia', *The Weekly Standard*, (20 July).

Aleksandrov, V. (1996), 'The Magic Seven: Who are They, The Saviors of Russia?' *Argumenty i fakt*, no. 1-2 (December).

Amann, R. and Cooper, J. (eds) (1986), *Technical Progress and Soviet Economic Development*, Basil Blackwell, Ltd, Oxford, UK.

Anderson, P. (1974), *Lineages of the Absolutist State*, NLB, London.

Angresano (1996), *Comparative Economic Systems*, 2nd Ed, Upper Saddle River, Prentice Hall, New Jersey.

Åslund, A. (1995), *How Russia Became a Market Economy*, Brookings, Washington, D.C.

Åslund, A. (1997), 'Observations on the Development of Small Private Enterprise in Russia', *Post-Soviet Geography and Economics*, vol. 38, no. 4, pp. 191-205.

Åslund, A. (1998), 'Russia's Financial Crisis: Causes and Possible Remedies', *Post-Soviet Geography and Economics*, vol. 39, no. 6, pp. 309-28.

Aukutsionek, S. (1998), 'Barter v Rossiiskoi promyshlennosti (Barter in Russian Industry),' *Voprosy ekonomiki*, vol. 70, no. 2, pp. 51-60.

Balzer, H. (1998), 'A Shadow Middle Class for A Shadow Economy', *Post-Soviet Affairs*, vol. 14, no. 2, (April-June), pp. 165-86.

Blasi, J.R, Kroumova, M. and Kruse, D. (1997), *Kremlin Capitalism: Privatizing the Russian Economy*, Cornell UP, Ithaca, NewYork.

Boettke, P.J. (1990), *The Political Economy of Soviet Socialism: The Formative Years, 1918-1928*, Kluwer Academic Publishers, Dordrecht, Netherlands.

Boone, P. and Johnson, S. (1999), 'Russia After Yeltsin: Economic Alternatives – Boom or Bust or Both?', manuscript presented at 'Russia Post-Yeltsin' Conference, Wye River Conference Center (19-20 August).

Boycko, M, Shleifer, A. and Vishny, R.W. (1995), *Privatizing Russia*, MIT Press, Cambridge Massachussets.

Brock, G. (1998), 'Public Finance in the ZATO Archipelago', *Europe-Asia Studies*, vol. 50, no. 6, pp. 1165-81.

Brock, G. (2000), 'The ZATO Archipelago Revisited - Is the Federal Government Loosening Its Grip? A research Note', *Europe-Asia Studies*, vol. 52, no. 7, pp. 1149-60.

Bunin, I. (1994), *Biznesmeny Rossii*, AO OKA, Moscow.
Clarke, S, Fairbrother, P. and Borisov Bizyukov, V. (1994), 'The Privatization of Industrial Enterprises in Russia: Four Case Studies', *Europe-Asia Studies*, vol. 46, no. 2, pp. 179-214.
Davis, S.J. and Haltiwanger, J.C. (1996), *Job Creation and Destruction*, MIT Press, Cambridge, Massachussets.
Ellerman, D. and Stiglitz, J. (2000), 'New Bridges across the Chasm: Macro- and MicroStrategies for Russia', paper presented at ECAAR Panel, ASSA Convention, Boston (January).
Ericson, R.E. (1991), 'The Classical Soviet-Type Economy: Nature of the system and Implications for Reform', *Journal of Economic Perspectives*, vol. 5, no. 4, pp. 179-214.
Ericson, R.E. (1999), 'The Structural Barrier to Transition Hidden in Input-Output Tables of Centrally Planned Economies', *Economic Systems*, vol. 23, no. 3 (September), pp. 199-224.
Friebel, G. and Guriev, S. (2000), 'Should I Stay or Can I Go? Worker Attachment in Russia', CEFIR Discussion Paper (November), available at CEFIR website www.cefir.org/papers2.html.
Frye, T. and Shleifer, A. (1997), 'The Invisible Hand and the Grabbing Hand', *American Economic Review*, vol. 87, no. 2 (May), pp. 354-8.
Gaddy, C. (1996), *The Price of the Past*, Brookings, Washington, DC.
Gaddy, C. and Ickes, B.W. (1998), 'Russia's Virtual Economy', *Foreign Affairs* (September-October), pp. 53-67.
Gaddy, C. and Ickes, B.W. (1998a), 'To Restructure or Not to Restructure: Informal Activities and Enterprise Behavior in Transition', *WDI Working Paper no. 134* (February).
Gaddy, C. and Ickes, B.W. (1999), 'An Accounting Model of the Virtual Economy in Russia', *Post-Soviet Geography and Economics*, vol. 40, no. 2, pp. 79-97.
Gaidar, E. (1996), *Dni porazhenii i pobed*, Vagrius, Moscow.
Gaidar, E. (1998), *Ekonomika perekxodnogo perioda*, IET, Moscow.
Goldman, M. (1998), 'Leading Russian Industrialists', *Economic Newsletter*, Davis Center for Russian Studies, Harvard University, vol. 23, no. 10 (24 June).
Gregory, P.R. and Stuart, R.S. (1998), *Russian and Soviet Economic Performance and Structure*, 6th Ed, Addison-Wesley, Reading, Massachussets.
Grossman, G. (1963), 'Notes for a Theory of the Command Economy', *Soviet Studies*, vol. 15, no. 2, pp. 101-23.
Gustafson, T. (1999), *Capitalism Russian-Style*, Cambridge UP, Cambridge, UK.
Hedlund, S. (1999), *Russia's "Market" Economy*, UCL Press, London, UK.
Hellman, J. (1998), 'Winners Take All: The Politics of Partial Reform in Post-communist Nations', *World Politics*, vol. 50, no. 2, pp. 203-34.
Hendley, K. (1998), 'Struggling to Survive: A Case Study of Adjustment at a Russian Enterprise', *Europe-Asia Studies*, vol. 50, no. 1, pp. 91-119.
Hendley, K, Ickes, B.W., Murrell, P. and Ryterman, R. (1997), 'Observations on the Use of Law by Russian Enterprises', *Post-Soviet Affairs*, vol. 17, no. 1, pp. 19-41.
Hough, Jerry (1969), *The Soviet Prefects*, Harvard University Press, Cambridge, Massachussets.
Ickes, B.W., Murrell, P. and Ryterman, R. (1997), 'End of the Tunnel? The Effects of Financial Stabilization in Russia', *Post-Soviet Affairs*, vol. 13, no. 2 (April-June), pp. 105-33.

IET (1997), 'Russian Enterprises in 1996-7', *The Russian Economy: Tendencies and Prospects*, Institute of Economic Transition, Moscow.

Johnson, J. (1997), 'Russia's Emerging Financial-Industrial Groups', *Post-Soviet Affairs*, vol. 13, no. 4 (October-December), pp. 333-65.

Karpov, P.A. (1997), 'On the Causes of Low Tax Collection (Arrears in the Fiscal System), General Causes of the 'Arrears Crisis' and Opportunities for the Restoration of Solvency of Russian Enterprises', Report of Interdepartmental Balance Commission, IBC, Moscow (December).

Khakamada, I. (1999), 'Quasi-Taxes for a Quasi-Feudal State', *Kommersant Daily* (19 March).

Khlebnikov, P. (2000), *Godfather of the Kremlin: Boris Berezovsky and the Looting of Russia*, Harcourt, New York.

Kornai, J. (1992), *The Socialist System: The Political Economy of Communism*, Princeton UP, Princeton, New Jersey.

Kranz, P. (1997), 'Russia's Most Powerful Man', *Business* Week, International Edition (24 November).

Kryshtanovskaya, O. (1997), 'The Real Masters of Russia', *Argumenty i Fakty*, no. 21 (May).

Kuboniwa, M. and Gavrilenkov, E. (1997), *Development of Capitalism in Russia: The Second Challenge*, Maruzen Co, Tokyo.

Latynina, Y. (1999), 'Holy Roman Empire', *Izvestiia* (23 April).

Lavigne, M. (1999), *The Economics of Transition*, 2nd Ed, MacMillan Press, London.

Linz, S.J. (1997), 'Russian Firms in Transition: Champions, Challengers and Chaff', *Comparative Economic systems*, vol. 39, no. 1, pp. 1-36.

Linz, S. and Krueger, G. (1998), 'Enterprise Restructuring in Russia's Transition Economy: Formal and Informal Mechanisms', *Comparative Economic Studies*, vol. 40, no. 2, pp. 5-52.

Mau, V. (2000), 'Russian Economic Reforms as Perceived by Western Critics', Chapter 6 in T. Komulainen and I. Korhonen (eds), *Russian Crisis and Its Effects*, Kikimora Publications, Helsinki, pp. 91-132.

National Intelligence Council (1999), 'Federalism in Russia: How is it Working?', *Conference Report: 9-10 December 1998*, NIC 99-02 (February).

OECD (1995), *OECD Economic Surveys: Russian Federation 1995*, OECD Publications, Paris.

OECD (1997), *OECD Economic Surveys: Russian Federation*, OECD Publications, Paris.

Peresvet, A. (1999), 'The Electorate's Votes will Flow by the "Pipe" ', *Rossiia* (9 July).

Postan, M.M. (1973), *Essays on Medieval Agriculture and General Problems of the Medieval Economy*, At the University Press, Cambridge, UK.

Postan, M.M. (1975), *The Medieval Economy and Society*, Penguin Books, Harmondsworth, UK.

Pryor, F.L. (1980), 'Feudalism as an Economic System', *Journal of Comparative Economics*, vol. 4, no. 1 (March), pp. 56-77.

Radaiev, V. (1998), 'On the Role of Force in Russian Business Relationships', *Voprosy ekonomiki*, no. 19 (October).

Rader, T. (1971), *The Economics of Feudalism*, Gordon and Breach, New York.

Ryterman, R. and Weber, B. (1996), 'The Role of Attitudes in the Performance of the Legal System: Evidence from a Survey of Russian Firms', The World Bank, October 1996.

Sachs, J.D. and Pistor, K. (eds) (1997), *The Rule of Law and Economic Reform in Russia*, Westview, Boulder, Colorado.

Shlapentokh, V. (1996), 'Early Feudalism - The Best Parallel for Contemporary Russia', *Europe-Asia Studies*, vol. 48, no. 3, pp. 393-411.

Shleifer, A. (1997), 'Government in Transition', *European Economic Review*, vol. 41, no. 3-5, pp. 385-410.

Solnik, S. L. (1998), *Stealing the State*, Harvard, Cambridge, Massachussets.

Stiglitz, J. (1999), 'Whither Reform?', speech at ABCDE Conference, World Bank, Washington, DC (April).

Sutela, P. (1998), *The Road to the Russian Market Economy*, Kikimora, Helsinki.

Sycheva, L. and Mikhailov, L. (1998), 'Moscow Banks' Balance Sheet Portfolios in 1995-97', *IET@online.ru* (June).

Verdery, K. (1996), 'A Transition from Socialism to Feudalism? Thoughts on the Postsocialist State', *What was Socialism and What Comes Next?* , PUP, Princeton, New Jersey, ch. 8, pp. 204-28.

Woodruff, D. (1999), *Money Unmade: Barter and the Fate of Russian Capitalism*, Cornell, Ithaca, New York.

Zisk, K.M. (1997), *Weapons, Culture, and Self-Interest: Soviet Defense Managers in the New Russia*, Columbia University Press, New York.

Chapter 2

Corruption and Organized Crime in the Russian Transition

Jim Leitzel

Abstract

Much of the perceived increase in corruption and organized crime in transitional Russia represents a more open version of activity that was commonplace during the pre-reform era. The partial nature of reforms, reflected in excessive government intervention in the economy and poor public provision of protection and contract law, has been a major source of new economic crime. Simultaneously, the costs imposed by corruption and organized crime have gone up, largely due to their relative disorganization and the general economic uncertainty during the reforms. The benefits of corruption and economic crime in transitional Russia likewise are higher than they would be in advanced Western market economies, because the alternatives are less attractive. Standard measures for combating corruption, including increased development and enforcement of the law combined with further liberalization, will be helpful in reducing the amount of economic crime. The social costs of the remaining corruption can be reduced via stabilization, political steadiness, and increases in accountability arising from a free press, an independent judiciary, and a watchdog legislature. The overall approach to corruption control should be one of harm reduction, not a generalized "crackdown", because efforts to fight corruption can themselves be quite costly, and potentially counterproductive.

Introduction

The extensive economic crime in transitional Russia is by now sobering but old news. Stories abound of organized criminal groups, contract killings, corruption at the highest levels, and police bribery and extortion.[1] What is relatively new is the Russian president, Vladimir Putin, who like his predecessor, has declared that the establishment of the rule of law is a high priority. Also new is the extent to which anticorruption has become a global crusade. The UN, the OECD, the Council of

Europe, and the EU have all adopted anticorruption declarations or conventions in recent years. The anticorruption message now permeates the IMF and is being "mainstreamed" by the World Bank. Transparency International, a Germany-based non-profit organization, takes as its mission the empowering of civil society to combat corruption.[2]

The purpose of this paper is to examine Russian corruption and, to a lesser extent, organized crime, and to suggest methods for dealing with these phenomena during the transition. The framework of analysis, drawn from Leitzel (1995), focuses attention on the pre-reform conditions, which included pervasive, though repressed, mafia-style activity and corruption. The emergence and transformation of crime during the transition have led to significantly higher costs, even as the problems of corruption and organized crime in transitional Russia often are vastly overstated. Standard policy measures will reduce the amount of economic crime: increased enforcement of the law should be combined with further liberalization and the development of publicly-provided contract law. The social costs of the remaining crime can be lowered through macroeconomic stabilization, political steadiness, and increased accountability for government officials. The overall approach to corruption control should be one of harm reduction, not a generalized "crackdown", however, because attempts to control corruption are themselves costly, and potentially counterproductive.

"Corruption" has a host of meanings. One important distinction is whether the scope of corruption is limited to government officials, or whether private parties can be considered to be corrupt, too. (In transitional Russia, of course, the distinction between state officials and private parties is not altogether clear). For the purposes of this paper, we will consider only official corruption, and will adapt Klitgaard's (1991, p. 221) description of corruption as "the misuse of office for private ends", by restricting attention to public office. Such a description immediately suggests the need to distinguish between legitimate and illegitimate uses of public office. There are legal notions of legitimate uses of public offices, but there are also ethical notions, as well as norms associated with standard practices.[3] These distinctions will not be important in the analysis that follows, however, so we can safely adopt the legal standard for legitimate use of a public office.

The term "Mafioso" is bandied about quite loosely in Russia; it can be used to identify any business person, any government official, any criminal, any rich person who does not sufficiently hide his wealth, or even anyone the speaker does not care for. Following Gambetta (1994), I will consider a mafia member to be someone who engages in the private (non-state) provision of protection, and further, I will employ "organized crime" as a synonym for mafia activity. The protection can be offered against other would-be protectors, petty criminals (e.g. protection against theft), contracting partners who might be tempted to renege on a deal or not pay a debt, or, in the worst case of pure extortion, protection against the protectors themselves. Mafia members may be involved in a host of legal and/or illegal endeavors, but it is the provision of protection that distinguishes a mafia from, say, a ring of thieves. Of course, private protection can be provided by

Western-style security firms, too, so to differentiate between a mafia and such a security firm, a further condition is required: the difficulty of exit. A security firm can be fired by a client and another hired in its place with little difficulty; mafia protectors generally cannot be replaced at a client's whim. A saying associated with entry into Soviet Military Intelligence (the GRU) applies just as well to dealing with the mafia: it is a ruble to get in, but two to get out.[4]

The phrase "the Russian mafia" is often used in ways that suggest a unitary and structured organization along the lines of the Sicilian mafia – an analogy that is quite misleading. What exists in Russia is thousands of "organized criminal groups", most of them consisting of just a handful (often two or three) members, and with no overarching hierarchy. The heroic Italian anti-mafia crusader, Judge Falcone, noted the difference between the Sicilian and the Russian mafias before his assassination in 1992, in terms that largely remain applicable:[5]

> Even if the Russian Mafia (and those of the other countries of the ex-Soviet bloc) do pose serious problems ... in the East an organisation comparable to Cosa Nostra does not exist. Without doubt the collapse of state and ideological structures will inevitably cause a growth in illegal trafficking and criminality, but the criminal organisations of the ex-Soviet Union, for the moment, are above all a phenomenon of generalised administrative corruption. There is no sense in calling something a Mafia when it is not...

In many instances, corruption and organized crime are intimately related, often in a complementary fashion. Corrupt officials can ensure that the state does not interfere with mafia organizations (or that the state does interfere with a rival to a favored mafia group, or a reluctant client of that group), and they can channel state procurements towards mafia clients; mafia revenues can be donated to the election campaigns of corrupt officials, or to illegally undermine the integrity of balloting. By establishing a long-term, repeated relationship with the government, organized criminal groups can combine with corrupt officials to find the best ways to manipulate the system to their mutual benefit. In some respects, however, the state and the mafia are substitutes, and even competitors. Known connections with high ranking government officials can provide a business with disproportionate access to public protection (i.e. access to police and the courts can itself be partially privatized), and organized criminal groups might be deterred from approaching potential clients so protected. In the extreme, whether they cooperate or compete, it might be very difficult to differentiate government officials from mafiosi – an overlap that frequently is noted in the case of Russia.[6]

The remainder of the paper is organized as follows. Section 2 presents a framework for analyzing economic reform issues, which is then applied in the following sections to the analysis of corruption and organized crime. Section 3 provides a description of the pre-reform situation with respect to economic crime in Russia, while section 4 examines the changes wrought by reform. Section 5 explores the costs and benefits of corruption and organized crime in the reform era, and considers the possibility that Russia will become mired in a high-corruption, low-growth equilibrium. Section 6 offers some policy suggestions aimed at combating organized crime and corruption in transitional Russia, while section 7 contains brief conclusions.

A General Approach to Transitions from Socialism[7]

Three elements in any reform process are the starting point for reforms, the desired destination, and the connecting path. In the case of Russian economic transition, the desired destination within the political mainstream has been a "normal" market economy, at least since the failed putsch of August 1991.[8] Alternatively, the starting point for Russian economic reform is known with surprisingly little precision, despite its importance for both the design and assessment of reforms. Much of this lack of precision is inherent in centrally-planned economies. Fixed prices, for example, render most statistics expressed in value terms (rubles) to be more-or-less arbitrary. Incentives to exaggerate output limit the reliability of statistics in terms of gross output, and even growth rate statistics are largely subjective. In pre-reform Russia, the substantial underground economy was almost completely absent from official measures of economic activity, and most information concerning the sizable defense sector was suppressed. Much of the variation among assessments of the impact of Russian reform to this day can be traced to strongly divergent views over the economic achievements of Soviet central planning.

During a transition from socialism to capitalism, many elements of the economy that previously were hidden, implicit, or repressed, become explicit or open. As a result, they might be newly counted in the statistics, even though the underlying economic substance has not changed. Inflation presents the classic example of the movement from repressed to open varieties of economic phenomena during transition. With fixed prices in the state sector, inflation under central planning takes a repressed form, which manifests itself as lessened availability of goods within the state sector, longer lines when goods are available, lower quality of goods, or higher prices on parallel markets. Standard price indices for state-sector goods, then, are not a reliable indicator of inflation under central planning, because such price indices will only change when state authorities make explicit alterations to the controlled prices. In a market economy, alternatively, inflation generally takes the open form of higher prices for goods. During a transition, most price controls are lifted, inflation changes from repressed to open form, and price indices suddenly begin to offer a reasonable measure of inflation. The initial jump in the recorded price level that occurs with price liberalization, however, does not represent new inflation, but rather the belated recognition in the price index of the previous repressed inflation. The change from repressed to open form during transition applies to many other elements of the economy, including unemployment, monopoly power, the system of taxation, and the social safety net.

This simple framework for examining transition suggests three general observations. First, many of the costs that frequently are associated with reform are not new; rather, they are more open forms of costs that previously were incurred in a somewhat hidden manner.[9] The large jump in the price index that occurs with price liberalization, but does not measure current inflation, is one instance of this phenomenon, as is the transition from hidden unemployment (such as employees involved in the production of worthless "goods") to open unemployment. Nevertheless, there are indeed some new costs that are generated during the reform process, leading to a second observation that these costs have their source in ill-conceived, partial reform measures. One example of inconsistent reforms resulting in high costs is the institution of hard budget constraints in an environment with substantial distortions, such as a very low fixed price for energy. In this case, socially-valuable firms could go bankrupt, while negative value-added enterprises could prosper, potentially making the economy worse off than in the previous setting of soft budget constraints and widespread official price controls. The third observation is that changes during transition cannot be measured against standards that would be appropriate for advanced Western market economies. Consider a perceived increase in monopoly power. In a market economy, such a development would probably signal a worsening of the economic situation, because monopolies are inefficient relative to the alternative of competitive firms. But in transitional Russia, the starting point is not one of competitive markets. An increase in monopoly power therefore is ambiguous with respect to its overall effects on the economy, given that the relevant alternative is not competitive markets, but rather something that potentially is worse than monopolies operating in a distorted environment.[10]

Having laid out a general framework for examining transitions from socialism, I will now suggest that both corruption and organized crime can be analyzed usefully within this structure. First, there were significant amounts of corruption and organized crime prior to reform, and one effect of reform has been to make this pre-existing activity more open, while simultaneously changing the character of crime. Second, to the extent that corruption and organized crime indeed have increased during transition, much of the increase can be attributed to inappropriate, partial reform measures. And third, Western standards cannot blindly be applied to the Russian transition. While a large perceived increase in corruption or organized crime almost certainly would be detrimental in mature market economies, the impact of such an increase is decidedly more ambiguous under the conditions prevailing in Russia.

The Pre-Reform Setting

The limitations on the availability and reliability of economic information in the USSR were even more severe in the case of illegal activity. Nevertheless, qualitative assessments are possible. The economic and political system of the

Soviet Union led to pervasive corruption and organized crime. The legal and the illegal sectors of the Soviet economy were intertwined, and they were both riddled with economic crime. As leading analysts of the Soviet second economy noted, "An international committee of experts charged with compiling a list of conditions that maximize the potential for a large underground economy would invent the Soviet Union".[11]

Consider the illegal sector. The extensive restrictions on private economic activity and the shortcomings of the planned economy created a large demand for illegally produced goods and services. Illegal activity then created its own demand for private protection, since the official state channels of protection (police, contract law) were not available to those behaving illegally. (For this reason, organized crime in the West tends to be most prevalent in illegal sectors, such as narcotics, prostitution, and gambling.) The monopoly on power established by the Communist Party of the Soviet Union (CPSU), enshrined in the constitution and implemented via control over the police, judiciary, and all important economic posts (the *nomenklatura*) made state officials, operating informally, the natural providers of that protection. That is, there was a close affinity between mafia activity and official corruption, and bribes tended to flow up the CPSU hierarchy. Here is one description of the system of protection for illegal economic activity in the Soviet Union:

> The patron, often some official, grants his permission, or at least his forbearance, and extends some measure of conditional protection. The client pays in cash or kind, and not infrequently buys his way into the particular niche. Indeed, second economy operations of even modest size require multiple and periodic payoffs - to administrative superiors, party functionaries or secretaries, law-enforcement personnel, innumerable inspectors and auditors, and diverse actual or potential blackmailers.[12]

Nor was it the case that bribes were restricted to the illegal sector of the economy. Managers of state enterprises were forced to engage in bribery and second economy wheeling and dealing to get the materials that they had a supposed legal claim to through the plan. Theft of materials and time by state workers was so institutionalized that it represented an expected and condoned part of compensation.[13] The whole system of corruption was well-organized, and for decades, quite stable. Those who refused to go along with the informal exchange mechanisms were subject to selective prosecution, because the official organs of justice were controlled by the same corrupt officials.

Robert Klitgaard (1991, p. 225) provides a heuristic equation that can be used to indicate the amount of corruption that will be supplied by government officials: Corruption = Monopoly + Discretion-Accountability. Communist Party officials had a monopoly on power, great discretion over what they could choose to overlook, and little accountability for their illegal actions. Corruption was promoted further by the system of central planning. First, there was significant demand for corruption by illegal economic actors, whose activity was itself fostered by the extensive controls and weaknesses in the official sector. Second, price controls and generalized excess demand implied that legal markets were not the mechanism that was employed to allocate scarce goods and services. As a result, state officials throughout the hierarchy, from truck drivers and retail clerks to state ministers, frequently had control over determining who would receive desirable commodities. The alternative to allocation by legal markets, in many cases, became corrupt allocation in illicit markets.

Reform

As with other types of crime, the systemic corruption and protection payments in the USSR were understood widely, but not acknowledged officially. Individual incidents of corruption would be reported in the Soviet press (often when it was to the political advantage of the rulers, as when some of Brezhnev's associates were discredited following his death), but the extent to which corruption permeated the system (indeed, almost defined the system) went unreported.[14]

It is not unusual for analysts to note the distinction between crime and the perception of crime, though such notice is often rather perfunctory, a minor qualifier in interpreting crime statistics and social concerns with crime. In transitional circumstances, however, partly because of the suppressed situation pre-reform, the role of perceptions is greatly enhanced. With the advent of *glasnost'* under Gorbachev and the further liberalization of the press under Yeltsin, crime and corruption became major topics for public discussion, and there often were novel incentives to offer sensationalized accounts. Repressed corruption (or at least repressed discussion of corruption) was becoming open. Even had there been no increase in the amount of corruption or mafia-style activity, this liberalization of the media would have resulted in heightened perceptions of economic crime. Furthermore, media revelations of corruption during systemic reform have an intensified impact on peoples perceptions, because the relevance of information gleaned from experience with the old system simultaneously is devalued.

Perceptions can influence reality. Potential "demanders" of corruption, such as those apprehended by the police for minor crimes, are more likely to offer bribes if they believe that bribery is common. With respect to corruption, Say's Law would seem to apply: supply creates its own demand, or perhaps more precisely, the perception of supply creates its own demand.[15] Likewise, potential "suppliers" also are more likely to become corrupt if they believe that it is the social norm, and that all of their colleagues are corrupt: the perception of supply creates its own supply, too. Further, combined with no increase in enforcement resources, a perception of higher crime reduces the subjective probability of being caught, and may result in more individuals choosing to behave illegally.[16] For all of these reasons, widespread perceptions of an increase in economic crime are, to some degree, self-fulfilling.

In creating perceptions of Russian crime – particularly in the West – the singular role of Moscow should be noted. As the capital and largest city in the former Soviet Union, vastly disproportionate resources were devoted to policing the capital: eight percent of the nation's policemen were assigned to Moscow, which contained three per cent of the population.[17] Further, structural factors in the old USSR, including the prohibition on released convicts settling in major cities, and the inability of young, single males to receive residence permits in large urban centers, served to reduce crime in the capital.[18] The ending of these special conditions contributed to increased crime in Moscow during transition, and the extraordinary status of Moscow as a media center gives it disproportionate weight in the news.[19]

The reform era in Russia liberalized more than just the media, however. There also was an extremely far-reaching liberalization of private economic activity, from cooperatives to individual enterprises and to Western-style firms. Entirely new markets, such as the financial market, developed – bankers, who often have access both to substantial funds and to information concerning wealthy firms and individuals, became favored targets for business-related crimes – and other markets grew from primitive roots in the underground economy.

The market-oriented reforms were incomplete, however, and the partial nature of the reforms led to increases in economic crime. The reforms were partial in three senses. First, taxes and restrictions were extensive enough that it was almost impossible, as many Russian business people would testify, for a business to obey all the laws and still earn a profit.[20] Second, local governmental officials retained considerable discretion over what the rules were, and over who could do what. Government control of the local commercial real estate market provided one important lever to manipulate private businesses, for example, and multiple approvals and licenses were necessary to receive local services.[21] Third, the public provision of protection, in terms of both police and business law, was inadequate. The result of the extensive, yet incomplete liberalization was a surge in the demand for corruption and private protection, for which there was a ready supply. In early 1997, there were 9,800 officially registered private security firms in Russia, with some 155,000 employees.[22]

Such partial reforms would provide fertile soil for economic crime anywhere, but Russia was particularly susceptible. Corruption and organized crime often are discussed under the more general rubric of "rent seeking", since the attractiveness of these activities is associated with the capture of rents. The rents that are available come in a variety of forms. Corruption frequently is associated with rents that accompany artificial scarcities arising from anti-competitive government policies, such as import licenses or price controls. The provision of protection (a good that has a strong natural monopoly element) can in itself create "protection rents", which can flow to organized criminal groups or the state.[23] But another source of rents is natural resources, which can fetch prices well in excess of the costs of extraction. Russia is uniquely well-endowed with natural resources. Liberalization of foreign trade during transition has increased greatly the potential for those with access to resources to capture rents through exporting. Not surprisingly, a good deal of alleged corruption and criminal activity has been associated with such resources: for example, there are frequent references to the aluminum mafia, the tin mafia, etc., and the far eastern parts of Russia, which are home to many of the resources, appear to harbor extensive organized criminal activity. Russia's bounty of natural resources, which probably prolonged the lifespan of the notoriously inefficient Soviet economy by years, if not decades, combined with the decentralization of power and access to world markets to provide a major impetus to economic crime during the transition.[24]

Costs and Benefits of Corruption and Organized Crime in the Reform Era

The transition not only has seen an increase in corruption and organized crime, and increased publicity for such activity, but also has changed the nature of these phenomena. Most notably, the organization and stability of corruption and protection in the old regime has collapsed with the CPSU, leaving contending protection agencies and uncertainty over whom to pay. One result has been a massive increase in violence. Just as illegal drug markets are most dangerous during turf wars that establish precedence, competition to replace the former CPSU monopoly greatly has increased the costs of economic crime in transitional Russia. The extreme economic uncertainty that characterizes the transition also has raised the costs of economic crime, as effective time horizons are shortened. Private protection agencies, then, behave as if the future existence of either their own organization or their clients is doubtful, creating a situation closer to extortion than to that characterizing Western security firms.[25] Homicide statistics provide one measure of the increase in violent activity. In 1996, there were approximately 29,700 premeditated murders or attempted murders in Russia, compared with 15,600 in 1990: an increase of more than 90 per cent.[26]

Nor is the distribution of the costs of economic crime during transition the same as it was in the pre-reform era. Foreigners, new businesses, and small firms are at a relative disadvantage in operating in a high corruption, mafia-infiltrated environment. In illegal markets, establishing a "connection" typically is much more difficult than in legal transactions – particularly if the corrupt environment is not well organized.[27] Those who are not already well-connected, then, face higher obstacles to doing business. One result is that old relationships are favored relative to new business ties, militating against the sorts of changes in business practices intended by reform. In transitional economies, furthermore, new firms and, to a degree, foreign investors, are an important element of growth, so discouraging these actors is particularly detrimental.[28]

Despite the conditions that tend to raise the costs of mafia-style activity during the transition, organized crime also provides some benefits. Successful mafia groups actually do provide protection, and as noted, that protection need not merely be against their own threats. Mafia protectors with sufficiently long time horizons are in some sense partners with their clients, often making them willing to provide services that increase their clients' profits, such as contract enforcement, debt collection, and dispute resolution. For many, if not most Russian businesses, security represents a normal business expense, but it is not an overwhelming concern. Even firms with foreign investment do not tend to see the mafia as an important obstacle to business.[29] If the feasible alternative to mafia protection is effective, publicly-provided protection, then an increase in organized crime is almost certainly economically and socially detrimental. If, however, effective public protection is unavailable, then the presence of a mafia can be, on balance, a positive development, and can reduce the uncertainty facing a business.

While the violence that accompanies mafia activity immediately suggests that organized crime, even with its benefits, comes at high cost, the costs of corruption are much less obvious. Some countries, such as South Korea, Thailand, and Japan, have reputations for high levels of corruption but nevertheless have achieved enviable economic growth – and China would be a recent addition to this list – though there is some evidence that on balance, corruption inhibits growth.[30] Dealing in a high-corruption environment is certainly unpleasant, and is often unfair, since access to corrupt officials is not distributed evenly. Other negative features of corruption are listed in Table 2.1.

Corruption, though, is not without its potential benefits, some of which also are listed in Table 2.1. The main benefit of corruption is that it allows business people to avoid or evade bad laws and regulations. While the rules governing private economic activity in transitional Russia are much more conducive to economic growth than they were in the pre-reform setting, the incomplete nature of reform still leaves a good deal of room for Pareto-improving corruption. But even good rules do not preclude benefits from corruption: first, because even good rules can benefit from some flexibility in certain circumstances, and second, because some marginalized groups may not be able to secure equal access to the rules in the absence of corruption.[31] Of course, other forms of corruption, such as bribery of the police that allows violent criminals to operate with impunity, are far from Pareto improvements, and it may be impossible to tolerate "good" corruption without simultaneously providing a green light to "bad" corruption.

The heightened level of violence presents an enormous cost. Abstracting from the violence (if that is possible), however, the overall economic impact of corruption and organized criminal activity in Russia is not so obvious. The difficulty in making a definitive pronouncement ("corruption is bad") is that the relevant alternative in Russia is far from a well-oiled, market-style system. But such a pronouncement is not required, either. Much of the concern over economic crime is aimed not at static calculations of costs and benefits, but rather at the influence that mafia-style activity and corruption will have on the course of transition. Does Russia run the risk of becoming mired in a long-term, high economic crime equilibrium? How salient is Robert Putnam's concern, that "Palermo may represent the future of Moscow"?[32]

The danger clearly exists. Officials growing wealthy off of corrupt incomes have little reason to push for liberalizations that will reduce their illicit gains, and they may even seek to establish more roadblocks that business people will pay to avoid. It often is quite difficult to break away from a situation of high corruption; a police officer who would like to stop taking bribes, for instance, might still be expected to pass a share of the bribes to his superiors, and honest people will find police work less attractive than it is to those willing to accept bribes. (The officer's formal pay, in fact, may be quite low, in anticipation of the informal routes to higher income.) And as noted, one characteristic of organized crime is that its clients in general cannot exit from the relationship at will. Further, the extent and visibility of corruption and organized crime, even beyond their actual costs, can induce cynicism in the population. If the way to individual economic success frequently involves, as before, illegal or immoral behavior, then in this dimension at least, reform can appear to be a rather futile endeavor.

Nevertheless, there is room for hope that Russia can avoid a long-term, high economic crime equilibrium. One reason for this optimistic assessment relates to the very disorganization of the current crime scene; while the disorganization, as we have seen, is likely to raise the social costs of economic crime, it simultaneously suggests that the "criminals" cannot easily operate as a coherent political force, capable of stalling further reform. Consider the comparison with the pre-reform system. The Communist Party was very well-organized, with a monopoly on power virtually unequaled in political history, with control over the mass media, and with representatives in every nook and cranny of Soviet society. Further, CPSU officials frequently were the beneficiaries of illicit incomes that flowed from that power. Nevertheless, the CPSU was unable to prevent the loss of its power and the onset of massive economic reform. Could the 9,000 "organized criminal groups" in transitional Russia be more effective?

A second reason to believe that economic reform need not be permanently stalled by the rent seeking of corrupt officials is that such officials often do quite well in a liberalized environment – and particularly when they are helping to shape the rules of the new market regime. Evidence for this contention has been accumulating throughout the Russian reform era. The former *nomenklatura*, by and large, has been financially successful despite the extensive liberalization.[33] There is a significant overlap between the skills that were required to get ahead in the Soviet system (which, after all, included a large illicit market) and those that are rewarded in a market economy.

Table 2.1   Some potential economic consequences of corruption

Positive Features	Negative Features
Allows (even good) rules to be more responsive to individual circumstances: increases flexibility.	Promotes horizontal and vertical inequality (i.e. is unfair and possibly immoral).
Provides exemptions to regulations, taxes, possibly in an efficient manner.	Selects against honest people, foreign firms, small firms, and new firms.
Allows bad rules to be circumvented.	Allows breaking of rules even when it is not efficient (increases incentive to commit violent crime or to pollute, for example).
Provides incentives to officials to work hard.	Undermines economic statistics.
Lowers administrative and other costs; for example, a bribe might be socially less costly than the same size fine.	Serves as an inferior substitute for efficient reforms.
If visible, corruption provides information about the quality of laws, and promotes efficient reforms.	Efforts to control corruption might themselves be quite costly.
	Encourages government officials to set up and maintain inefficient roadblocks, to secure bribes.
Increases access to the government for some socially marginalized groups.	Creates uncertainty as to what the rules really are; engenders instability in the effective legal environment.
	Breeds cynicism, and undermines the establishment of the rule of law.
	Reduces tax revenues, potentially leading to increased rates on those who pay, or to higher inflation.
	Need for unrecorded income to pay bribes or to avoid corrupt officials drives businesses underground.
	Diminishes incentives to reduce costs, innovate, etc.

A third reason to suspect that there will be continued pressure to avoid the high-crime equilibrium is just the unpleasantness of it all. Business people in the current Russian environment often have had to dirty their hands in the course of their activity, but they are not proud of it, nor is that the environment that they want their children to inherit. And while individual exit is not easy, widespread incentives to legalize the business environment make the possibility of an evolution to more regular markets far from impossible, particularly in legitimate businesses (as opposed to illegal drugs, for instance). Further, much of the illegal activity was associated with one-time opportunities, such as the "primitive capitalist accumulation" of spontaneous privatization. Pressure to move towards a legal market economy (or at least to limit the social costs of corruption) would seem to be greater in relatively high-income countries like Russia, as opposed to some very low income countries. The high level of education in Russia, for example, raises the return to productive activity relative to rent seeking, thereby lessening the barriers to a transition to a low economic crime equilibrium.[34] Economic development, free trade, and a democratic tradition themselves help to lessen corruption.[35]

A related point is that, in stable settings, the extent of corruption depends on past levels of corruption.[36] A transitional environment has the advantage that perceptions of previous behavior have less weight in affecting current decisions. Corruption of the old planning apparatus need not lead people to believe that a new organization such as the revamped Audit Chamber or the Tax Police will be equally corrupt. Transition, and the new institutions that accompany transition, offers a slate that may not be perfectly clean, but at least is not as discredited as the previous system.

Fourth, widespread and visible corruption provides information to policy makers regarding where the rules and their associated enforcement regimes are not compatible with providing incentives to individuals to comply. This information then suggests that the rules or their enforcement should be changed. This may sound like meager compensation for economic crime, but it is preferable to no compensation. And the provision of such information is more important in a transitional setting, where policy makers have little familiarity with regulation of legal private economic activity.

Fifth, and finally, many of the steps that would seem to be part of a transition to a market economy, such as privatization and price liberalization, also would seem to be serve as anti-corruption measures in the long run. This complementarity is aided by other reform-related concerns. For example, Russia's interest in joining the OECD and the WTO will involve liberalization measures as well as the adoption of anti-corruption policies, and a low-corruption environment can also be a spur to foreign investment.[37]

Combating Corruption and Organized Crime[38]

The seeming pervasiveness of organized crime and corruption have led to repeated calls for crackdowns. In a sense, the standard response to perceived increases in corruption and mafia-style activity is to attack the supply side, to identify and prosecute the venal officials and the mafiosi, and to bring severe punishments to bear. In terms of Klitgaard's formulation (Corruption = Monopoly + Discretion - Accountability), the common call is for an increase in accountability. Such increased accountability has even been made a condition for assistance from international organizations.[39]

Increased accountability can be supplemented by legislated reductions in monopoly and discretion. Laws can be improved or eliminated to reduce bureaucratic obstacles to business, decreasing both monopoly power and the discretion of officials. Such changes can often be accomplished through minor alterations in rules and procedures; for example, internal regulations can prevent regular police officers from enforcing laws against minor vices, when enforcing such laws provides frequent opportunities for corrupt behavior.[40]

There undoubtedly is some merit to the "crackdown" approach. The penalties actually imposed on corrupt officials generally are quite low, typically not going beyond dismissal, and the clearance rate for business-related murders evidently is not high. Nevertheless, there are some problems with implementing an off-the-shelf crackdown on corruption. First, it is very hard to measure changes in corruption, since so much of it never comes to light. If aid is made conditional on lessened corruption, for example, how will the fulfillment of that condition be assessed – by fewer arrests or by more arrests for corruption? Second, charges of corruption frequently are baseless, and without adequate safeguards for defendants, a stepped-up campaign against corruption could become little more than a way of settling political scores, or even be used to persecute those officials who, in the eyes of their colleagues, are insufficiently corrupt. Third, and perhaps more important, there are benefits associated with organized crime activity and corruption, as discussed in the previous section. The "accountability" approach does not discriminate between reductions in the good and the bad types of economic crime. Fourth, a crackdown could be implemented by stricter controls over both government officials and private economic actors, threatening the continuation of economic reform.

The alternative (or rather, complementary) approach to corruption control can be characterized as "harm reduction", a terminology commonly used in drug policy. Here, the focus is not so much on reducing corruption *per se*, but on reducing the social costs of that corruption that does take place. Some forms of reducing corruption also are likely to reduce the social costs of corruption. Encouraging a free press, free elections, an independent judiciary, and a legislative branch with some oversight over the executive branch, as well as by promoting a civil society that has oversight over government more generally: these represent alternative routes to increased accountability, beyond a "crackdown" and augmented transparency in rules. Such forms of corruption control are good at targeting socially-detrimental corruption, because unlike beneficial corruption, socially-costly corruption frequently has tangible victims with incentives to complain, if they can do so in a manner that provides reasonable assurances against reprisals.[41] Free and competitive elections do not ensure that venal officials will not be elected and re-elected; nevertheless, they do make it likely that the social costs of that corruption that does take place are relatively minor, because those officials who engage in particularly costly corruption will have difficulty getting re-elected.

How should policy makers go about reducing the social harm from organized crime? The answers are standard and widely understood, and in part they relate to improving the partial reform measures that led to the increase in mafia activity in the first place.[42] Further liberalization and rationalization of the tax code are needed to allow profitable private businesses to operate legally. The public alternative to private protection, particularly the provision of contract law and improved police protection, also is part of the solution. Effective time horizons can be increased via macroeconomic and political stabilization. Macroeconomic stabilization in Russia has been slow in coming but now, after the financial crisis of August 1998, appears to be well along.

Policies that would be appropriate in a world of rule-abiding angels may be ill-advised in a world peopled by, well, people. And government officials are people, too. The potential for corruption, therefore, must be taken into account in designing public policy; indeed, this is the real key to limiting the social costs of corruption. Powers of officials must be restrained to reflect the possibility that powers will be corruptly misused. Nevertheless, considerations of corruption are often paid little heed at the stage of policy development: "the more usual practice is to choose the policies that would be best *if* the whole bureaucracy were dependable, and then to deplore its corruption, and condemn it for the failure of the policies chosen".[43]

One element of anti-corruption and anti-organized crime measures that is indispensable is a real commitment by leaders to seriously undertake such campaigns. Such commitment is surprisingly hard to come by, in part because the leaders themselves often emerge at the top without completely clean hands, and in part because the commitment can be both socially and personally costly.[44] Analysts of the Sicilian mafia frequently suggest that its long-term vitality is in part illusory, because of the absence of a sustained state campaign to combat the mafia. Despite the recurrence of public announcements of anti-corruption campaigns, it is still an open question whether top political levels in Russia are committed to the rule of law, much of which involves limitations on their own powers, particularly when the current deviations from legality are more likely to serve than to harm the political leaderships direct, short-term interests.

Conclusions

I have argued that much of the perceived increase in corruption and organized crime in transitional Russia represents a more open version of activity that was commonplace during the pre-reform era. The partial nature of reforms, particularly the greatly increased incentives to engage in private business, combined with continuing government intervention in the economy and poor public provision of protection and contract law, has been a major source of new economic crime. Simultaneously, the costs of corruption and organized crime have gone up, largely due to relative disorganization and the general economic uncertainty during the reforms. Likewise, the benefits of economic crime in transitional Russia are higher than they would be in advanced Western market economies, again because of overly-restrictive laws governing private economic activity and the poor development of public protection. Further liberalization and the development of publicly-provided contract law will help to reduce the amount of economic crime. The costs of the crime that does take place can be reduced via stabilization, political steadiness, and increases in accountability arising from a free press, an independent judiciary, and a watchdog legislature.

Russia has two economic crime problems, a "stock" problem and a "flow" problem. The stock represents the accumulated corruption and crime of recent years, while the flow represents the ongoing, daily additions to that stock. Past activity represents a sunk cost. While exacting retribution for some past activity often is worthwhile, in Russian circumstances, such a policy will undermine the more pressing concern, which is to lower the social costs of the future flows.

Let me explain. In Russia, every business or government official is at risk for having engaged in some sort of corrupt or illegal activity. In the words of "oligarch" Boris Berezovsky, "Only those people who have been asleep for the past 10 years have avoided willingly or unwillingly breaking the law"– and Berezovsky explicitly included high government officials in his indictment.[45] With nearly everyone guilty, enforcers have almost unlimited discretion to target whomever they (dis)like. The appearance of unfairness, then, can hardly be avoided when someone is selected for enforcement in such an environment. This perception of unfairness, however, itself undermines the deterrence of future bad behavior that is the social gain from a crackdown: prosecutions are viewed as being based on political unpopularity, and not on behavior. When the crackdown also inhibits the working of a free press, one of the established bulwarks against corruption, then it is doubly ill-advised.[46] The retribution for some previous crime and corruption comes at the expense of providing improved incentives for the future.

Notes

[1]   Criminal and corrupt acts by Russian officials numbered 53,700 in 1999, a 35.6 per cent increase over 1998, according to the First Deputy Interior Minister Vladimir Kozlov. RFE/RL Newsline, March 2, 2000.

2   In the 2000 Corruption Perceptions Index computed by Transparency International, Russia tied for 82nd out of the 90 countries ranked, where being ranked nearer the bottom indicates greater corruption. See www.transparency.org/documents/cpi/2000/cpi2000.html.

3   Noonan (1984, pp. xi-xii) notes different standards underlying the notion of bribery.

4   See Suvorov (1986, p. 1).

5   Falcone (1993, p. 102). For the recent structure of mafia elements in the Russian city of Perm', see Varese (1997).

6   See, e.g., Handelman (1995).

7   This framework is adopted from the introduction of Leitzel (1995), and a more extensive discussion of this approach can be found in that source.

8   There is a good deal of variance among normal market economies, of course, but the differences are largely inconsequential for Russian reforms at this stage. Further, political gains by anti-market groups could put the desired destination in doubt, though major opposition groups in Russia tend to suggest that they are not against market-oriented reform, but rather, in favor of a slower or more controlled transition.

9   The distribution of the costs may change during reform, however. It also should be noted that a similar observation applies to some of the benefits associated with reform; for example, the legalization of the second economy will allow pre-existing underground businesses to surface, and be newly counted in measures of economic activity.

10   Another way to motivate the second and third observations is by an appeal to the theory of the second best. The pre-reform conditions are woefully distorted, so there is little *a priori* basis for knowing whether marginal changes either in the direction of competitive markets or in the opposite direction are socially desirable.

11   Grossman and Treml (1987, p. 285).

12   Grossman (1989, p. 81).

13   See Gaddy (1991) and Treml (1990). Leonid Brezhnev was reported to have said, "No one lives on wages alone. I remember in my youth we earned money by unloading freight cars. So, what did we do? Three crates or bags unloaded and one for ourselves. That is how everybody lives...." Quoted in Treml (1990, p. 2), from F. Burlatskiy, *Literaturnaya Gazeta*.

14   Simis (1982) details the systemic nature of Soviet corruption.

15   On the applicability of Say's Law to corruption, see Andvig and Moene (1990). A common illustration arises from foreign travel: it is not unusual to hear stories of individuals traveling abroad who would never consider attempting to bribe a police officer in their native country, but who are quick to offer bribes to police in some foreign countries, solely on the country's reputation for police corruption.

16   Sah (1991).

17   Shelley (1996, p. 85).

18   Shelley (1996, p. 162). See also Alexeev, Gaddy and Leitzel (1995, p. 687), for a discussion of the Moscow bias.

19   Frisby (1998, p. 35), notes that Moscow's crime rate now exceeds the national average.

20   This point is commonly made; see, e.g., Goldman (1996, p. 43). In many instances, laws are contradictory, so it is not even possible to be in business and be law-abiding – a situation reminiscent of the era of central planning.

21   In one survey of Moscow shop managers, the average number of inspections reported was more than 18, double the amount reported in Warsaw. See Shleifer (1997).

22   OMRI Daily Digest, March 12, 1997. It is easy to overlook the large role that private security plays in Western market economies. In 1996, there were more than 155,000 licensed private security guards in the state of California alone, excluding off-duty public police officers who often moonlight as security guards. Sklansky (1999, p. 1174, n. 28).

23   On protection rents, see Lane (1958); this concept has been applied to Russian organized crime in Lotspeich (1996).

24   On the windfall from oil and natural gas in the 1970s, see Grossman (1998).

25   Shleifer and Vishny (1993) analyze some of the differences between stable and more competitive forms of corruption.

26   The 1990 figure is from Rossiyskaya Federatsiya v Tsifrakh v 1992 Godu [1993], and the 1996 figure (actually a decline of some 2,000 from 1995) was announced by the Interior Minister, as reported in OMRI Daily Digest, January 20, 1997. A further decline was reported in the first quarter of 1997; see RFE/RL Newsline, April 21, 1997. Note also that these figures include attempted murders, and therefore are not directly comparable with homicide statistics from many Western countries.

27   Wei (1997) provides cross-country evidence of how uncertainty in corruption (beyond the existence of corruption itself) dissuades foreign investment.

28   Johnson and Loveman (1995) document the importance of new firms in the Polish transition.

29   See Halligan and Teplukhin (1995, pp. 119-121), and OMRI Daily Digest, March 21, 1997. The surveys reported in these source involved foreign firms that had already invested. Fears of crime or the mafia might be more important in preventing initial investments.

30   Mauro (1995).

31   In a model involving "good" rules, Acemoglu and Verdier (2000) show that some corruption might still be tolerated, because it is too costly to suppress corruption entirely.

32   Putnam (1993, p. 183). The statement would look considerably less foreboding if placed at a higher level of aggregation: Italy may represent the future of Russia.

33   Los (1998, p. 80).

34   See Acemoglu (1995, pp. 31-32).

35   See Treisman (2000).

36   Tirole (1996).

37   Wei (1997a).

38   An earlier version of this section appeared in Leitzel (1996).

39   Michel Camdessus, the Managing Director of the IMF, indicated that a reduction in corruption was necessary to ensure continued IMF assistance to Russia. RFE/RL Newsline, April 4, 1997. See also the World Bank's efforts at "mainstreaming" anti-corruption, at www1.worldbank.org/publicsector/anticorrupt/mainstreaming.htm.

40   See Sherman (1978, p. 250).

41   See the discussion of steps that potential or actual victims of corruption might take to shield themselves from costs imposed by corruption in Alam (1995).

42   Similar suggestions for combating the mafia can be found in such otherwise dissimilar analyses as Goldman (1996) and Layard and Parker (1996, pp. 167-172).

43   Leff (1989, p. 402).
44   Insinuations of corrupt activity from his previous employment in St. Petersburg have
been made against President Putin. See, for instance, Matt Bivens, "Waiting for
Vladimir Putin," TheMoscowTimes.com, March 26, 2000, at
www.themoscowtimes.com/stories/2000/03/26/001.html, accessed on June 15, 2000.
Further, substantial questions have been raised about the integrity of the March,
2000, presidential balloting; see
www.themoscowtimes.com/stories/2000/09/09/119.html.
45   Berezovsky was quoted in "Tycoon Resigns from Duma as relations with Kremlin
Cool," by Amelia Gentleman, *The Guardian*, July 18, 2000, p. 12.
46   See, for instance, Matt Bivens, "Back to the USSR," *Brill's Content*, at
www.brillscontent.com/August2000/russia_0700.html, accessed on July 1, 2000.
Measures taken in recent months against oligarch Vladimir Gusinsky, former
television anchorman Sergei Dorenko, and others, seem to threaten media freedoms
in Russia.

References

Acemoglu, D. (1995), 'Reward Structures and the Allocation of Talent', *European Economic Review*, vol. 39, pp. 17-33.
Acemoglu, D. and Verdier, T. (2000), 'The Choice Between Market Failures and Corruption', *American Economic Review*, vol. 90, no. 1, pp. 194-211.
Alam, M. S. (1995), 'A Theory of Limits on Corruption and Some Applications', *Kyklos*, vol. 48, no.3, pp. 419-35.
Alexeev, M, Clifford, G. and Leitzel, J. (1995), 'Economic Crime and Russian Reform', *Journal of Institutional and Theoretical Economics*, vol. 151, no. 4, pp. 677-92.
Andvig, J. C. and Moene, K. O. (1990), 'How Corruption May Corrupt', *Journal of Economic Behavior and Organization*, vol. 13, pp. 63-76.
Falcone, G. with Padovani, M. (1993), *Men of Honour*, Warner Books, London.
Frisby, T. (1998), 'The Rise of Organised Crime in Russia: Its Roots and Significance', *Europe-Asia Studies*, vol. 50, pp. 27-49.
Gaddy, C. (1991), 'The Labor Market and the Second Economy in the Soviet Union', *Berkeley-Duke Occasional Papers on the Second Economy in the USSR*, no. 24, (January).
Gambetta, D. (1994), *The Sicilian Mafia*, Harvard University Press, Cambridge.
Goldman, M. I. (1996), 'Why is the Mafia so Dominant in Russia?', *Challenge*, pp. 39-47 (January-February).
Grossman, G. (1989), 'The Second Economy: Boon or Bane for the Reform of the First Economy', in S. Gomulka, Y. Ha and C. Kim (eds), *Economic Reforms in the Socialist World*, Armonk, M. E. Sharpe, New York.
Grossman, G. (1998), 'Subverted Sovereignty: Historic Role of the Soviet Underground', in Stephen S. Cohen et al. (eds), *The Tunnel at the End of the Light*, University of California–IAS, Berkeley.
Grossman, G. and Treml, V.G. (1987), 'Measuring Hidden Personal Incomes in the USSR', in S. Alessandrini and B. Dallago (eds), *The Unofficial Economy*, Gower Publishing Company Ltd, Aldershot, England.
Gustafson, T. (1999), *Capitalism Russian-Style*, Cambridge University Press, Cambridge.

Halligan, L. and Teplukhin, P. (1995), 'Investment Disincentives in Russia', in *Russian Economic Trends*, Centre for Economic Reform, Whurr Publishers, vol. 4, no. 1.

Handelman, S. (1995), *Comrade Criminal*, Yale University Press, New Haven.

Johnson, S. and Loveman, G.W. (1995), *Starting Over in Eastern Europe: Entrepreneurship and Economic Renewal*, Harvard Business School Press, Boston.

Klitgaard, R. (1991), 'Gifts and Bribes', in Richard J. Zeckhauser (ed), *Strategy and Choice*, MIT Press, Cambridge.

Lane, F.C. (1958), 'Economic Consequences of Organized Violence', *Journal of Economic History*, vol. 18, pp. 401-410.

Layard, R. and Parker, J. (1996), *The Coming Russian Boom*, The Free Press, New York.

Leff, N.H. (1989), 'Economic Development through Bureaucratic Corruption', *American Behavioral Scientist*. vol. 8. pp. 8-14. (1964). Reprinted in A.J. Heidenheimer. M. Johnston, and V.T. LeVine (eds), *Political Corruption: A Handbook*, Transaction Publishers, New Brunswick.

Leitzel, J. (1995), *Russian Economic Reform*, Routledge, London.

Leitzel, J. (1996), 'Corruption in the Russian Transition', *Eurasia Economic Outlook*, The WEFA Group, pp. 1.7-1.9, (May).

Los, M. (1998), ' "Virtual" Property and Post-Communist Globalization', *Demokratizatsiya*, vol. 6, pp. 77-86 (Winter).

Lotspeich, R. (1996), 'An Economic Analysis of Extortion in Russia', Working paper, Indiana State University, Department of Economics, (November).

Mauro, P. (1995), 'Corruption and Growth', *Quarterly Journal of Economics*, vol. 111, pp. 681-712 (August).

Noonan, J.T.Jr. (1984), *Bribes*, Macmillan, New York.

Putnam, R. (1993), *Making Democracy Work*, Princeton University Press, Princeton.

Sah, R.K. (1991), 'Social Osmosis and Patterns of Crime', *Journal of Political Economy*, vol. 99, no. 6, pp. 1272-95.

Shelley, L. I. (1996), *Policing Soviet Society - The Evolution of State Control*, Routledge, London.

Sherman, L.W. (1978), *Scandal and Reform: Controlling Police Corruption*, University of California Press, Berkeley.

Shleifer, A. (1997), 'Government in Transition', *European Economic Review*, vol. 41, pp. 385-410.

Shleifer, A. and Vishny, R.W. (1993), 'Corruption', *Quarterly Journal of Economics*, vol. 108, no. 3, pp. 599-617.

Simis, K. (1982), *USSR: The Corrupt Society*, Simon and Schuster, New York.

Sklansky, D. A. (1999), 'The Private Police', *UCLA Law Review*, vol. 46, pp. 1165-1287 (April).

Suvorov, V. (1986), *Inside the Aquarium - The Making of a Top Soviet Spy*, Macmillan, NewYork.

Tirole, J. (1996), 'A Theory of Collective Reputations', *Review of Economic Studies*, vol. 63, pp. 1-22.

Treisman, D. (2000), 'The Causes of Corruption: A Cross-National Study', *Journal of Public Economics*, vol. 76, pp. 399-457.

Treml, V.G. (1990), 'Study of Employee Theft of Materials from Places of Employment', *Berkeley-Duke Occasional Papers on the Second Economy in the USSR*, no. 20 (June).

Varese, F. (1997), 'The Structure of Criminal Groups Compared: Perm, Sicily and the USA', Paper prepared for BASEES Annual Conference, Cambridge, UK *(12-14 April)*.

Wei, S-J. (1997), 'Why is Corruption So Much More Taxing Than Tax? Arbitrariness Kills', NBER Working Paper, no. 6255 (November).

Chapter 3

Strong Institutions are more Important than the Speed of Reforms

Vladimir Popov

Introduction

Ten years ago, on the eve of transition, economic discussion in the profession was dominated by the debate between shock therapists, who advocated radical reforms and rapid transformation, and gradualists, justifying a more cautious and piecemeal approach to reforms. Shock therapists pointed out to the example of East European countries and Baltic states – fast liberalizers and successful stabilizers, that experienced a recovery after two to three years fall in output, while their CIS counterparts were doing much worse. Gradualists cited the example of China, arguing that the lack of recession and high growth rates is the direct result of the step by step approach to economic transformation. Shock therapists were arguing that "one cannot cross the abyss in two jumps", that rapid liberalization allows to avoid painful and costly period, when the old centrally planned economy (CPE) is not working already, while the new market one is not working yet.

As time passed, there appeared statistics that allowed to test the predictions of theories. Quite a number of studies were undertaken with the intention to prove that fast liberalization and macro-stabilization pays off and finally leads to better performance (Sachs, 1996; De Melo, Denizer and Gelb, 1996; Fisher, Sahay and Vegh, 1996; Åslund, Boone and Johnson, 1996; Breton, Gros and Vandille, 1997; Fisher and Sahay, 2000). To prove the point, the authors tried to regress output changes during transition on liberalization indices developed by De Melo et al. (1996) and by EBRD (published in its Transition Reports), on inflation and different measures of initial conditions.

The conventional wisdom was probably summarized in the 1996 World Development Report *From Plan to Market*, which basically stated that differences in economic performance were associated mostly with "good and bad" policies, in particular with the progress in liberalization and macroeconomic stabilization: countries that are more successful than others in introducing market reforms and bringing down inflation were believed to have better chances to limit the reduction of output and to quickly recover from the transformational recession. "Consistent policies, combining liberalization of markets, trade, and new business entry with reasonable price stability, can achieve a great deal even in countries lacking clear property rights and strong market institutions" – was one of the major conclusions of the WDR 1996 (p. 142). The conclusion did not withstand the test of time, since by now most economists would probably agree that because liberalization was carried out without strong market institutions it led to the extraordinary output collapse in CIS states. Liberalization may be important, but the devil is in details, which often do not fit into the generalizations and make straightforward explanations look trivial.

Take the example of Vietnam and China - two countries that shared a lot of similarities in initial conditions and achieved basically the same results (immediate growth of output without transformational recession) despite different reform strategies. While Chinese reforms are normally treated as a classical example of gradualism, Vietnamese reformers introduced Polish style shock therapy treatment (instant deregulation of most prices and introduction of convertibility of dong) even before Poland did, in 1989, and still managed to avoid the reduction of output.[1]

Or, take the example of the differing performance of the former Soviet Union (FSU) states. The champions of liberalization and stabilization in the region are definitely Baltic states (cumulative liberalization index by 1995 - 2.4-2.9), whereas Uzbekistan (with the same index of 1.1) is commonly perceived to be one of the worst procrastinators. However in Uzbekistan the reduction of output in 1990-95 totaled only 18 per cent and the economy started to grow again in 1996, while in the Baltics output fell in the early 1990s by 36-60 per cent and even in 1996, two years after the bottom of the recession was reached, was still 31 per cent to 58 per cent below the pre-recession maximum.

At a first glance, there seems to be a positive relationship between liberalization and performance (Fig.3.1), but a more careful consideration reveals that the link is just the result of sharp difference in the magnitude of the recession in EE countries, as a group, and FSU states, also as a group (Fig.3.1). Within these groups there is no correlation whatsoever.

Overall, attempts to link differences in output changes during transition to the cumulative liberalization index and to macro stabilization (rates of inflation) have not yielded any impressive results: it turned out that dummies, such as membership in the ruble zone (i.e. FSU) and war destruction, are much more important explanatory variables than either the liberalization index or inflation (Åslund, Boone and Johnson, 1996). Other studies that tried to take into account a number of initial conditions (repressed inflation -monetary overhang before deregulation of prices, trade dependence, black market exchange rate premium, number of years under central planning, urbanization, overindustrialization, and per capita income) found that in some cases liberalization becomes insignificant as well (De Melo, Denizer, Gelb and Tenev, 1997, p. 25; Heybey and Murrel, 1999; Popov, 2000).

Figure 3.1 Liberalization and output change

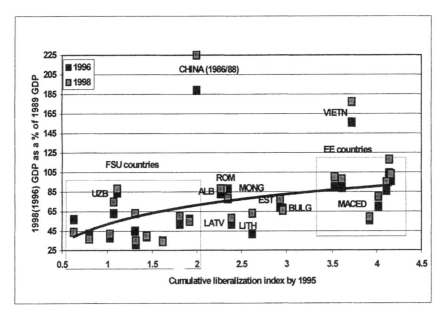

This implies that there is still no good explanation even for the basic stylized facts, such as the ability of China and Vietnam to avoid the recession completely, or such as the markedly greater magnitude of the recession in FSU as compared to East European (EE) countries, not to speak about differing performance of countries belonging to the same geographical region.

This paper starts by separating the transformational recession (the deviation of actual output from potential) from the process of economic growth (recovery from the transformational recession). It is argued that the former (the collapse of output during transition) can be best explained mostly by distortions in industrial structure and trade patterns accumulated during the period of central planning, and by inflation and the strength of the state institutions during transition period, while the speed of liberalization does not seem to play a major role. The latter process (recovery) should be treated as a normal growth process: it could be modeled by using conventional production functions and in the long run may demonstrate the ability to capitalize on liberalization by increasing factor efficiency (Shmelev and Popov 1989; Popov, 1998a, 1999).

Non-policy Factors: Distortions in Industrial Structure and Trade Patterns

The explanation accepted in this paper as a working hypothesis is based on the most conventional approach to the transformational recession: it is viewed as a supply-side phenomenon, as a structural adjustment process resulting from the need to overcome disproportions inherited from the centrally planned economy (CPE) - high militarization, overindustrialization and underdevelopment of the service sector, "under-openness" of the economy, the perverse structure of trade among former Soviet republics and among socialist countries. The greater the magnitude of these distortions inherited from the centrally planned economies, the more pronounced the reduction of GDP during the transformational recession.[2]

The supply-side explanation implies that the reallocation of resources (restructuring) due to market imperfections is associated with the temporary loss of output. Thus, the decline in the production of non-competitive enterprises and industries is not offset immediately by an increase in the production of competitive industries and enterprises due to barriers to capital and labor flows such as poorly developed banking system and securities markets, uncertain property rights, the lack of easily enforceable and commonly accepted bankruptcy and liquidation procedures, the underdevelopment of land market, housing market and labor market infrastructure, and so on.

Attempts to separate non-policy from policy factors by running multiple regressions produce some statistically satisfactory and economically meaningful results.[3] Though there is a relationship between the magnitude of output decline on the one hand and the liberalization index and inflation on the other ($R^2 = 65\%$), this weakens greatly or even disappears completely once variables that characterize objective conditions are factored in. It is noteworthy that nearly 70 per cent of the variations in the magnitude of the decline of output may be explained by only two dummy variables (both significant at the one per cent level) that account for membership in the FSU and for wars. It is even more remarkable that the addition of liberalization variable to the equation does not seem to make any difference: the correlation coefficient does not increase when liberalization is taken into consideration; to make matters worse, the coefficient of the liberalization index is not statistically significant and has the unexpected sign: the greater the liberalization, the larger the decline of output. Inflation variable is always significant and has the predicted (negative) sign, but this cannot be considered as an important finding: the link between macroeconomic stabilization and economic growth was demonstrated more than once for a much greater group of countries (see for instance: Bruno, 1995; Bruno and Easterly, 1995).

These results suggest that the usual argument linking the better performance of EE, especially the Central European countries (as compared to the FSU, especially the CIS countries), to better economic policies (greater liberalization) does not necessarily hold. Indeed, the identification and decomposition of the "FSU effect" may be carried out more effectively by bringing into the equation not policy variables, but non-policy factors, such as the relative magnitude of the distortions in trade and industrial structure.

To avoid the multicolinearity problem, we have constructed an aggregate indicator of distortions (summing up all the distortions mentioned above, since they are expressed as a per cent of GDP). There is a fairly strong correlation between aggregate distortions in industrial and trade structure before transition and the subsequent performance during transition, as measured by the GDP change (Fig. 3.2). Among countries with minor aggregate distortions (less than 30 per cent of GDP) are three former Yugoslav republics (Slovenia, Croatia, Macedonia), the Czech and Slovak republics, Hungary, China and Vietnam. All these countries, with the exception of war-affected Macedonia, are doing better than most other transition economies. On the other hand, among countries with most distorted economies (aggregate distortions of over 50 per cent of GDP) we find all the former Soviet republics, except Russia (where aggregate distortions amounted to only 39 per cent of GDP). In fact, aggregate distortions alone may explain 32 per cent of output variations during transition and about 50 per cent of variations if the economies affected by war are excluded. Taking into account the other two non-policy factors characterizing the initial conditions, we obtain statistically sound and robust results: over 60 per cent of the variations in performance may be explained by (1) the advantages of backwardness, (2) aggregate distortions, and (3) the war dummy variable.

Figure 3.2   Aggregate distortions in industrial structure and external trade before transition and GDP change during transition

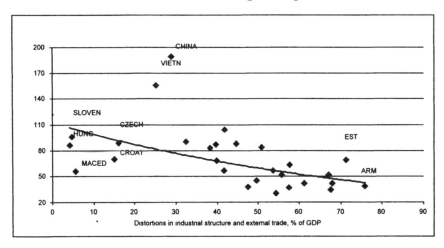

The addition of the FSU dummy to the equation leads to the absorption of the aggregate distortions variable (the FSU dummy thus plays the role of a proxy for distortions), while the impact of the level of economic development and war remains statistically significant. Adding inflation as an explanatory variable allows to improve the results, but the inclusion of liberalization index only deteriorates T-statistics and does not increase the explanatory power of the regression at all. To put it differently, the observed differences in performance may be explained *mostly* by the unequal initial conditions, while the role of traditional "good policy" factors appears to be quite limited.

Such an interpretation suggests, among other things, that recent research aimed at providing some empirical evidence for the conventional wisdom (greater liberalization and stabilization lead to better performance) may not reach this goal by demonstrating that countries, which are more advanced in liberalization and in fighting inflation are doing better than others. Once the pre-transition initial conditions are taken into account, it turns out that conventionally monitored policy factors, such as the degree of liberalization and the rates of inflation, do not really explain much. Differences in economic performance in post-communist countries during transition appear to be associated predominantly not with chosen reform paths, but with the magnitude of initial distortions in industrial structure and trade patterns, and with the initial level of economic development.

This is not to say that government policy in general does not affect performance, but to admit that conventional understanding of the policy factors (progress in liberalization and macroeconomic stabilization) is not enough to account for all of them. It may well be that most important policy factors that affect performance are not associated, despite popular beliefs, with the speed of liberalization and macro-stabilization. Rather, these are the policy measures that preserve or create strong and efficient institutions facilitating the functioning of the market economy.

Policy Factors: Institutions, Rule of Law and Democracy

The decline of the institutional capabilities contributed a great deal to Russia's and CIS poor economic performance. If regression equations that account for initial conditions only are used to predict economic performance (GDP change), it turns out that China and Vietnam did much better than expected, EE and Baltic states on average did not so good, but still a bit better than expected, whereas most CIS states did much worse than expected. Exceptions within CIS prove the rule: Uzbekistan and Belarus, i.e. exactly those countries that are not only known for proceeding with slow reforms, but are also believed to have the strongest state institutions among all CIS states.[4] Ukrainian example, on the other hand, proves that it is not the speed of reforms *per se* that really matters: being a procrastinator, it did nevertheless worse than expected due arguably to the poor institutional capabilities (trust in political institutions in Ukraine is markedly lower than in Belarus).

The efficiency of state and non-state institutions is not easily measurable. In most FSU and Balkan countries the collapse of the institutions is observable in the dramatic increase of the share of the shadow economy; in the decline of government revenues as a proportion of GDP; in the inability of the state to deliver basic public goods and appropriate regulatory framework; in the accumulation of tax, trade, wage and bank arrears; in the demonetization, "dollarization" and "barterization" of the economy, as measured by high and growing money velocity, and in the decline of bank financing as a proportion of GDP; in poor enforcement of property rights, bankruptcies, contracts and law and order in general; in increased crime rates; etc. Most of the mentioned phenomena may be defined quantitatively with a remarkable result that China and Vietnam are closer in this respect to EE countries than to CIS. However, the construction of the aggregate index of the efficiency of institutions is problematic because the rationale for choosing weights is not clear.

One possible general measure is the trust of businesses and individuals in various institutions - here FSU states rank much lower than East European countries in all available surveys. In the global survey of firms in 69 countries on the credibility of the state institutions, CIS had the lowest credibility, below that of Sub-Saharan Africa (World Bank, 1997a, pp. 5, 35). Especially striking was the gap between EE and CIS countries: differences in credibility index between South and Southeast Asia and EE were less pronounced than differences between Sub-Sahara Africa and CIS.

Another good proxy for measuring institutional capacity of the state is the financial strength of the government - the share of state revenues in GDP. Though much have been said about "big government" and too high taxes in former socialist countries, by now it is rather obvious that the downsizing of the government that occurred in most CIS states during transition went too far. This argument has nothing to do with the long-term considerations of the optimal size of the government in transition economies – it is true that in most of them government revenues and expenditure as a share of GDP are still higher than in countries with comparable GDP per capita. But whatever the long term optimal level of government spending should be, the drastic reduction of such spending (by 50 per cent and more in real terms) cannot lead to anything else but institutional collapse.

Before transition in former socialist states not only government regulations were pervasive, but also the financial power of the state was roughly the same as in European countries (government revenues and expenditure amounted to about 50 per cent of GDP). This allowed the state to provide the bulk of public goods and extensive social transfers. During transition tax revenues as a proportion of GDP decreased markedly in most countries. However, Central European countries and Estonia managed to arrest the decline, while Russia (together with Lithuania, Latvia, and several Southeast Europe and Central Asian states) experienced the greatest reduction. In Vietnam the share of government revenues in GDP grew by 1.5 times in 1989-93. Chinese government revenues as a percentage of GDP fell by over 2 times since the late 1970s, but it looks more like a conscious policy choice rather than a spontaneous process (authoritarian regimes have always better powers to collect tax revenues, if they choose to do so, as did all governments in the CPE's before the transition).

In most CIS states the reduction of the government expenditure occurred in the worst possible way - it proceeded without any coherent plan and did not involve the reassessment of government commitments. Instead of shutting down completely some government programs and concentrating limited resources on the other with an aim to raise their efficiency, the government kept all programs half-alive, half-financed, and barely working.

This led to the slow decay of public education, health care, infrastructure, law and order institutions, fundamental R&D, etc. Virtually all services provided by the government - from collecting custom duties to regulating street traffic - are currently the symbol of notorious economic inefficiency. There were numerous cases of government failure which further undermined the credibility of the state since many government activities in providing public goods were slowly dyeing and were only partly replaced by private and semi-private businesses.

Three major patterns of change in the share of government expenditure in GDP,[5] which generally coincide with the three major archetypes of institutional developments, and even broader - with three most typical distinct "models" of transition, are shown in Fig. 3.3. Under **strong authoritarian regimes** (China) cuts in government expenditure occurred at the expense of defense, subsidies and budgetary financed investment, while expenditure for "ordinary government" as a percentage of GDP remained largely unchanged (Naughton, 1997); **under strong democratic regimes** (Poland) budgetary expenditure, including those for "ordinary government", declined only in the pre-transition period, but increased during transition itself; finally, **under week democratic regimes** (Russia) the reduction of the general level of government expenditure led not only to the decline in the financing of defense, investment and subsidies, but to the downsizing of "ordinary government", which undermined and in many instances even led to the collapse of the institutional capacities of the state.

Figure 3.3 Government expenditure, % of GDP

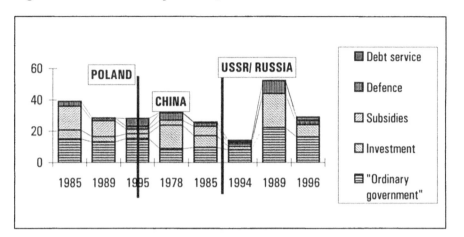

While in China total budgetary expenditure and that for "ordinary government" are much lower than in Russia and Poland, they were sufficient to preserve the functioning institutions since the financing of social security from the government budget was traditionally low. In Russia, however, though expenditure for ordinary government seem to be not that much lower than in Poland, the pace of their reduction during transition exceeded that of GDP: to put it differently, given the various patterns of GDP dynamics, while in Poland "ordinary government" financing grew by about one third in real terms in 1989-95/6 (and while in China it nearly doubled), in Russia it fell by about three times! The Russian pattern of institutional decay proved to be extremely detrimental for investment, and for general economic performance.

After adding the decline in government revenues variable to the ones that characterize initial conditions (level of development and distortions) and external environment (war dummy variable), the explanatory power of the regression increases to 75 per cent with the excellent T-statistics (28 observations). And it is quite remarkable that the inclusion of liberalization variables at this point does not improve regression statistics. Factoring in inflation allows to improve the explanatory power to 85 per cent. The correlation coefficient rises further up to 92 per cent, if other indicators of the institutional capacities, such as the share of shadow economy, are added, though the number of observations in this case is only 17 because of the lack of data (Table 3.1).

There was only one group of transition economies, where the share of state revenues in GDP remained relatively stable during transition – Central European countries. Outside Central Europe there were only four countries where the share of government revenues in GDP did not fall markedly – Belarus, Estonia, Uzbekistan, Vietnam. The first three are also the top three performers in the FSU region, whereas Vietnam's performance is second to only that of China. It is noteworthy that Belarus and Uzbekistan, commonly perceived as procrastinators, nevertheless show better results than most more advanced reformers. On the other hand, this is the alternative explanation of the Estonian success in economic transformation as compared to most CIS states and even to neighboring Baltic states: the usual interpretation focusing on the progress in liberalization may overlook the impact of strong institutions.

It is precisely this strong institutional framework that should be held responsible for both - for the success of gradual reforms in China and shock therapy in Vietnam, where strong authoritarian regimes were preserved and CPE institutions were not dismantled before new market institutions were created; and for the relative success of radical reforms in East European, especially in Central European countries, where strong democratic regimes and new market institutions emerged quickly. And it is precisely the collapse of strong state and institutions that started in the USSR in the late 1980s and continued in the successor states in the 1990s that explains the extreme length, if not the extreme depth, of the FSU transformational recession.

Table 3.1 **Regression of change in GDP on non-policy and policy-related factors (all coefficients are significant at five per cent level except those in brackets)**
Dependent variable = log (1996 GDP as a % of 1989 GDP)

For China - all indicators are for the period of 1979-86 or similar

Equations, Number of Observations / Variables	1, N=28	2, N=28	3, N=28	4, N=28	5, N=17	6, N=17
Constant	5.23	4.96	5.55	5.71	5.91	6.07
Distortions, % of GDP[a]	-.01	-.01	-.01	-.01	-.00	-.00
1987 PPP GDP per capita, % of the US level	-.01	-.02	-.01	-.01	-.02	-.01
War dummy[b]	-.63	-.58	-.40	-.40	0.26^c	0.27^c
Decline in government revenues as a % of GDP from 1989-91 to 1993-96	-.01	-.01	-.01	-.01		
Liberalization index		(.07)		(-0.4)		(-.05)
Log (Inflation, % a year, 1990-95, geometric average)			-.12	-.14	-.12	-.14
Shadow economy as a % of GDP in 1994					-.02	-.02
Adjusted R^2, %	75	75	85	84	92	91

[a]Cumulative measure of distortions as a % of GDP equal to the sum of defense expenditure (minus three per cent regarded as the 'normal' level), deviations in industrial structure and trade openness from the 'normal' level, the share of heavily distorted trade (among the FSU republics) and lightly distorted trade (with socialist countries) taken with a 33 per cent weight (see Appendix for details).

[b]Equals one for Armenia, Azerbaijan, Croatia, Georgia, Macedonia, and Tajikistan and zero for all other countries.

[c]Significant at eight per cent level.

To put it differently, Gorbachev reforms of 1985-91 failed not because they were gradual, but due to the weakening of the state institutional capacity leading to the inability of the government to control the flow of events. Similarly, Yeltsin reforms in Russia, as well as economic reforms in most other FSU states, were so costly not because of the shock therapy, but due to the collapse of the institutions needed to enforce law and order and carry out manageable transition.

To sum up, there is enough evidence that differing performance during transition, after factoring in initial conditions and external environment, depends mostly on the strength of institutions and not so much on the progress in liberalization *per se*.

Finally, there is a difficult question what leads to the institutional collapse and can it be prevented. Using the terminology of political science, it is appropriate to distinguish between strong authoritarian regimes (China, Vietnam, Uzbekistan), strong democratic regimes (Central European countries) and weak democratic regimes (most FSU and Balkan states – Fig. 3.4). The former two are politically liberal or liberalizing, i.e. protect individual rights, including those of property and contracts, and create a framework of law and administration, while the latter regimes, though democratic, are politically not so liberal since they lack strong institutions and the ability to enforce law and order (Zakaria, 1997). This gives rise to the phenomenon of "illiberal democracies" - countries, where competitive elections are introduced before the rule of law is established. While European countries in the XIX century and East Asian countries recently moved from first establishing the rule of law to gradually introducing democratic elections (Hong Kong is the most obvious example of the rule of law without democracy), in Latin America, Africa, and now in CIS countries democratic political systems were introduced in societies without the firm rule of law.

Authoritarian regimes (including communist), while gradually building property rights and institutions, were filling the vacuum in the rule of law via authoritarian means. After democratization occurred and illiberal democracies emerged, they found themselves deprived of old authoritarian instruments to ensure law and order, but without the newly developed democratic mechanisms needed to guarantee property rights, contracts and law and order in general (upper left quadrant in Fig. 4). No surprise, this had a devastating impact on investment climate and output.[6]

As Fig. 3.5 suggests, there is a clear relationship between the ratio of rule of law index on the eve of transition to democratization index, on the one hand, and economic performance during transition, on the other, although the positive correlation for authoritarian countries is apparently different from that for democracies. To put it differently, democratization without strong rule of law, whether one likes it or not, usually leads to the collapse of output. There is a price to pay for early democratization, i.e. introduction of competitive elections of government under the conditions when the major liberal rights (personal freedom and safety, property, contracts, fair trial in court, etc.) are not well established.

Figure 3.4   Indices of the rule of law and political rights (democracy), 0-10, higher value represent stronger rule of law and democracy

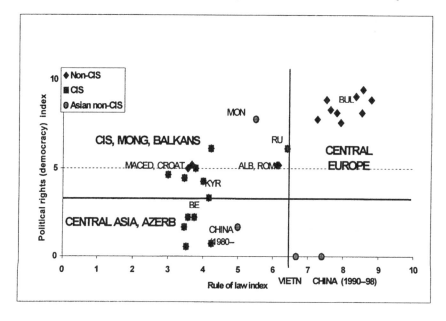

Figure 3.5 Ratio of the rule of law to democracy index and output change

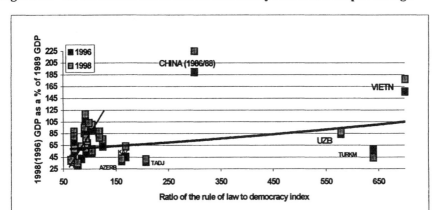

If the rule of law and democracy indices are included into the basic regression equation, they have predicted signs (positive impact of the rule of law and negative impact of democracy) and statistically significant (Table 3.2, Equation 1), which is consistent with the results obtained for larger sample of countries. The best explanatory power, however, is exhibited by the index that is computed as the ratio of the rule of law index to democracy index: nearly 80 per cent of all variations in output can be explained by only three factors – pre-transition distortions, inflation, and rule-of-law-to-democracy index (Table 3.2, Equation 2). If liberalization variable is added, it turns out to be not statistically significant and does not improves the goodness of fit (Equation 3). At the same time, the ratio of the rule of law to democracy index and the decline in government revenues are not substitutes, but rather complement each other in characterizing the process of the institutional decay. These two variables are not correlated and improve the goodness of fit, when included together in the same regression, to 88 per cent (Equation 5) - better result than in regressions with either one of these variables. The liberalization index, when added to the same equation, only deteriorates the goodness of fit, is not statistically significant, and has the "wrong" sign.

Institutional Change in Transition Economies

Table 3.2   **Regression of change in GDP in 1989-96 on initial conditions, policy factors, and rule of law and democracy indices (all coefficients are significant at nine per cent level except those in brackets)**
Dependent variable = log (1996 GDP as a % of 1989 GDP)
For China - all indicators are for the period of 1989-96 or similar

Equations, Number of Observations / Variables	1, N=28	2, N=28	3, N=28	4, N=28	5, N=28	6, N=28
Constant	5.33	5.26	5.26	5.40	5.41	5.50
Distortions, % of GDP[a]	-.004	-.004	(-.003)	-.006	-.007	-.007
1987 PPP GDP per capita, % of the US level				-.007	-.009	-.008
War dummy[b]				-.19	-.36	-.37
Decline in government revenues as a % of GDP from 1989-91 to 1993-96					-.011	-.011
Liberalization index			(.015)			(-.018)
Log (Inflation, % a year, 1990-95, Geometric average)	-.19	-.20	-.20	-.17	-.13	-.14
Rule of law index, average for 1989-97, %	.(007)[c]					
Democracy index, average for 1990-98, %	-.007					
Ratio of the rule of law to democracy index		.088	.090	.060	.048	.046
Adjusted R^2, %	76	79	79	82	88	87

[a] Cumulative measure of distortions as a % of GDP equal to the sum of defense expenditure (minus three per cent regarded as the 'normal' level), deviations in industrial structure and trade openness from the 'normal' level, the share of heavily distorted trade (among the FSU republics) and lightly distorted trade (with socialist countries) taken with a 33 per cent weight (see Appendix for details).

[b] Equals one for Armenia, Azerbaijan, Croatia, Georgia, Macedonia, and Tajikistan and zero for all other countries.

[c] Significant at 14 per cent level.

Concluding Remarks

Differences in performance during transition depend strongly on the initial conditions, in particular, on the pre-transition levels of GDP per capita and distortions in industrial structure and external trade patterns. The higher the distortions (militarization, overindustrialization, "under-openness" of the economy and the share of perverted trade flows), the worse is the performance as measured by the GDP change. And the higher was GDP per capita before transition, the greater were distortions embodied in fixed capital stock, the more difficult it was to overcome these distortions to achieve growth.

By focusing on liberalization and macroeconomic stabilization as key policy variables in transition economies the conventional wisdom overlooked the impact of strong institutions. Accounting for uneven initial conditions sheds new light on the relative importance of various policy factors. Macroeconomic stability continues to matter a great deal - the inclusion of the inflation variable improves the coefficient of correlation from 63 to 78 per cent, but liberalization index does not appear to be important - the coefficient is not statistically significant and in most cases has unexpected sign. On the contrary, changes in the institutional capabilities of the state have dramatic impact on performance.

In a sense, the importance of preserving strong institutional capacity of the state for ensuring good performance may be considered as the main finding of this paper with strong policy implication. After allowing for differing initial conditions, it turns out that the fall in output in transition economies was associated mostly with poor business environment, resulting from institutional collapse. Liberalization alone, when it is not complemented with strong institutions, can not ensure good performance.

Moreover, the process of the collapse of output in transition economies is best described by the supply side recession model, where the key determinants are initial conditions and the strength of institutions, while the impact of liberalization is hardly noticeable. It follows that the debate about the speed of the liberalization (shock therapy versus gradualism) was to a large extent misfocused, whereas the crucial importance of strong institutions for good performance was overlooked.

Institutional capacities in turn, depend to a large extent on the combination of the rule of law and democracy: the data seem to suggest that both - authoritarian and democratic regimes with the strong rule of law can deliver efficient institutions, whereas under the weak rule of law authoritarian regimes do a better job in maintaining efficient institutions than democracies. To put it in a shorter form, the record of illiberal democracies in ensuring institutional capacities is the worst, which predictably has a devastating impact on output.

Notes

[1] While Vietnamese industry, excluding constantly and rapidly growing oil production, experienced some downturn in 1989-90 (-6 per cent in 1989 and 0 per cent in 1990) agricultural growth remained strong, so that GDP growth rates virtually did not fall (5-6 per cent a year).

[2] Kornai (1994) puts forward at least five general reasons for the transformational recession: (1) the need for enterprises to adjust to the replacement of a sellers market by a buyers market causes the reduction of output even when relative prices do not change; (2) the transformation of the real structure of the economy resulting from the change in relative prices; (3) the disruption of co-ordination resulting from the transition from bureaucratic to market institutions; (4) the hardening of the budget constraints of firms, leading to bankruptcies and cuts in output; (5) the backwardness of the financial sector, posing difficulties for the proper operation of market stimuli. While some of these factors overlap and others deserve a closer scrutiny and should be broken down into sub-factors, none of them depends on the transitional path chosen and can be eliminated by government policy in the short and medium term.

[3] More detailed description of the data and regressions is in Popov (2000).

[4] The decline in government revenues as a per cent of GDP in these countries was less pronounced than elsewhere in CIS.

[5] Data for China (World Bank, 1996b), Russia (Goskomstat) and Poland (Rocznik Statystyczny 1990, Warszawa; and data from Institut Finansow provided by G. Kolodko) do not include off-budget funds, which are very substantial in all three countries and are used mostly for social security purposes. Defense expenditure are from official statistics, i.e. lower than Western estimates, which is likely to lead to overstatement of spending for investment and subsidies at the expense of defense outlays. For USSR/Russia investment and subsidies are shown together.

[6] The **democracy** index is taken from Freedom House (www freedomhouse org/rankings.pdf), but inverted and calibrated, so that complete democracy coincides with 100 per cent, whereas complete authoritarianism with 0 per cent. The rule of law index is taken from (Campos, 1999) and for China, Vietnam and Mongolia – from International Country Risk Guide, 1984 to 1998, and calibrated, so that 100 per cent corresponds to the highest possible rule of law.

References

Åslund, A., Boone, P. and Johnson, S. (1996), 'How to Stabilize: Lessons from Post-Communist Countries', *Brookings Papers Econom. Activity*, vol. 1, pp. 217-313.

Breton, P., Gros, D. and Vandille, G. (1997), 'Output Decline and Recovery in the Transition Economies: Causes and Social Consequences', *Economics of Transition*, vol. 5, no. 1, pp. 113-30.

Bruno, M. (1995), 'Does Inflation Really Lower Growth?', *Working Paper*.

Bruno, M. and Easterly, W. (1995), *Inflation Crisis and Long-Run Growth*, Unpublished, World Bank.

Campos, N.F. (1999), 'Context is Everything: Measuring Institutional Change in Transition Economies', *Working Paper*, Prague.

De Melo, M, Denizer, C. and Gelb, A. (1996), 'Patterns of Transition From Plan to Market', *World Bank Economic Review*, vol. 3, pp. 397-424.

De Melo, M., Denzier, C., Gelb, A. and Tenev, S. (1997). 'Circumstance and Choice: The Role of Initial Conditions and Policies in Transition Economies', The World Bank, International Financial Corporation.

Fisher, S., Sahay, R. and Vegh, C. A. (1996), 'Stabilization and Growth in the Transition Economies: The Early Experience', *Journal of Economic Perspectives*, vol. 10, no. 2, pp. 45-66.

Fisher, S. and Sahay, R. (2000), 'The Transition Economies After Ten Years', SSRN Working Paper.

Heybey, B. and Murrell, P. (1999), 'The Relationship between Economic Growth and the Speed of Liberalization During Transition', *Journal of Policy Reform*, vol. 3, no. 2.

Kornai, J. (1994), 'Transformational Recession: The Main Causes', *J. Comp. Econom.*, vol. 1, pp. 39-63.

Naughton, B. (1997), 'Economic Reform in China: Macroeconomic and Overall Performance', in Lee, D. (ed), *The System Transformation of the Transition Economies: Europe, Asia and North Korea*, Yonsei University Press, Seoul.

Popov, V. (1998a), 'Investment in Transition Economies: Factors of Change and Implications for Performance', *Journal of East-West Business*, vol. 4, no. 1/2, pp. 47-98.

Popov, V. (1998b), 'Will Russia Achieve Fast Economic Growth?', *Communist Economies and Economic Transformation*, no. 4.

Popov, V. (1999), 'Investment, Restructuring and Performance in Transition Economies', *Post-Communist Economies*, no.3.

Popov, V. (2000), 'Shock Therapy versus Gradualism: The End of the Debate (Explaining the Magnitude of the Transformational Recession)', *Comparative Economic Studies*, vol. 42, no. 1, pp. 1-57.

Shmelev, N. and Popov, V. (1990), *The Turning Point: Revitalizing the Soviet Economy*, Doubleday, New York.

World Bank (1996), 'From Plan to Market', World Development Report, Oxford University Press, New York.

World Bank (1997a), 'The State in A Changing World', World Development Report, Oxford University Press, New York.

Zakharia, F. (1997), 'The Rise of Illiberal Democracies', *Foreign Affairs*, vol. 76, no. 6, pp. 22-43.

Chapter 4

An Evolutionary Analysis of Russia's Virtual Economy

Clifford Gaddy and Barry W. Ickes

Abstract

The hybrid system that the Russian transition has evolved into has been called the virtual economy. This paper analyzes the evolution of the virtual economy. We pay particular attention to the interaction of economic reform policies and the adaptive behavior of enterprise directors.

Introduction

Despite grand expectations Russian economic reform has not followed the path that most reform advocates anticipated. Rather than becoming a normal market economy, Russia has evolved into a new system - *a virtual economy* (Gaddy, and Ickes, 1998; Gaddy and Ickes, 1999; Gaddy and Ickes (forthcoming); Ericson, 1999) - that is stable in the near term, but threatens also to lock the country into a path that is ultimately unsustainable. In order to understand the future development of the Russian economy, one must first analyze how the economy got stuck. This is the primary question posed by the Russian experience for the economics of transition. Some argue that the virtual economy is just a continuation of the Soviet economy. This is not quite right. While there are important legacies from the Soviet period, it is important to understand how agents have *adapted* their behavior.

In this paper we study the evolution of the virtual economy from its Soviet roots. This enables us to understand how behavior adapted to the conditions that transition presented. By studying the evolution of this peculiar system we gain insight into the stability of the system. The behaviors that constitute the virtual economy - barter, nonpayments, investments in relational capital - are viewed as mutations. We then study how transition afforded selective advantages to certain mutations, and how this governed the dynamic evolution of the system. In particular, we analyze how policies that may have led to successful market reform can become derailed if there is a sufficient population of mutants.

Institutions and Transition

Explaining the difficulties of transition in Russia analysts focus on two explanations. Some analysts focus on errors of policy - primarily inadequate and insufficient implementation of market reforms (e.g. Aslund, 1999). Other analysts argue that Russia's difficulties stem from an inadequate institutional environment. Advocates in the latter camp argue that Russia lacked the institutions appropriate to the market, and this caused market reform to become derailed (e.g. Stiglitz, 1999). A more gradual pace of reform was needed to allow market institutions to develop.

It is important to note that the key differences between the two arguments is not the importance of market institutions, but rather the manner in which these develop. Implicit in their arguments are very different theories of the development of economic institutions. The former camp essentially adopted the 'field of dreams' approach; that is, 'if you build (markets) they (institutions) will come.' The latter camp implicitly assumes that Russia began market reform with an institutional vacuum; hence, institutional development must precede structural reform.

Despite the seemingly stark differences between the two views of Russian reform, the two camps share a common approach. Both explain the vagaries of the reform process in terms of policy settings. One camp sees inadequate implementation of economic reform. The other camp views the problem as too accelerated a pace of economic reform. What is relatively neglected in both views is the role of initial conditions in explaining the course of Russian economic development. Hence, neither camp analyzes the role of the inherited structure in generating economic institutions. The implicit assumption is that the demise of the Soviet system wiped out the economic institutions of the planned economy. While this may be true to some extent for the formal institutions of the planned economy - e.g. *Gosplan, Gossnab* - informal economic institutions survived and played an important role in transition. The distinction between formal and informal institutions is an important one, and we discuss this below [section 4].

Soviet Roots of the Virtual Economy

The roots of the virtual economy lie in the largely unreformed industrial sector inherited from the Soviet period. At the heart of the phenomenon are the large number of enterprises that still produce goods but destroy value.[1] This is perhaps the most important legacy of the planning system. As Rick Ericson has noted, 'a structure of production - location, capital, employment, materials and energy use, etc. - has been created, without any regard for economic opportunity costs, in an environment free of economic valuation and only subject to consistency in arbitrarily measured accounting units' (Ericson, 1997).[2] The central implication of this legacy is that value and output measured in Soviet prices convey no information about the actual market viability of an economic enterprise. Because decisions were made without regard to opportunity cost criteria, arbitrary pricing was not a handicap to planning. But it meant that the structure of production was such that non-viable enterprises could survive indefinitely. The arbitrary pricing system hid the value transfers required to make these enterprises appear viable. The nature of Soviet accounting meant that prices covered some notion of the cost of production; the problem was this was not the *economic* notion of costs. It is due to this history of decision-making independent of opportunity cost that an industrial structure replete with value-destroying enterprises emerged. This is the central feature of the Soviet legacy for the transition; hence, it is worth some further discussion.

At minimum, value destruction implies that the value of output is less than the costs of producing it, including the contributions from the factors of production.[3] Of course, many enterprises may incur such losses temporarily and still be viable. This might be the case, for example, in a recession. Hence, the assertion that an enterprise is value destroying refers to such activity on a *persistent* basis.[4]

Notice that value destruction requires that the costs of production are covered by some other activity. Hence, two conditions are required for its persistence. First, economic actors are not held responsible for covering the actual costs of production; and, second, value is transferred from other activities to support this one. In Soviet practice it was the first condition that was most critical. Enterprise directors were responsible for fulfilling plans, not for covering true costs. Of course, the pricing system under planning made it impossible to ascertain true costs anyway. Moreover, the pricing system generated automatic transfers between activities. In the post-Soviet transition, however, enterprises are ostensibly required to be viable; hence, a value transfer is necessary to enable the activity to survive.[5]

To understand the phenomenon of value destruction it is important to begin with Soviet pricing. Although prices were set arbitrarily, they were not random. Rather systematic biases predominated. Raw material inputs were underpriced in the Soviet economy.[6] Their prices were based on the operating costs of extraction, ignoring rent (that is, disregarding the opportunity cost of using the resources now rather than in the future). No doubt this harmonized with the goal of increasing production today; scarcity pricing might have induced more conservation, which mitigates against maximizing current production. This bias in raw material prices fed into the system of industrial prices. Heavy consumers of energy were, in effect, subsidized. So too were heavy users of capital, thanks to the absence of interest charges. In short, costs of production were calculated on the basis of an incomplete enumeration of costs. This led to lower prices for inputs than for final uses, and thus an understatement of the share of gross output used in production, and hence, an overstatement of net output (Ericson, 1997; Gaddy and Ickes, 1998).

In addition to incomplete cost-based pricing, the system was biased towards certain users. The same commodity would carry a different price if it were used by heavy industry or light industry. This would then feed into the calculation of costs of production of these goods, so that high priority sectors would appear to have lower costs of production than low priority sectors. This meant that the apparent distribution of productivities at the onset of transition, what we may think are efficient sectors, was liable to mask the true picture.[7]

The fact that the pricing system disguised the relative efficiency of various activities means that only with economic liberalization would the true viability of these activities become apparent.[8] Many sectors that appeared to be creating value turned out to be destroying value once prices moved to reflect costs.[9] The extent to which the Soviet economy produced the 'wrong things in the wrong way' could only be gauged after liberalization. This effect was magnified by the move to world prices.[10] Many industrial enterprises could not cover costs once prices moved to market-clearing levels.

Recognition of the non-viability of value destroying enterprises is confused by the argument that failed reform policies are the cause.[11] Much of the change in the sectoral distribution of output that has occurred since the end of planning is due more to price liberalization than to real changes in the economy.[12] The Russian economy remains a hyper-industrialized system composed of enterprises that would not be viable in a market economy, supported by transfers from energy and raw materials sectors.

There is one other key difference between the Soviet economy and the current Russian economy that should be discussed here. Under Soviet conditions the transfer of value from energy and raw materials to industry was merely an accounting convenience. There was no operational economic implication. Industry appeared more productive than was actually the case, but this was immaterial to the operation of the system. In the Russian economy, on the other hand, the transfer of resources from energy and raw materials to industry must be *induced*. The transfer of value is no longer simply an accounting convenience. It now reflects a redistribution of income. To maintain this the owners of assets that are contributing value must be induced to do so.[13] To the extent that the payment necessary to induce the value transfer leaves the system (e.g., in the form of capital flight), the Russian economy has less total value with which to support government consumption compared with the Soviet economy.

Insights from Institutional Analysis

It is increasingly popular to attribute the failure of shock therapy in Russia to the lack of attention paid to institutions. The argument is that reformers paid too much attention to macroeconomic policy and changes in property rights and not enough attention to the creation of the foundations of a market economy. While superficially appealing, this characterization misses much of the point. The real issue is not the importance of market-based institutions, but rather how they are created. Reformers hoped that if the macroeconomic setting was correct market-based institutions would develop from below. The critics argue that failure to create such institutions created a vacuum in which reforms were hijacked. Common to both arguments, however, is the notion that post-Soviet transition takes place in an institutional vacuum. In this section we present an alternative formulation.

The demise of the planning system constituted a dramatic change in the formal structure of the economic system. The primary means of economic coordination and formal authority were replaced by the market mechanism. It is a mistake, however, to focus exclusively on formal mechanisms. As North has argued, in revolutionary circumstances:

> the formal rules change, but the informal constraints do not. In consequence, there develops an ongoing tension between informal constraints and the new formal rules. An immediate tendency ... is to have new formal rules supplant the persisting informal constraints. Such change is sometimes possible, in particular in a partial equilibrium context, but it ignores the deep-seated cultural inheritance that underlies many informal constraints. Although a wholesale change in the formal rules may take place, at the same time there will be many informal constraints that have great survival tenacity because they still resolve basic exchange problems among the participants, be they social, political, or economic. The result over time tends to be a restructuring of the overall constraints - in both directions - to produce a new equilibrium that is far less revolutionary (North, 1990; Hewett, 1990).

The importance of informal constraints is critical to understanding developments in Russia. The importance of informal mechanisms in the Soviet system was the key idea in Grossman's model of the command economy.[14] These informal mechanisms developed because the formal planning system alone could not cope with the economic problems of a complex economy. Because a consistent feasible central plan was impossible to produce, decisionmakers, especially enterprise directors, had to choose *which* elements of the plan they would have to violate so that other elements could be fulfilled. Hence, an enterprise director had to resort to informal means in order to survive.[15]

In the late Soviet period the importance of informal mechanisms intensified as *perestroika*-era reforms further weakened the effectiveness of the formal system. Enterprises, and especially their directors, developed relationships to insure supplies of inputs and to protect against interference. These relationships not only survived the end of the Soviet era, but their value was enhanced by the elimination of many formal mechanisms that they competed with.[16] Thus enterprise directors were highly skilled at adapting to survive in an environment where adherence to the rules of the game were not a feasible survival strategy.

There is a general point here: organizations develop to meet the problems created by the institutional framework. Thus, North notes that in an unproductive institutional framework, 'The organizations that develop in this framework will become more efficient - but more efficient at making the society even more unproductive and the basic institutional structure even less conducive to productive activity. Such a path can persist because the transaction costs of the political and economic markets of those economies together with the subjective models of the actors do not lead them to move incrementally toward efficient outcomes' (North, 1990; Ericson, 1997).

The important lesson from this discussion is that institutions develop in accord with problems faced by agents in the economy. In the Russian case these are dominated by the structural problems that are the legacy of the Soviet period. These institutions were robust to the formal changes in the environment brought on by the reform process. But this also means that an alternative approach to transition that was more gradual would still have to cope with the structural problems that the informal mechanisms are solving. Slowing reform down so that institutions could catch up neglects the fact that there was no institutional vacuum, and that behavior was adaptive.

The Nature of Reforms

The central idea of economic reform is to influence enterprise behavior via the budget constraint.[17] The goal of market reform is to focus attention on the bottom line; to force enterprises to increase revenues or cut costs to satisfy the budget constraint. This is the natural way for economists to view reform. Enterprise behavior is fully characterized by the budget constraint. A profit-maximizing firm will respond to the budget constraint in appropriate ways; either by reducing costs or increasing revenues.

Budget Constraint

An enterprise can relax the pressure from its budget constraint in several ways. First, it can increase efficiency, raising the amount of output that it can obtain from given inputs. Second, it can reduce the amount of inputs purchased (although this may also reduce revenue if these inputs are needed for production). Third, the enterprise may increase sales through better marketing, obtaining a better price for output. Fourth, the enterprise can also forego investment. If capital depreciates, however, this has long-run consequences for production, since the capital stock in period $t + 1$ will be lower than in period t.[18] Fifth, the enterprise can also borrow, if credit is available. Thus if the enterprise can transform itself to make it more attractive to investors it able to relax its budget constraint. Notice that borrowing today implies that repayments will be higher in future periods.

The budget constraint is hardened by reducing subsidies or increasing tax payments. In Soviet times subsidies were a central feature of a regime that required production of goods independent of cost considerations.[19] In transition, most explicit subsidies have been reduced, though implicit subsidies often remain, and tax offsets and other special deals are a key feature of the environment. What is crucial at present, however, is that one can easily conceptualize how a hardening of the budget constraint - via elimination of direct and indirect subsidies and through collecting taxes - forces the enterprise to meet the budget constraint through market methods.

Market Distance

Reform via the budget constraint is premised on the assumption that the only dimension for survival is profits. If enterprises cannot earn profits, they cannot survive. Hence, tightening the budget constraint would force enterprises to increase efficiency. Of course, this weakens all enterprises on impact. But such a policy is also intended to have a *differential* effect on enterprises based on their relative efficiency. The key idea is that the weakest enterprises will be the most severely impacted by the policy, while the stronger enterprises will survive and, presumably, get stronger.[20]

The underlying notion here is *monotonicity* of reform. Reform is monotonic if its impact on an enterprise is related to its degree of inefficiency. A profits tax is likely to be monotonic, if profits are monotonically related to efficiency. A random monitoring of enterprises will not be a monotonic policy, however. Policies that are monotonic may be preferable, because their impact is directly related to a characteristic of the enterprise that we are interested in. But we need an index of efficiency with which to characterize the enterprise. A useful measure is the distance an enterprise must traverse to produce a marketable product.[21] Let $d_i \in (0, D)$ be the distance of enterprise i. An enterprise that produces a product it can sell in world markets has $d_i = 0$ while a completely inefficient enterprise has $d_i = D$. Transition starts with some initial distribution of enterprise distance.[22] The greater is d the less viable the enterprise. Suppose that $\underline{d}$ is the cutoff point for viability: that is, all enterprises with $d_i > \underline{d}$ are not financially viable.

Notice that d_i is a state variable that describes the conditions of the enterprise. At the start of transition it is inherited. During transition, however, it is an endogenous variable. If an enterprise restructures it can reduce its d_i.[23]

Now consider the effect, for example, of an increase in tax collection. This tightens the budget constraint for all enterprises, essentially increasing d_i for all i. Those enterprises that were closest to the breakeven point, $\underline{d}$, are pushed beyond it. The pressure to restructure is greatest for enterprises closest to this point, but all feel the pressure. The more inefficient, the greater the shock. The most inefficient may be wiped out by the shock, but healthier enterprises will grow stronger as a result of the intervention.

This uni-dimensional view of restructuring - reform means reducing d_i - lies at the heart of much reform advice.

Relational Capital

Now suppose that the organism has another survival mechanism. Enterprises also differ in their inherited stock of relational capital. Some enterprises (directors) have better relations with local and/or federal officials than others. Relations with other enterprises (directors) will also vary. The stock of these relationships determines the types of transactions that can be supported (barter versus cash, pre-payment, etc.). Relational capital is goodwill that can be translated into informal economic activity.[24]

Let r_i be the stock of relational capital of enterprise i. The actions that an enterprise takes can affect its stock of r. Just as investment augments the physical capital stock, enterprises can invest in relational capital as well.[25] An enterprise can, for example, perform services for the local government. This action may enhance the enterprise's relationships with local officials, and thus increase its capacity to conduct informal activities in the future. It is important to recognize that augmenting relational capital is costly.

The key point is that relational capital can aid enterprise survival. Enterprises that have high d may survive by exploiting relational capital, r_i. Thus if we ρ_{t+1} be the probability that an enterprise in operation at time t will survive to time $t+1$, we can now write $\rho_{t+1} = \rho\ (d_{it},\ r_{it})$. The uni-dimensional view of restructuring ignores the effect of r on this probability. We can also consider that the enterprise chooses to invest in reducing d and in increasing r in order to increase this probability.

R-D Space

Once we take into consideration the importance of relational capital it is evident that the initial conditions that characterize enterprises in transition are two-dimensional. We can illustrate this with Fig. 4.1 (taken from Gaddy and Ickes, 1998) which we refer to as the *R-D* space diagram.

Figure 4.1   R-D space diagram

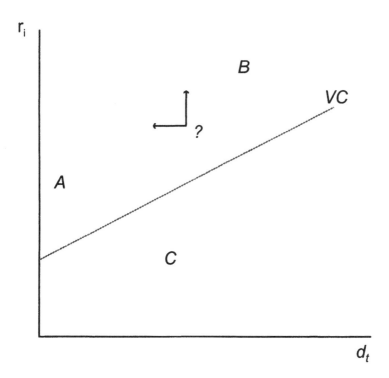

Although relations can allow an enterprise to compensate for large distance, some enterprises have such poor initial combinations of r and d that they are not viable. Not only are these enterprises situated far from the market, but the quality of their relations with officials and other enterprises is so poor that they cannot be relied on for survival. Clearly, the minimum level of relations needed to survive is increasing with distance. So we can imagine a boundary (VC in Fig. 1) that separates the region of viable enterprises from those that are not viable.[26] It is clear that the larger the distance to the market, the greater is the minimum level of relations necessary to survival. This implies the positive slope of the VC line. How steep VC will be depends on the institutional setting.[27] In a fully transparent economy relations may compensate very little for large distance. If officials are more corrupt, then relations may be much more important.

In this two-dimensional environment, the effects of market-type reforms need not be monotonic. That is, tightening of the budget constraint does not necessarily put the most pressure on those enterprises that are most inefficient (have the highest d). Those that inherited and/or invested in r are relatively better off. If investment resources are limited then the relevant issue for an enterprise is the relative return to investing in distance reduction and relational capital.[28] What is critical for our analysis is that these relative returns will depend on the nature of reforms and on the choices of enterprises.

Privatization of Relational Capital

One of the most important, but rarely emphasized, results of economic reform in Russia was the privatization of relational capital.[29] In Soviet times, personal relations, connections, and influence (*blat*),[30] had important value to the functioning of the system. The primary benefit to the director lay in increased ability to fulfill the plan. In the highly distorted regime of central planning supply failures were a constant feature of economic life. Relations with local party officials and with other enterprise directors were often crucial to obtaining scarce inputs. In late *perestroika* and even more during economic reform the autonomy of the director increased as the force of the plan weakened. One consequence of this was that directors obtained the capability appropriate the returns to the relationships they had developed.

In order for directors to appropriate these returns, the enterprises had to continue to operate. Much of the relational capital was enterprise specific. The primary form of these connections is in relationships with directors of other enterprises, often in related lines of activity. The director cannot cash this out. Instead, to appropriate these rents it is crucial to keep the enterprise operating.

To appropriate these rents the director utilizes relationships to obtain inputs and find customers. If the enterprise produced marketable products these relationships would be of less importance. Hence, workers would be less content to see a portion of the income of the enterprise diverted by directors. But for an unviable enterprise the alternative to director appropriation is enterprise closure. Faced with this tradeoff, workers are more willing to accept the personal enrichment of a director who is also able to obtain resources necessary to keep the operation going.

The privatization of relational capital is thus an important part of the explanation of why directors fight to keep open enterprises that have few prospects in the market economy. Notice the symbiotic relationship between the workers and directors. Workers need the director to keep the unviable enterprise afloat. Directors need the enterprise in order to exploit their relational capital.

Relational Capital and Reform

In the Soviet system as it actually operated informal relations were central. A key role was played by officials - primarily *obkom* and *raikom* officials - who mediated this process. Informal relations increased flexibility in the Soviet system, but some system of mediation was needed to impose some notion of social efficiency in a system where prices could not provide that information. Officials played that role. Relational capital in the Soviet system involved relationships with *Gossnab*, *obkom* officials, and enterprise directors. In transition, the privatization of relational capital means, essentially, that *Gossnab* and the *obkom* officials are out. But the enterprise relations remain. Thus reform removed the formal rules of the old system (which had already eroded under Gorbachev), but left much of the informal system intact, but without the mediating aspects.

The paradox then, is that under the Soviet system Communist party officials had mediated and limited the use of relational capital. In transition the role of relational capital was enhanced by the formal changes in the system.

The elimination of mediation made it easier (more economical) to invest in relational capital. The director has more power than before. There are now less people to please. Returns to investment in relational capital are now all appropriated by the director. To some extent it could be argued that the tax service still takes it, but liberalization makes it easier for director to evade the state. Hence, the director has more incentive to invest in r.

Had the relational capital not previously existed privatization-"Russian style" would have had different effects. The initial conditions facing enterprises would have been such that the only survival strategy would have been to invest in reducing d. Privatization of relational capital altered the outcome.

Relational Capital and Increasing Returns

The ability of an enterprise to use relational capital to circumvent the strictures of the budget constraint will depend on the strategies employed by other enterprises. If all other enterprises eschew relational capital the ability of an enterprise to exploit it may be attenuated. This may seem paradoxical: if enterprise i is the only one to possess relational capital surely its return ought to be higher as it is more scarce. This seems plausible, but it ignores the means by which relational capital is utilized.

The more enterprises eschew relational capital the more transparent is economic activity. This makes it more difficult to use the strategies that enterprises utilize - such as barter and tax offsets - to circumvent the budget constraint. When all other enterprises act like firms in a market economy the one that tries to exploit relational capital stands out. This raises the cost of getting officials to help; especially as they must also use non-transparent means to provide resources. In using informal activities to survive there is strength in numbers. This may lead to economies of scale in using relational capital.

Consider, for example, the use of barter. If most enterprises do not use non-monetary transactions then it will be hard for an enterprise to employ barter. The costs of finding a partner to transact with will be harder. When barter is widespread, on the other hand, it is easier to find such partners. Barter thus is an example of a thick-market externality. The fact that others use barter increases the return to me from using it.[31]

Increasing use of relational capital results in reduced transparency. This lowers the cost of using relational capital. It may thus enhance the net return to investing in relational capital, even if it means that more agents are seeking resources. When transactions are transparent it is difficult to transfer value via a non-monetary exchange. The reason is that stakeholders can readily see the subsidy element contained in the transaction. This vitiates the point of the transaction. To engage in such a transfer in a transparent economy would then require more resources to buy off those now privy to the real deal. When the economy is opaque, on the other hand, the value transfer is hidden from view. This may mean that more resources are available to be redistributed.[32] Hence, the cost of implementation is lower. Consequently, the return to using relational capital must increase with the number of enterprises employing such strategies.

It is useful to consider the analogy to rent seeking. The greater the number engaged in a contest over rents the smaller is the expected return. But this is because the size of the rent is fixed, so that a greater number of contestants means a lower probability of achieving the given prize (or a smaller share). With relational capital this may no longer be the case. When the economy is transparent government resources must be used for their official uses. Government officials may find it very difficult to divert tax to enterprises. In an opaque economy, on the other hand, the cost of diverting resources decreases, as it is harder to follow the transactions. In a transparent economy a tax offset is a clear subsidy to an enterprise, and an official will have to answer for his action in allowing it. In an economy where these are widespread, however, granting an offset no longer appears out of the ordinary.

This increasing returns phenomena turns out to plan an important part in the following analysis.

Mutation and Resistance: An Evolutionary Analysis

An enterprise that exploits its relational capital to circumvent the budget constraint can be thought of as a mutation. This follows because the enterprise is utilizing strategies that were previously not available. For example, the enterprise has adopted strategies - barter, tax offsets - that were not available to market-like firms.[33] This view of enterprise behavior fundamentally contradicts that of reformers who designed the Russian privatization. They viewed Soviet-type enterprises as potential 'market-like' enterprises encumbered by political controls. The notion was that without government control, and with hard budget constraints, enterprises in Russia would behave like 'normal' enterprises.[34] That is, once political controls were lifted they would maximize shareholder value like any firm in the west.

This conventional view ignores the fact that due to the mutation of the enterprise it has survival strategies unavailable to the 'normal' enterprise.[35] The enterprise in the virtual economy can produce goods that can be used for barter or for tax offsets but that cannot be sold on the market. It can also procure inputs at a lower cost because it exploits relations to allow it to pay in non-monetary means. The cost of employing these extra strategies is a lack of transparency which necessarily ensues. This may make it impossible to attract external funds for restructuring.[36] Hence, the enterprise that uses these strategies finds it prohibitive to reduce distance, while the market-oriented enterprise cannot engage in virtual survival strategies.[37]

Shock therapy produced a sudden change in the environment facing enterprises.[38] Formal subsidization from the state budget was eliminated, and enterprises were supposed to cover their own costs.[39] In the absence of mutation, the enterprises that were inefficient - had high d - would be less fit. The importance of mutation is that the effects of the environment shift were *not* monotonic. High d enterprises may have have higher survival probabilities if they had invested sufficiently in relations. Enterprises that chose transparency would be at a competitive disadvantage to those that invested in, or had initially high, relational capital. Shock therapy is supposed to impact on enterprises via the effect on the budget constraint. Hence, those enterprises that had invested in alternative means of survival would be less effected by the shock. These enterprises are 'effectively' immune from the therapy, even if the therapy was designed precisely to attack them.

Notice that the proportion of enterprises that follow these 'virtual' strategies is not limited by the frequency of mutation. Enterprises can *imitate* behavior that they observe to be successful. If some enterprises in the virtual economy are able to survive without undertaking costly restructuring, then other enterprises may choose to follow this behavior.[40] Hence, once virtual strategies appear to be working the system may rapidly tip.[41]

This is not necessarily an argument that reforms were ill-conceived,[42] though excessive focus on the budget constraint may suggest that it was. It also refers to *implementation*. Reforms that would have shut down lossmaking enterprises were shunned because the consequences of these reforms were deemed intolerable.[43] Clearly, effective hardening of budget constraints was an implicit assumption necessary to the therapy of tight money and liberalization. The fact that hard-budget constraints were avoided through investment in relational capital means that reforms were not fully implemented.

Incomplete Therapy

Incomplete shock therapy failed to wipe out loss-making enterprises. A new mutant strain emerged with the survival strategies available in the virtual economy. This made it harder for new enterprises to compete. The greater the number of mutant enterprises that exploit these virtual strategies the greater the relative disadvantage for market-type enterprises, because mutant enterprises operate under different rules.

The process we are examining bears a relationship to the problem of multi-drug resistant (MDR) tuberculosis (TB). MDR strains of TB are never found in the wild. Rather, they are the product of human intervention. Genetic resistance to particular anti-TB drugs occurs naturally, but this is diluted by the overwhelming prevalence of drug-susceptible organisms. In the natural environment there is no evolutionary advantage to genetic resistance to antimicrobials which are introduced by man. The presence of antimicrobials provides the selective pressure for resistant organisms to become predominant. Human intervention that introduces antimicrobials creates the selective pressure in favor of MDR. The primary mechanism by which this happens is an *incomplete* regimen of treatment (or poor adherence to a proper regimen). The incomplete regimen wipes out the drug-susceptible organisms, leaving the field for the drug-resistant varieties.

The analogy with enterprise behavior is straightforward. In a competitive environment there is no selective advantage to investing in relational capital. Reducing market distance is the key to viability. Incomplete therapy in Russia, however, did not create such an environment. Relational capital continued to result in a positive payoff in terms of enterprise fitness and survival. For enterprises that possessed sufficient relational capital, the opportunity to survive via virtual strategies became a viable option. Hence, the greatest burden of shock therapy was felt by enterprises that did not have, or chose not to invest in, relational capital. Incomplete therapy imposed a *relative* burden on enterprises that chose to act in a "normal" manner. Hence, incompleteness provided selective pressure that favors the mutant enterprise. This is similar to the outcome for a TB patient who does not take the full complement of anti-TB drugs, or who fails to follow a multi-drug regimen.[44]

A Simple Evolutionary Model

One way to see the effects of incomplete shock therapy is to analyze the evolutionary process of enterprise behavior. Suppose that enterprises can choose to behave as market-like *(M)*, Soviet *(S)*, or virtual *(V)*.[45] The relative payoff for each of these strategies will depend on the conditions of that particular enterprise and on the choices of other enterprises. The former we have already characterized in terms of di and ri. Presumably the greater is the market distance for a given enterprise the lower the payoff to choosing the *M* strategy. Similarly, the payoff to choosing *V* would be less if an enterprise had a low level of r. But relative payoffs will also depend on how other enterprises behave, and that is our focus in this section.

Why would the payoff to a strategy depend on the choices of other enterprises? Consider, for example, barter. The cost to a given enterprise of eschewing cash will depend on the difficulty of finding other partners willing to use non-monetary exchange.[46] This suggests that there is a thick-market externality in choosing the *V* strategy. It may be that the market system is more efficient if all enterprises are market-like enterprises; indeed, this is the assumption we make in this section. But that is not the critical question for transition. Rather, we want to know if there is a path from the command system to the market economy. It may be that the market is more efficient if all enterprises are market-like. Nonetheless, it may be impossible for the market system to invade and overtake an economy that is populated primarily by Soviet-type enterprises.

A crucial question for transition is whether the market system can be approached gradually. A simple way to study this question is to see how the choices of strategies evolves based on the populations of the three types of enterprises. We study this question in the form of a simple model with three strategies: Soviet *(S)*, Market *(M)*, and Virtual *(V)*. The payoff that an enterprise receives depends on the strategies that other enterprises are playing. Let $\pi\,(i,\,j)$ be the payoff to an enterprise choosing strategy i when all other enterprises choose strategy $j(i,\,j = S,\,M,\,V)$. We assume that the payoff to being a market enterprise is greatest when other enterprises choose the market strategy, and it is lowest when all other enterprises follow the Soviet strategy.[47] Hence the payoff to the market strategy is:

$$\pi\,(M,\,M) > \pi\,(M,\,V) > \pi\,(M,\,S)$$

and similarly for the virtual and Soviet strategies:

$$\pi\,(V,\,V) > \pi\,(V,\,S) > \pi\,(V,\,M)$$
$$\pi\,(S,\,S) > \pi\,(S,\,V) > \pi\,(S,\,M)$$

Notice also that the market economy is assumed to be socially efficient and an economy fully populated by Soviet-type enterprises is least efficient. Thus, $\pi\,(M,\,M) > \pi\,(V,\,V) > \pi\,(S,\,S)$. It is important to recognize, however, that these payoffs refer to outcomes in the transition environment. This means that when all enterprises choose the soviet strategy they are playing in an environment without Soviet institutions. It is an economy where all enterprises play Soviet-type strategies (play by formal and informal Soviet rules), but where Soviet institutions such as *Gosplan* no longer exist.

An illustrative payoff matrix that shares these assumed payoffs is given by:

	Market	Soviet	Virtual	
Market	5	0	3	
Soviet	0	3	1	
Virtual	2	3	4	(*)

where the numbers are payoffs to a row strategy against a population of column strategies.

Hence, $\pi\,(M,\,M) = 5$, $\pi\,(M,\,S) = 0$, $\pi\,(M,\,V) = 3$, etc. Notice that the payoff matrix given above has the following features:

- The Soviet enterprise is (weakly) dominated by the Virtual enterprise: that is, the Virtual enterprise always does as well as the Soviet enterprise and sometimes better.

- Against a population of Soviet enterprises the Virtual enterprise does as well as the Soviet enterprise.

Most of the payoffs in (*) are straightforward. The fact π *(M, V)* < π *(V, V)* is worth comment. A market enterprise that operates in an economy with many virtual enterprises is under threat precisely because of the fiscal pressure from the government. With many virtual enterprises, enterprises that operate in the monetary economy are prey to the tax authorities. The relative situation of a market-like firm is decreasing in the number of virtual enterprises because the latter are able to barter and use tax offsets to reduce the real value of liabilities. One might also question the assumption that π *(M, V)* > π *(M, S)*. If the economy is dominated by Soviet enterprises the market enterprise would find it very difficult to procure inputs - much harder than with virtual enterprises. This is the logic behind the assumption. One may argue, however, that in the virtual economy the market-type enterprise will, again, be the prey of the tax authorities. This may suggest that it is plausible to also investigate the implications of assuming.[48]

Figure 4.2 Some evolutionary dynamics

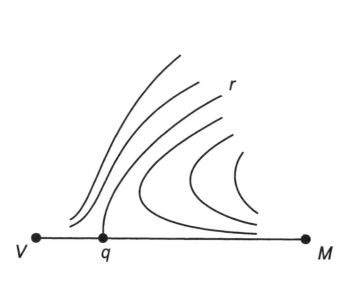

There are three pure strategy equilibria in this game. One consists of all Market enterprises; this is the most efficient. A second equilibrium consists of all Virtual enterprises. The last one consists of all Soviet enterprises but this is, of course, weakly dominated. In addition, there is also a mixed strategy equilibrium q with $^1/_4$ Market enterprises, no Soviet enterprises and $^3/_4$ Virtual enterprises.

Notice that if there were no Soviet-type enterprises we would not expect to see any virtual enterprises. The reason is that the 'all market' equilibrium dominates the 'all virtual' equilibrium. By assumption we have chosen the all-market equilibrium to be most efficient, and in an environment where the only two types of enterprises are M and V the system will end up in the 'all market' equilibrium. But when Soviet-type enterprises exist it is possible that the economy will end up in the "all virtual" equilibrium. The presence of Soviet-type enterprises affects where we end up, even though this strategy is dominated by the others.

To see this we assume that the population of each type of enterprise depends on its relative performance compared with the other types. Thus, let $p_i(t)$ be the proportion of enterprises that choose type $i = S$, M or V at time y. We can formulate the change in the population by:

$$p_i = p_i [e_i Ap - p^T Ap)]$$ (**)

where x is the vector of population shares (p_M, p_S, p_V), A is the 3×3 matrix of payoffs from (6.1), and e_i is the vector of payoffs for an enterprise choosing strategy i (i.e., $e_S = (5, 0, 3)$. The term in the brackets is the difference between the payoff from a particular strategy and the average for all enterprises given the current population shares. Thus the growth in the population of any type of enterprise depends on its *relative* performance compared to the average of all enterprises. For initial populations of the three types of enterprises we can see how strategies evolve. In particular, we can study how the basins of attraction are altered by the initial population shares.[49]

The results can be understood with the aid of Fig. 4.2. Suppose initially that all enterprises are Soviet-type. We are at the top of the simplex. Now assume that in period 0 a shock occurs that converts some proportion of these enterprises to market strategies. Further suppose that there is a mutation that creates a virtual enterprise. We can let the initial population of these enterprises be arbitrarily small (i.e. $p_V(0) = .001$). The resulting dynamics depend on how large is this shock. The critical value is $p_S(0) = r_S = .625$.[50] If the shock does not bring the share of enterprises choosing the Soviet strategy below this critical value, the dynamics take the economy to the 'all virtual' equilibrium. When the shock is greater than this, however, the economy successfully transits to the market. The critical boundary is labelled in Fig. 4.1 as the curve qr.

Another way to think about these dynamics is to consider the basins of attraction. There are two basins of attraction. One is the market economy. The other is the virtual economy. The choices of enterprises eventually take us to one of these basins. In our example, the basins of attraction are given by the regions Vq and Mq along the base of the simplex. As is apparent from Figure 4.1 the basin of attraction of the market economy is larger than that of the virtual economy. It is interesting, however, to ask what would happen if there was a constraint that the proportion of Soviet enterprises could not shrink to zero. That is, suppose that a political constraint requires the continued presence of state-owned enterprises. In a sense this was precisely the case early in transition, primarily with respect to defense enterprises. The effect of such a constraint is to increase the relative size of the virtual economy's basin of attraction. To see this, notice that such a constraint implies that the economy no longer ends up at the base of the simplex - where the share of Soviet enterprises is zero - but at some higher level. Essentially, the base of the simplex shifts up, with the boundary *qr* unchanged. Given the slope of *qr* it is apparent that the probability that a virtual mutation will take us to the virtual basin of attraction increases.

The market economy is evolutionarily stable. The system is immune to *small* mutations. The virtual economy is also evolutionary stable. The problem is large mutations. When there are both Soviet and Market enterprises the system is vulnerable to the virtual virus.

A key assumption is that when most enterprises are *M* then being a market enterprise dominates being a virtual one. But when there are a sufficient mass of non-market enterprises it pays to be virtual. The reason is that when most enterprises are operating with tax offsets and barter it is very costly to restrict to cash.

Remark 1. *Note that this is related to the rotation of the RB curve in R-D space. The RB curve separates the regions where enterprises choose to invest in relations from that where enterprises choose to reduce distance. If the boundary rotates counter-clockwise this increases the domain of attraction of the basin in the Northeast. The key to push market reform is to rotate it clockwise.*

Because the virtual economy is a basin of attraction, it may be stable to small perturbations. Thus reforms that might seem effective on market thinking may backfire. For example, tightening the cash constraint. See Gaddy and Ickes, 1998.

Behavioral Adaptation

In the biological world evolution relies solely on relative fitness. In social evolution, however, adaptation can occur not just through replication but through adaptation.[51] Enterprise directors can observe the success of other enterprises and adapt their behavior. This could lead to more rapid adjustment to the virtual equilibrium.

In the previous example it was assumed that enterprises were equally likely to interact with any type of enterprise. Payoffs were determined solely on the basis of population frequencies for the economy as a whole. This seems to be the logical assumption because the nature of the payoffs depends on the mixture of enterprises in the economy, not on particular interactions.

One could argue, however, that enterprises may be more likely to interact with like-minded enterprises. This could lead to further bifurcation. If agents tend to interact with like-minded agents, this may reinforce behavior.[52] Recall that the payoff to being a virtual enterprise increases is higher when interacting with other virtual enterprises. This suggests that the virtual trap could be strengthened by the presence of non-random interactions.

Evolution can also occur via cultural transmission. Most models in evolutionary game theory assume that agents interact randomly with other agents. But in structured environments, agents interact more often with agents that are similar to them. This can speed the adoption of certain equilibria. This is certainly relevant for transition economies, because enterprises in the production sector tend to interact with the same enterprises that they dealt with under central planning. The increased interaction with such a structured group can lead to a more rapid adjustment to the new equilibrium.

Policy Ineffectiveness

Notice that all of the shocks that have occurred since the start of transition have had greater relative impact on marketized enterprises. Attempts to increase the intensity of reform have all focused on hardening the budget constraint without any actions to reduce the payoff to investments in relations. Such policy measures illustrate the principle that in the virtual economy populated by mutant enterprises, conventional policy prescriptions will not work as expected. Here we consider two examples.

Transparency   The first illustrative example of a policy that has unintended consequences is increasing enterprise *transparency*. An essential element of market reform is that enterprises make their financial activities more transparent. The implicit bargain of market reform was that greater transparency would be rewarded by greater access to credit. Financial markets require transparency, as does foreign investment. Of course, transparency also makes problems more apparent. But if the only way to obtain external financing is to take the plunge to greater transparency, then enterprises will choose this costly option.

The problem with choosing transparency is two-fold. First, it precludes the use of strategies that rely on relational capital. Second, transparency is essentially irreversible. If there were no r then those enterprises with greater d would be disadvantaged. The move to greater transparency would have the greatest benefits for enterprises that are closest to the market. Hence, the fitness of the most efficient enterprises would be enhanced relative to lossmaking enterprises. The problem is that when relational capital is an available survival strategy those enterprises that chose transparency may be relatively *disadvantaged*.

Why are market-like firms relatively disadvantaged when r is an available survival strategy. The enterprise that eschews relations and tries to become more efficient will face more favorable market conditions if less efficient enterprises must meet budget constraints. When these enterprises exploit relations, however, then they can continue to produce even though they do not cover costs. The more transparent enterprises have undertaken costly restructuring but the payoff has been reduced by the continued operation of the less efficient.

This argument has important implications for discussions of the role of corporate governance. It has become almost commonplace to point out that inadequate corporate governance is a severe problem in Russia, one that inhibits investment, especially foreign investment.[53] The conventional view is that weak corporate governance is a key barrier to external finance for Russian enterprises. This is an important argument, but it is critical to keep in mind that the opposite is also true: the low probability of attracting external finance inhibits the development of good corporate governance. There are two parts to this. First, enterprises that have very high d see very little return to improving corporate governance. Even with very transparent relations they are unlikely to attract external financing, because the expected return is so low. Second, enterprises that may have higher expected returns face the twin problems of high interest rates and increased tax incidence. The fiscal problems of the Russian government prior to August 1998 increased the cost of external finance to enterprises through crowding out.[54] This automatically reduces the expected return to choosing transparency. In addition to this, an enterprise that chooses to reduce d faces increased relative tax incidence from entering the monetized part of the economy. This also reduces expected return. Hence, enterprises led by directors that fully understand the connection between good corporate governance and external finance may *choose* not to implement the former because the benefits are not sufficient.

The relative disadvantage faced by enterprises that chose transparency is the product of extremely high costs of external finance. Ignoring problems of corporate governance - these should be less severe in transparent enterprises - the fiscal policy of the Russian government has crowded out much investment. Transparent enterprises have not received the intended benefit, but they have paid the cost in terms of foreclosing the use of relational strategies. Those enterprises that chose transparency are now more vulnerable than before.

This effect is especially true when there is a tax crackdown. High tax rates that result from fiscal weakness and campaigns to increase tax collections mean that pressure falls greatest on those enterprises whose books are most transparent.

Tight money A second example of a policy that is rendered ineffective by the virtual economy is that of tight money. An essential element of shock therapy is a policy of tight money to stabilize the price level. Indeed, most critics of so-called shock therapy have pointed to tight monetary policies as one of the prime causes of the output fall.[55] Certainly, tight money is an essential element of the tightening of budget constraints. If credit is lax there is less pressure on enterprises to restructure.

Tighter credit is a perfect example of a policy that is supposed to hurt all enterprises and is supposed to have the greatest impact on the least efficient. The latter are most likely to suffer cash flow problems, and hence most likely to be pressured by an inability to borrow.[56] The policy of tight money is premised on the assumption that survival is uni-dimensional. If survival via investment in relational capital is feasible, then this assumption is not appropriate. Enterprises that invest in relational capital may insulate themselves against credit shocks. Tight money then has greater relative impact on those enterprises that invested in reducing distance. The 'fitness' of the latter enterprises is reduced relatively by the tight money policy. This induces imitation, and virtual behavior spreads.

Enterprises in Russia were able to use relational capital to insulate them from the stringencies of the budget constraint. The ability to pay for inputs and to pay taxes in kind, rather than in cash, provides them with an advantage compared to those that must use cash. Barter typically costs the paying enterprise less than an equivalent *nominal* amount of cash. Else, the enterprise would sell the output for money and pay with it.[57] Hence, once barter became more common even enterprises that could afford to pay with money chose to use barter.

We can put this in the context of our evolutionary analysis. The transition process was perturbed by the tightening of credit during 1995 and the ruble corridor. This induced a mutation in enterprise behavior. In particular, monetary tightening induced the use of barter. Lack of liquidity may have induced enterprises to engage in non-monetary behavior. Once this mutation occurred, the stability of virtual behavior implies that barter would persist even if the initial conditions that shocked the system are no longer present.

This account fits with some recent empirical work that studies barter. It has been argued by (Commander and Mumssen, 1998), for example, that barter became widespread in Russia in response to the monetary tightening of 1994-1995. Yet, as demonstrated in (Guriev and Ickes, 2000), barter does not seem to be related to the financial position of the enterprise. The latter study also shows that there is a lock-in effect of barter: once enterprises use barter it is cheaper to continue. We return to this below.

The key point is that the importance of relational capital and of networks of relationships among enterprises preceded the imposition of tight money. Hence, when tight money was imposed, resort to virtual strategies caused the policy to be ineffective. Tight money penalized the wrong enterprises. It reinforced barter - a phenomenon that clearly preceded the tightening of credit - and provided a relative advantage to those whose relations were sufficient to support barter. This leaves the interesting counterfactual: if tight money would have been imposed earlier - *before the mutation* - would it have been more effective because virtual behavior was not consolidated yet?

Conclusion

Note that institutions arise to meet the challenges posed to agents. If you change the rules, it had better be the case that new institutions will solve this better than the old. There is competition between the structures.

There are two critical factors in this story. First, there is the inherited structure of the games agents are involved with. This structure determines the suitability of institutions to help agents solve the problems they face. The second factor is that informal rules exist that developed when the old rules and the inherited structure were predominant. When the formal rules are changed, the informal rules provide an alternative lifeboat for those agents that cannot play by the new rules.

So in our game, if the market system is sufficiently advantageous it can invade and take over the Soviet environment. That means that the (new) formal rules are not too out of sync with the problems agents face. If the legacy from the old regime is so severe that the new rules are not consistent with the problems agents face then a change in the formal rules may not be sufficient to make the new rules dominate. In these circumstances, the informal rules may end up dominating; if the perturbation is not large enough then the virtual economy becomes the equilibrium.

Conquest recognizes the difficulty, but the metaphor is incorrect:

> It is not as if a country can, as it were, be put in dry dock and equipped with new institutions in a careful and considered way. The whole venture is more like trying to reequip a ship at sea, in stormy waters, with a new engine (Conquest, 200; Hewett, 1990).

This metaphor misses the point because it has the institutions replaced still in one fell swoop, but it is good because it explains that time does not sit still for the reformers, and that the key problem is the difficult environment in which the new institutions must take root.

In all transition economies new formal rules replaced the old, and in all these economies informal rules were also present. There are critical differences, however. These relate to the structure - which determines how ill-suited the new formal rules are to the problems agents face, and the capacity to solve the problems via the informal rules. Thus, in the case of Russia the inherited structure was so ill-suited to the market that the new formal rules threatened the very survival of a large share of industry. In addition, the large energy and resource sector made it feasible for inefficient enterprises to survive through informal rules.

In successful Central European Economies (CEEs) it is arguable how ill-suited the industrial sector was to the market, but the absence of the value pumps did render the informal rules less effective. One could argue, in fact, that the cut-off of Soviet supplied energy weakened the very system that supported value destroyers in these economies, so the informal rules were less suited to the new structure.

The point of this argument, it is important to emphasize, is not that the pace at which formal rules were changes was wrong in Russia. It is rather that changing the formal rules without consideration of the true structure necessarily deflects attention from the viability of the informal rules that can be a crutch for those enterprises threatened by the new environment. Relational capital that was inherited from the old regime was an important asset to enterprises that were placed under stress by market reform. Because reformers did not adequately assess the true inherited structure - they believed that more enterprises were potentially viable than was actually the case - they neglected the extent to which relational capital would be the only means of survival. Hence, they did not attack the informal rules sufficiently to insure that the formal rules would take root. That is why market reform proved less successful, and why the system evolved into the virtual economy.

Notes

[1]   For a fuller analysis of value destruction, see Gaddy and Ickes, forthcoming.

[2]   'The industrial base and network of interactions underlying the Russian economy was built over a period of more than 60 years in order to provide a specified bundle of goods and services deemed desirable by central planners and their subordinates in the industrial administrative hierarchy. While much effort was expended to maintain input-output consistency and balance in providing and expanding this configuration of outputs, there was virtually no consideration of economic valuation, opportunity cost or scarcity rents in determining the structure and level of economic activity' (Ericson, 1999).

[3]   This is the weak definition of value destruction. The strong version of value destruction implies that the value of output does not even cover the costs of purchased inputs. See the appendix in Gaddy and Ickes, 1999, for a discussion of value destruction.

[4]   To assess whether value is created or destroyed market prices are crucial. Notice that the same configuration of activities can produce value at one set of prices and destroy it at others. Thus the Soviet economy separated domestic prices from the world market. Given Soviet prices, which placed a high premium on defense output, economic activity produced value. It is compared with outside opportunities for using the same resources that the phenomenon of value destruction comes into play.

[5]   Explaining the nature and persistence of this value transfer is the purpose of the virtual economy hypothesis.

[6]   See Ericson, 1997, for a discussion of calculation of national income in the Soviet economy, and on the implications of pricing rules on the measurement of sectoral income.

[7]   See Ericson, 1997, for an analysis of the implications of arbitrary pricing on the apparent and actual production of value added in the Soviet economy. Ericson (1998) was the first study to formalize the dual nature of the Soviet economy in terms of priority (military) and nonpriority sectors.

[8]   As noted by Ericson: 'This legacy of the Soviet system constitutes a structure of capital and economic activity that is fundamentally non-viable in an environment determined by market valuation, and hence requires massive transformation at its very roots' (Ericson, 1997).

[9]   It is perhaps more correct to say that the end-users in the Soviet regime - the Communist Party - placed such a high value on the output of the defense sector the value was produced. The problem is that with the end of the regime the value of that production has shrunk dramatically, as it is now valued by the market.

[10] This point was emphasized in Bosworth and Ofer, 1995.

[11] This is exacerbated by the reform-induced recession common to even successful transition economies.

[12] This becomes apparent when sector output for the Soviet period is measured at world prices. Consider, for example, the contribution to industrial output from electrical energy, fuel, and forestry and timber products. In 1991 at Soviet prices these sectors contributed 17.1% of total output. At world prices, however, these sectors amounted to 51.6% of total output! See OECD, chapter 1.

[13] This relates to the notion of 'good leakage' discussed in Gaddy and Ickes, 1998.

[14] Hewett (1990, chapter 4) pays special attention to the analysis of informal mechanisms in the Soviet economy.

[15] As Hewett noted, '[t]he successful "entrepreneur" in this system is not a person who develops new products and new technologies, but one who successfully develops a workable relationship with the government and party authorities supervising his enterprises' (Hewett, 1990, 199).

[16] Especially party and state organs, at lower levels, such as the *obkoms* and *raikoms*.

[17] A related aspect of this was the following bargain: become transparent and the cost of borrowing will be reduced. Because credit is more likely to flow to enterprises which have more transparent books, and because firms in transition suffer from credit constraints, there should be great incentive to clean up the books to attract credit. Of course, this only works if credit is actually available, as we discuss below.

[18] This is clearly a popular strategy employed by many Russian enterprises.

[19] The soft-budget constraint of a Soviet-type enterprise (Kornai, 1992) involved *ex post* subsidies. In transition, soft-budget constraints are often transformed into tax arrears and arrears to other enterprises.

[20] The image suggested is that of a vaccine, which introduces minute amounts of a virus in order to trigger the immune system to produce antibodies. The rationale for hardening budget constraints represents an attempt to stress the organism to induce it to restructure its behavior to increase long-run viability.

[21] The notion of market distance is discussed at length in Gaddy and Ickes, 1998.

[22] Let μ_i be i's share of GDP (or employment), then $\Omega = \int_i (d_i \mu_i) \, di$ is a measure of the average distance of the economy. It thus represents the initial level of the gap that must be overcome in transition. An important point about Russian initial conditions is that Ω was larger than in other transition economies.

[23] But distance depends not only on the decisions within the enterprise but also on what is happening in world markets.

[24] It is important to note that relations aid in production. Hence, investing in relations is *not* the same activity as rent-seeking. The extent to which relational capital has positive or negative impacts on the economy depends on the environment. In a transparent market economy, r may reduce transaction costs -- acting like trust. In an opaque environment, such as Russia's Virtual Economy, however, r may be used to circumvent fiduciary responsibilities.

[25] 'Organizations will also encourage the society to invest in the kinds of skills and knowledge that indirectly contribute to their profitability. Such investment will shape the long-run growth of skills and knowledge, which are the underlying determinants of economic growth' (North, 1990, 79).

26   Notice that the position of the *VC* line will depend on how open is the economy. Enterprises that would be unviable (for given *d*) in an open economy may be viable if the economy is autarkic.

27   As *d* increases, we may further suppose that the minimum *r* necessary to survival increases at an increasing rate.

28   The analysis of enterprise decisions to reduce distance and invest in relations is analyzed in Gaddy and Ickes, 1998.

29   Although this process was not his concern, North noted that property rights will not develop in a socially efficient manner if transaction costs are high: 'If political transaction costs are low and the political actors have accurate models to guide them, then efficient property rights will result. But the high transaction costs of political markets and subjective perceptions of the actors more often have resulted in property rights that do not induce economic growth, and the consequent organizations may have no incentive to create more productive rules' (North, 1990, 52).

30   See Ledeneva, 1998.

31   See Guriev and Ickes, 2000, for empirical evidence of economies of scale in the use of barter in Russia.

32   This may offset the effect of more contestants for the pie. The pie may increase with greater non-transparency.

33   It is inappropriate, but probably inevitable, that these should be termed *virtual* strategies.

34   This was articulated clearly by some key architects of Russian privatization. For example: 'In our view, controlling managers is not nearly as important as controlling politicians, since managers' interests are generally much closer to economic efficiency than those of the politicians' (Boycko, Shleifer and Vishny, 1996, 65).

35   A 'normal' enterprise can increase its profits by increasing revenue or reducing costs. It does not have alternative means for survival. Of course, this 'normal' enterprise is an ideal type. Firms in market economies may also engage in bribes and rent-seeking.

36   The non-transparent enterprise has financial records that are difficult to assess, hence outside investors are reluctant to invest.

37   In practice the boundary is rarely so sharp. See Gaddy and Ickes, 1998 for a discussion of *Igor's* rules for successful enterprise management in Russia.

38   Or, a change in the formal rules of the system in the terminology of institutional analysis.

39   In practice, this took several steps which we ignore for simplicity.

40   This points to a generic problem in transition, pooling. For example, once enterprises that lack liquidity are able to barter other enterprises will pretend they are illiquid to share in the benefits of barter. This pooling makes it difficult to target policies that ameliorate the conditions of enterprises and households that suffer in the transition. The ability to engage in such pooling is clearly dependent on the initial distribution of agents in distress.

41   In section 6.2 we provide an example of an evolutionary game where such tipping can occur. Starting from an economy populated only by Soviet enterprises, the evolution to the market can detour to the virtual economy if enough Soviet-type enterprises survive.

42   That argument has been made quite often, recently, most notably in Stiglitz, 1999.

43   This argument is developed further in Gaddy and Ickes, forthcoming, using the concept of 'impermissibility.'

44   In fighting TB it is crucial to follow a multi-drug regimen, because the virus mutates sufficiently so that a unitary drug regimen is ineffective.

45   This is a poor use of terminology. The virtual economy refers to an economic system, not a particular type of enterprise. The virtual economy contains both inefficient manufacturing companies and *Gazprom*. But it is simpler to refer to enterprises that use barter and offsets as virtual enterprises, as a second-best type of shorthand.

46   For some empirical evidence on the presence of economies of scale in using barter in Russia, see Guriev and Ickes, 2000.

47   This is somewhat counter to the analysis of partial reform, ala Murphy-Shleifer-Vishny. In their analysis, market-like invaders can prosper in an environment of state-owned enterprises by purchasing inputs from state-owned enterprises at below market prices. The case is not directly related, however, because there is no discussion of how the surplus (bribes) is distributed, so we cannot really discuss relative fitness.

48   Notice that we can do this without altering the pure-strategy equilibria. For example, we can use the alternative payoff matrix:

	Market	Soviet	Virtual
Market	5	0	3
Soviet	0	3	1
Virtual	2	3	4

We have investigated the evolutionary dyanamics with this payoff matrix using replicator dynamics, as in the example studied in the text. The qualitative behavior remains similar - there are still two basins of attraction - but the likelihood of getting stuck in the virtual economy is smaller than with the original payoff matrix, in the sense that we need a larger initial mutation of virtual enterprises, $pv(0)$ and the critical value to reach the market economy is lower.

49   The dynamics specified in (**) is known as the "replicator dynamics" in evolutioary game theory. See, for instance, Weibull (1995) for a further discussion and interpretation.

50   Of course the specific shares are dependent on the chosen payoffs in the matrix A.

51   This has been studied in different contexts by Boyd, 1997, and Young, 1998.

52   For example, Young, 1998, has shown that if agents interact in sufficiently small, close-knit groups, then the expected waiting time until the evolutionary process comes close to its asymptotic distribution is bounded independently of the number of agents or of the initial state.

53   See, for example, Blasi, Kroumova and Kruse, 1997, 176-181, for a discussion of the problems of corporate governance on the prospects of attracting investment. This issue has recently been taken up by Stiglitz (1999).

54   After the crisis and default raising external finance may be even more difficult. Certainly, foreign investment is more difficult to attract. Interest rates remain high, and domestic financial institutions engage in very little lending to the commercial sector of the economy.

⁵⁵ Which does not mean that this argument is correct.
⁵⁶ This is not necessarily the case. It is possible that more efficient enterprises have borrowed to finance restructuring so that they are burdened by a shortage of credit. But less efficient enterprises may have to borrow for working capital.
⁵⁷ This is not quite correct. There are other costs of using cash. It may attract criminal groups if it is know that the enterprise possesses cash. There may also be tax advantages of using barter. In addition, an enterprise that signals that it has cash may find it harder to delay wage payments to workers. For further discussion, see Gaddy and Ickes, 1998.

References

Aslund, A. (1999), 'Why Has Russia's Economic Transformation Been So Arduous?' Paper presented at the World Bank's Annual Bank Conference on Development Economics, Washington, D.C., April, pp. 28-30.

Blasi, J.R., Kroumova, M. and Kruse, D. (1997), *Kremlin Capitalism: Privatizing the Russian Economy*, Cornell University Press, Ithaca, New York.

Bosworth, B. and Ofer, G. (1996), *Reforming Planned Economies in an Integrating World Economy*, Brookings, Washington, DC.

Boycko, M., Shleifer, A. and Vishny, R. (1996), *Privatizing Russia*, MIT Press, Cambridge, Massachussets.

Boyd, R. (1997), *Population Structure, Equilibrium Selection and the Evolution of Norms.* To be published in proceedings volume for conference on Economics and Evolution held at the International School for Economic Research, University of Siena, June. Ugo Pagano, ed., Cambridge University Press, Cambridge, UK.

Commander, S. and Mumssen, C. (1998), 'Understanding Barter in Russia', EBRD Working Paper no. 3, London, UK.

Conquest, R. (2000), *Reflections on a Ravaged Century*, Norton, New York.

Dewatripont, M. and Roland, G. (1995), The Design of Reform Packages under Uncertainty, *American Economic Review*, vol. 85, no. 5, December.

Ericson, R. E. (1988). Priority, Duality, and Penetration in the Soviet Command Economy, *RAND Note N-2643-NA*, RAND Corporation, Santa Monica, California.

Ericson, R. E. (1999), The Post-Soviet Russian Economic System: An Industrial Feudalism? mimeo, January, Columbia University, New York.

Ericson, R. E. (1999), The Structural Barrier to Transition: A Note on Input-Output Tables of Centrally Planned Economies, *Economic Systems*, vol. 23, no. 3, September, pp. 199-224.

Ericson, R. E. (1999), Comment on an Accounting Model of Russia's Virtual Economy, *Post-Soviet Geography and Economics*, vol. 40, 2, March, pp. 103-109.

Ericson, R.E. and Ickes, B.W. (1999). "An Equilibrium Model of the Virtual Economy", *Working Paper*, William Davidson Institute, Michigan.

Gaddy, C. and Ickes, B.W. (1998), Russia's Virtual Economy, *Foreign Affairs*, September/October, vol. 77, no. 5.

Gaddy, C. and Ickes, B.W. (1998), To Restructure or Not to Restructure: Informal Activities and Enterprise Behavior in Transition, Working Paper, May, William Davidson Institute, Michigan.

Gaddy, C. and Ickes, B.W. (1999), A Simple Four-Sector Model of Russia's Virtual Economy, *Post-Soviet Geography and Economics*, vol. 40, no. 2, March, pp. 79-97.

Gaddy, C. and Ickes, Barry W., *Russia's Virtual Economy*, Washington: Brookings, forthcoming.

Grossman, G. (1963), Notes for a Theory of the Command Economy, *Soviet Studies*, vol. 15, no. 2, pp. 101-23.

Guriev, S. and Ickes, B.W. (2000), Barter in Russia, in P. Seabright (ed.), *The Vanishing Ruble: Barter and Currency Substitution in post-Soviet Societies*. Cambridge University Press, Cambridge, UK.

Hewett, E.A. (1990), *Reforming the Soviet Economy: Equality versus Efficiency*, Brookings, Washington.

Kornai, J. (1992), *The Socialist System: The Political Economy of Communism*. Princeton University Press, Princeton, New Jersey.

Ledeneva, A.V. (1998), *Russia's Economy of Favours*, Cambridge University Press, Cambridge, UK.

North, D.C. (1990), *Institutions, Institutional Change and Economic Performance*. Cambridge University Press, Cambridge, UK.

Organization for Economic Cooperation and Development (1995), *Russian Economic Survey*, OECD, Paris.

Stiglitz, J.E. (1999), Whither Reform: Ten Years of the Transition, *Annual Bank Conference on Development Economics*, The World Bank, Washington DC.

Young, P. (1998), Diffusion in Social Networks, mimeo, Johns Hopkins, Baltimore, Maryland.

Chapter 5

Russia's Economic Policy at the Beginning of the New Phase

Vladimir Mau

Political and Economic Stability

The main feature that distinguished the year 2000 was the stability and even predictability of the main characteristics of Russia's economic and political development. The last surprise of 1999: B. Yeltsin's early resignation at the same time launched the process of establishing a system of steady relationships between the main political players. This, in turn, became one of the most important factors of economic stability.

Such a development bears out repeated conclusions of our economic reviews about the political nature of the Russian economic crisis. The main source of economic instability throughout the nineties was the permanent political crisis, the failure of the leading political forces and interest groups to come to terms on the fundamental issues and goals of economic policy. The overcoming of a political crisis should, of course, lead to economic stabilization. However important and complex are the problems of structural adaptation of the old Soviet system to the requirements of the market, however important are external shocks, the very ability of economic agents to adequately respond to them depends on the ability of the political elite to come up with clear and stable "rules of the game" – and secure practical implementation of those.

The first signs of political stabilization came as early as 1999. Already the firing of Ye. Primakov's government that passed off without trouble despite the backing of this government by the Duma majority, the failure of the impeachment attempts, ease with which new premiers (S. Stepashin and V. Putin) were appointed, indicated the new realities of political life. Still, those events might have meant only the change of tactics by the opposition parties that had lost interest in the Kremlin intrigues and decided to focus on the preparation for more important events: the parliamentary and presidential elections.

However, the Duma election campaign showed that there were more serious grounds for the intensity of the conflicts to decline. Pre-election documents of the leading political groups demonstrated doubtless convergence of their stands on the main issues of social and economic development, including microeconomic and fiscal policies, property relations, etc.[1] While their approaches and proposals could be widely different, the parties represented at the Duma stayed within the paradigm of the market economy, and distinctions between them never transcended the range of differences inherent to the positions of the right and left ends of the political spectrum.

Such a trend rested on an objective economic foundation. One of the important consequences of the 1998 financial crisis and a sharp devaluation of the rouble was the resolution of the conflict between the exporting sector of the Russian economy and the industries that had a potential of import substitution. The favourable conditions in the world market helped to boost exports, while the low exchange rate protected the Russian producers in the domestic market, thus encouraging their development. Conflict that seemed impossible to resolve in the mid-nineties and constituted the greatest danger to the stability of the post-Communist Russia virtually ceased to exist. That had an inevitable impact on the positions of the political forces that acted in the interests of economic groups.

The December 1999 parliamentary elections resulted in the emergence of the State Duma with a structure that enables the executive branch to vote any bill it needs through the lower house. The spectrum of the political parties and blocs represented in the Duma may be broken down into three parts roughly equal in strength: the left-wing, pro-government and the center with the right-wing. In such a situation, practically any proposal by the President or the government is bound to get the backing of the Duma: the pro-government factions vote for it almost automatically with either the right wing or the left-wing's votes added. Difference between the right wing and left-wing factions matters only when a constitutional majority is required to pass a bill. However, even in these cases the executive powers always succeed in finding a common language with the Duma. Thus, the kind of parliamentary mechanism has developed in Russia that in the Western political practice is referred to as the "voting machine" (not to be confused with the rubber-stamp parliament of the Soviet times).

This was shown as early as the first sessions of the State Duma in January 2000, when the key posts in the lower house were carved up between the left-wing and pro-government factions, with the interests of the right-wing and the center all but ignored. At that time such a development caused concern that this alliance would end up as a long-lasting bloc reflecting the political preferences of the new administration, but this concern proved to be unfounded. Throughout that year the executive branch was striking up temporary coalitions, now with these factions, now with those, achieving what they wanted to. Moreover, there was a pattern behind forming the coalitions: in resolving the social and economic issues the executive powers relied on the center and center right forces, while with regard to the "symbolic" issues they looked to the left wing.[2]

Such political maneuvering is in principle only natural for a regime that is pulling out of a long period of instability.[3] It drastically decreases the political and financial costs of passing the bills, as in most cases there is no need to work out compromises in getting the ideological opponents to vote for the proposed document. Practically all the groups can vote consistently with their ideological preferences. This system is conducive to taking responsible economic decisions, which was evidenced by the voting on the Tax Code and the 2001 budget: it was for the first time in the post-Communist period that the budget was approved without support from the Communist Party and the Agrarian Party, i.e., the very forces, whose votes previously had to be secured at the expense of macroeconomic stability.

At the same time, the current situation is fraught with danger, as decisions that were approved automatically may turn into obstacles once the political conditions or goals change. For example, the compromise reached in forming the governing bodies of the current Duma, when all the committees on the social issues were handed to the left-wing factions, seriously impeded work on the relevant laws, including such important ones as the Labour Code and the pension legislation.

One could also say that the development of federative relations is entering a new phase, where the stabilization of political processes is the main trend. The main features of change in this area are, first, the equalization of conditions in which the regional political institutions operate, second, the enhancement of federal control over the situation in the regions and establishment of the uniform "rules of the game", third, a clearer division of responsibilities and levels of government. The political crisis of the nineties gave rise to "special relations" of some regions with the federal center, with the price that the politically weak center had to pay for political support being the violation of the federal legislation, the expansion of its responsibilities to the extent that often ran counter to the Constitution. These practices were formalized through the adoption of bilateral agreements ("agreements on the division of responsibilities") between the federal center and the regions, which was made possible by the first chapter (not subject to amendment) of the RF Constitution.

An important step towards the development of a stable economic and political system is the establishment of equal economic conditions for all regions. What is meant is not absolute equalization of these conditions, for, according to the regions' status, they should be allowed sufficient room to compete for investors. Rather, it is equalization as opposed to the situation where some regions enjoyed more favourable treatment than others, such as special tax regimes for Tatarstan and Bashkiria, which, unlike other regions, were allowed to retain a greater proportion of tax revenues than the other regions. This situation, which quite recently seemed impossible to resolve, was changed in March 2000. What is more, the leaders of those republics initiated the revision of their special status ostensibly by themselves.

General regulation and stabilization of relations between the center and the regions called for deeper political reforms. Those became the object of the first laws the President initiated during his first month in office. Constitutional bills that changed the rules for making up the Federation Council and entitled the President to depose the regional leaders and dissolve their legislatures if those violated the federal legislation, had two important potential consequences. First, the regions were encouraged to act on their own to bring their laws in line with the federal legislation, as there were too many of those laws for the center to be able to revise. Second, the heads of the regional administrations were stripped of immunity and were allowed to be deposed for failure to comply with lawful decisions of the federal authorities.

The uniformity of law was to be further enhanced by the institute of the President's representatives in the federal okrugs (consolidated regions) formed simultaneously with the reform of the upper house. Initially, the achievement of this uniformity was deemed to be the primary goal of establishing them. In addition, the representatives of the President were to coordinate the activities of the federal authorities in the regions, taking them out of the regional authorities' control. This was one of the most serious political and economic problems of the nineties, for the regional leaders, who had a lot of political clout, were able to influence the operation of the institutions that were supposed to be out of their sphere of influence in principle (in the first place, those were courts, prosecutors' offices and the tax authorities).

Finally, the President himself began to act much more actively, initiating the cancellation of undoubtedly unlawful decisions that had been taken by the authorities of some regions (Archangel, Vladimir, Orenburg, Voronezh, Tver). This was to demonstrate the federal authorities' commitment to bringing the regional legislations in line with the federal legislative framework. Characteristically, the majority of the repealed laws reflected the desire of the regional authorities to impose excessive and unlawful restrictions on businesses.

The reform of fiscal relations between the center and the regions is also crucial. The federal government has renounced the practice of expanding "the non-financed mandates", which is a code-name for shifting the responsibility for financing certain expenditures (social, as a rule) to the regions. The federal center took upon itself the implementation of the programs that were prescribed by the legislation but accompanied this with substantially increasing the share of taxes going to the federal coffers. It is noteworthy that the legislators proved willing to go along with such redistribution of the financial resources.

At the same time, the reform of fiscal relations between the center and the regions is accompanied by actions that are to supposed to alleviate the effect of the drastic measures for some of the regional authorities. In parallel with the change of Tatarstan and Bashkiria's fiscal status, special mechanisms (programs) are being adopted that allow those regions to adapt to the reduction in the tax revenues that remain at their disposal. With this in view, the federal government pledged to return to them at the first stage of the reform most of the financial recourses transferred to the federal budget and approve special programs of those republics' development. In addition, amendments to the legislation that effectively extend the terms of office for a number of influential regional leaders (including the president of Tatarstan) for almost a decade, have been approved. A mild procedure for the rotation of the Federal Council has been adopted. Finally, the State Council made up of the regional governors has been established, which is meant to cushion the blow of losing the parliamentary status for them.

Stabilization has changed the role of privatisation, its place in Russia's political and economic life. On the one hand, privatisation has shed its importance as a major factor of securing political support for the regime, i.e., the one that was predominant throughout 1992-1997. On the other hand, the favourable economic situation and the tax revenue growth have sharply decreased the importance of the fiscal function of privatisation, which was especially essential in 1997-1998. As a result, it has become possible to focus on the economic objectives of privatisation, on implementing it for the purpose of increasing the efficiency of the economic system. In 2000, discussions about approaches to further privatisation were going on, but the element of political fighting was hardly discernible in them.

Finally, stabilization has caused substantial shifts in the structure of the Russian elite, changed the balance of economic and political influence groups, the role and status of "oligarchs". One of the distinctive features of the 90s was direct influence of economic interest groups on the executive branch, exerted, in contrast to stable democracies, without relying on political intermediates (parties, parliament). Now the situation is changing. Political institutes are acquiring a weight of their own and are gradually becoming equal parties to a dialogue with business, or even beginning to play the leading role in this dialogue. To a certain extent, this is part of a general trend towards the strengthening of the political system but this transformation also rests on a serious macroeconomic basis.

In the second half of the 1990s, inability of the authorities to balance the budget and the need to constantly rely on the resources of the financial market to stop the gap, made them vulnerable to the main players of the financial market. The fate of the government and even the stability of the political system hinged on the situation in the GKO market, which in practice meant their dependence on the actions of a few owners of major financial entities. The way they operated in the financial markets, - primarily, their decisions to buy or sell securities could have brought about the fall of the rouble, the Cabinet or the entire political system of the country. This is just what made them oligarchs. Thus, dependence on the oligarchs was not only personal but also institutional, and each new budget that ran a deficit strengthened the oligarchs' effective control over the authorities' course of actions.

Now this has all ceased to exist - the balanced budget has put an end to the authorities' dependence on business, banks' political role has weakened substantially. The government, at long last, has proved capable of promising what it can really provide, hence there is no need to run into debt. Thus, the government has necessary leeway now. Social support is, of course, important, but now there is an opportunity to lean on various interest groups, taking advantage of conflicts between them to stabilize political power.

Of course, all this does not mean the abatement of corruption or opportunities to maintain "special relations" between business and authorities. Now, however, this problem is more of a personal rather than institutional nature.

What is a different story is whether business is able to act in an organized way to lobby for its corporate interests (which was the case when it fought against the government's proposals for changing the corporate profits tax in the autumn of 2000). After the crisis of the "old oligarchy", a new, more adequate system of relations between the authorities and business began to take shape. The acquisition by the business elite of the "trade mark" of the Russian Union of Industrialists and Entrepreneurs was an important step in legalizing these relations, which may take the form of the French patronate in future.

The new political environment means that a new phase of Russia's social and economic development has begun, which paves the way for developing a new program of the nation's social and economic development.

Strategic Program of Russia's Social and Economic Development

An immediate impulse to the development of the new strategic program of Russia's development and reform was given by the emergence of a new administration with V. Putin at the head. There were, however, deeper causes, which are associated with the actual (not only formal) completion of the first stage of the post-Communist reform and the emergence of objective and subjective circumstances that point to the beginning of a new phase.

The first program of the post-Communist reform was outlined in 1991-1992 and reflected the Gaidar government's general intentions with respect to the reform of the Russian economy. The main goals set by this program were the liberalization of the economy (primarily, of the prices and foreign trade), macroeconomic stabilization (fiscal and monetary), and, finally, privatization, which was regarded to be the most important goal of institutional transformation as part of the development of a market economy. The implementation of this program took much longer than was originally planned, but by the end of the nineties the goals of the program had been achieved. This set the stage for moving on to the next phase of the post-Communist development: that of the structural and institutional reform securing sustainable growth.

Political stabilization, gradual overcoming of the power crisis and the consolidation of power, the convergence of the elite groups' stances on the fundamental issues, made it possible to start a discussion on the issues of Russia's long-term development to be started, which was reflected in the drawing up of the Strategic Conception, also known as the Gref Program. It was supposed to set the main goals of Russia's social and economic development, identify the key mechanisms of achieving a rate of growth that allows bridging the gap between Russia and the most advanced countries of the world. In other words, the program was supposed to set the goal of securing high rates of growth in the situation of the post-industrial challenges.

In the course of the economic and political discussions of 1999-2000, three main approaches to addressing these issues took shape.

First, the etatist model typical of the left-wing groups. Under this model, the state is the main economic agent, and only this agent can assume responsibility for investment. This implies utmost concentration of resources in the hands of the state (primarily, the rent and export revenues) and their redistribution to suit the national priorities. Protectionism is no less important in this model as a way of defending the domestic producers from the competition of stronger foreign companies.

Second, growth based on the encouragement of business and the government's proactive policy of establishing environment favourable for investors - both domestic and foreign. This requires the establishment of an adequate system of institutes, including the appropriate legislation and efficient enforcement.

Third, an approach involving drastic cuts in budget spending as a share of the economy, making it comparable with the parameters typical of the countries with a similar level of development (the reduction of the budget share of the economy from 35-36 per cent to 20-22 per cent of GDP based on the "enlarged government").

The development of the new Strategic Program involved the discussion of all possible alternatives of the concept, including the etatist approach (and even its mobilization-oriented version). This is the principle of the new administration that is willing to consider all kinds of proposals without rejecting them on ideological or political grounds.[4] However, after some discussion the etatist approach was rejected for the following reasons:

- The government has proved to be an inefficient decision-maker as far as investment is concerned. It can concentrate resources but they are highly likely to be used in a manner which is far from efficient.
- This approach runs counter to the federalist set-up of Russia, as it implies a drastic concentration of resource management in one center.
- This is hardly compatible with democracy and property rights.
- And, finally, it does not in the least meet challenges of the post-industrialist era in which the stability of property rights and encouragement of entrepreneurship is a *sine qua non*.

The discussion mainly unfolded between the adherents of the second and third approaches. This fact in itself became a significant event in the political and economic life of the post-Communist Russia. Both approaches are closely related and are in effect liberal. The establishment of a new institutional environment implies a certain reduction of budget spending as a share of GDP, as in such conditions economic agents have more resources left for investment. The reduction of budget spending as a share of GDP as a key problem of growth, in turn, implies the establishment of the same kind of institutional environment, that is, environment characteristic of a market-based democracy (property rights guarantees in the first place). Throughout the nineties, the difference between these two approaches was practically indiscernible on the political level, for their adherents were united in opposing the etatist (and populist) alternative. Only as late as 2000, their separation in the framework of the liberal model became evident to everyone and moved from the plane of the purely economic debate into the political sphere.

The beginning of this debate itself indicated the new phase of the Russian economic reform. The focus of the economical and political debate shifted to the right (liberal) end of the spectrum, whereas the doctrines of the left were increasingly displaced from the sphere of practical discussion to the area of abstract speculation.

The Gref program was mainly drawn up in the first half of 2000. The key feature of this document was its political and ideological consistency - for the first time since the 1992 program. The key concept of this document is the establishment of institutional environment conducive to entrepreneurship as a basis of sustainable growth.

Approval by V. Putin of the fundamental approaches of the Strategic Program in April 2000 meant that the conceptual choice was made in favour of the politico-economical model proposed by this document. The full text of the program was not approved as an official document then. However, it was used as a basis of more technological documents, such as the Program of Measures for a period of 18 months, i.e., years 2001-2003, and government-drafted laws and regulations.

Such a development is only natural. It is not only thanks to its formal approval that an ideologically consistent document can lend credibility to the prospects of a policy. It also depends on how accurately it reflects actual trends in the development of social and economic processes.[5] At the same time, a formal approval implies tedious coordination between numerous agencies, which either protracts the process substantially or results in inconsistency. The latter is inevitable and only natural in the situation of a real political process seen as a result of interaction between various interest groups.

The Strategic Program centers on a package of institutional and structural reforms, including political ones, implemented as overall macroeconomic stability (primarily, fiscal and monetary stability) is maintained.

The key components of the institutional reforms that, under the Gref Program, Russia is to carry through, are as follows:

- Tax reform and alleviation of tax burden.
- Reform of the budgetary system. What is meant is not formal spending cuts but deep structural reforms of the public sector that would secure more efficient management of public funds.
- Deregulation of business or, which is the same thing, improving the efficiency of the government regulation of business. It involves lowering barriers to entry, simplifying the systems of registration, licensing and supervision of private businesses, simplifying the implementation of investment projects.
- Guaranteeing property (including intellectual property) rights. Improving the efficiency of state property management.
- Lowering and unification of customs tariffs.
- Development of the financial market and financial institutions. Increasing the stability and efficiency of the banking sector is a special problem.

- Reform of natural monopolies, to improve their investment attractiveness, which involves splitting up the monopoly and competitive sectors, the enhancement of their transparency and encouragement of competition to the maximum possible extent.
- Reform of the social support system to concentrate resources on providing benefits to the poor.
- Reform of the pension system along the lines of developing savings-based pension provision.

The key feature of the Strategic Program is that it does not envisage any sectoral priorities, which is the most important characteristic of the document aimed at addressing the problems of the post-industrial era. In fact, two circumstances are recognized here. First, the time has not come yet to speak about comparative advantages of the Russian economy in terms of specific industries. Only practical activities will show in which particular industries Russia will be able to hold its own in competition with the world's most advanced producers. Second, it might be individual companies rather than industries that will prove to be the most competitive. The latter is generally more characteristic of the countries facing the challenges of the "catching-up industrialization".[6]

Finally, the Strategic Program aims to deal with a number of key issues that go beyond the socio-economic policies as such. Two of them are especially important: the administrative and judiciary reforms. The achievement of practically all economic goals hinges on the reform of these two systems, as entrepreneurial activity will be impeded by corruption among the government official and unfair court rulings. The recognition of this fact also means that in the current Russian situation the problem of enforcement comes to the fore, being even more important than the adoption of new laws and regulations.

Economic Program and Economic Policy

Practical implementation of the Strategic Program had begun even before it was formally approved. As early as 2000, the most important bills that aimed to reform the tax system fundamentally were introduced to the Duma. The 2001 budget drafting was also based on these laws.

Tax Reform

The nature of the tax legislation package and its relation to the budget projections reflected some important features of the new administration's course of action. Those features are worthy of special mention. Traditionally, the tax ideas of the Russian authorities were based on the effective recognition of the so called Laffer curve, that is, expectations that tax revenues will increase if tax burden on the economy is alleviated,[7] even though no serious empirical justification of this assumption has been provided to date.

Having proposed tax cuts in 2000, the government decided against building the expectations of higher revenues into the next year's budget projections, in spite of the criticism by some deputies. It is not so much skepticism about the Laffer curve or even conservatism of the new government's budget planning, as a demonstration of firm commitment to the idea of alleviating tax burden on the economy. In other words, alleviation of the tax burden as a factor of encouraging economic growth is one of the government's key goals.

Another peculiarity of the tax reform is that it is oriented to bringing financial demands in line with the actual potential of tax collection. The proposed system (the flat personal income tax and the unified payroll tax) recognizes as a given the scantiness of the administrative resources available to the weak state. In other words, the authorities are trying to avoid laying claims which they are clearly unable to enforce.

The new tax system clearly targets certain social groups. It is undoubtedly attractive to the public at large but is especially important to the entrepreneurs, on whose support the government counts in the first place.

Finally, the new tax system may have important political implications. The radical cut of the personal income tax and renunciation of the progressive principle set the stage for the emergence in future of a political force oriented towards social democracy. Up until recently, Russia had no economic basis for the emergence of a party whose platform would be requiring tax increases with a view to using the additional revenues for social and economic purposes (which is what social-democrats' economic program is all about). The heavy tax burden induced everyone, including the far left, to call for its alleviation, which made the left's platform extremely inconsistent. Now the situation is changing, and it will not be long before political forces emerge whose platform will put the main emphasis on establishing a "fairer" tax system.

Customs Regulation

Action taken to reform import tariffs was based on similar logic. It was decided to cut the number of tariff rates and amalgamate commodity items as much as possible. This approach is inconsistent with the prevailing world trends, for, thanks to the development of information systems, there are now new opportunities for monitoring goods crossing borders and, accordingly, for using more subtle and diversified methods of customs regulation. However, the limited administrative resources of the Russian authorities do not allow them so far to exercise efficient customs control, and the government is demonstrating willingness to concede this in its customs policies.

Discussion around the new customs tariffs has testified to somewhat contradictory position of the government in the system of economic interests being formed. Proposals for customs tariff cuts received wide support from the political elite. The government had no influential forces in its ranks that would insist on the "protection of domestic producers" through customs regulation. That might have been due to two circumstances. First, the still low real exchange rate of the rouble which is a barrier to foreign goods. Second, the nascent economic growth made the import of technologies, equipment and components vital to many companies. Hence, the importance of cutting tariffs on the relevant products.

However, the developments of the autumn of 2000 were not as straightforward as that. The delays in the final approval and publication of the new customs regulations resulted in heightening of pressure from groups that were not interested in the liberalization of foreign trade policy. It became clear that those groups included companies operating in Russia under investment agreements (car assembly) and the light industry. This pressure was mounting in direct proportion to the real appreciation of the rouble.

The prospects of the official approval of (or failure to approve) the new import tariffs will be an important test that will allow both economic goals and the political strength of the government to be appraised.

Budget Expenditures Reform

Whereas in 2000 the revenue base issues (the tax reform, revision of revenue sharing between the federal and regional budgets) were the focal point of the financial system reform, in 2001 the restructuring of the federal budget spending should come to the fore.

So far, budget spending has never been reformed in a systematic way. Expenditures are planned, to a large degree, on an ad hoc basis and are oriented to possible revenues instead of being part of a thought-out system of economic and political priorities or a vision of the nation's strategic development. Practice demonstrates convincingly that without systemic transformation of this area, not only the budget but the entire economic, social and political life of the country will remain potentially (and actually) unstable. Which means that the system of budget spending is a complex theme in which all the problems of macroeconomic policy and structural reform as well as political problems proper are intertwined.

On the one hand, the transformation of the system of expenditure planning and management is a prerequisite of overcoming Russia's dependence on the fluctuations of the world economic conditions and alleviating debt burden on the economy. Without such transformation, even budget balancing cannot be carried through, as the budget will remain vulnerable to all kinds of unfavourable circumstances.

On the other hand, this reform paves the way for improving business climate and is one of the components of structural reform. It will put things into the right perspective for budget recipients, and, more importantly, set priorities of using the state's financial resources in the medium term.

The change and refinement of the mechanisms of budget funds allocation is another area of this reform. If that is achieved, the reform will help to combat corruption and improve business climate in Russia.

Finally, the reform of budget expenditure involves the resolution of a number of political problems. The establishment of strategic priorities and transparent procedures of budget financing should put a restraint on the populist tendencies in the authorities' course of action, especially in situations where additional resources become available to them thanks to favourable economic conditions.

Business Climate and Deregulation

A major test of the government's efficiency is whether it will be able to secure the official approval and practical implementation of the deregulation program. This program was outlined in the Strategic Program, with top priority activities set forth in the list of priority measures. At the end of 2000, the first package of laws and regulations was drafted and presented for the government approval. It deals with simplifying rules and procedures for business registration, licensing, and supervision by inspecting authorities. Each of these areas is important from both economic and political standpoints.

It is important from the economic standpoint because this is where the most serious obstacles to entrepreneurship are concentrated. The absolute power of bureaucracy is primarily reflected in the barriers that a business runs into when started, and is also displayed when all kinds of inspections are held. There are about three dozen inspecting authorities, the duration and periodicity of inspections are not specified by regulations, requirements are often impossible to meet, while penalties and fines are so heavy that they may cause a business to close down. Small and medium-sized businesses are, of course, especially vulnerable, not only because of bureaucratic pressure and bribe extortion. Excessive regulation may also be used for squeezing competitors out of the market and squaring the authorities' accounts with entrepreneurs who are not loyal enough.

From the political standpoint, the prospects of the deregulation package are important because its fate will be an indicator of the government's ability to concentrate political will on the priority areas and to attain its goals, overcoming the bureaucracy's resistance. Despite the overall awareness of the importance of the proposed measures, each of them will meet with serious bureaucratic resistance, as they all trespass on the rights of a host of important agencies, both on the federal and the regional level.

Also of interest is what name will be used for the relevant package of the approved documents. In this context deregulation may as well be regarded as a package of measures to improve the efficiency of the government regulation of the economy. Of course, the measures themselves are more important that the name. However the name that will be predominantly used will also be an indicator of tendencies currently prevalent in Russia.

Reform of Natural Monopolies

In 2000, a fundamentally new tendency emerged in this sector. While earlier the management of the relevant sectors of the national economy put up strong resistance to the government's attempts to implement their restructuring, now they are themselves becoming the driving force of change. In the first place, this applies to the railway system and electric utilities. We do not at all mean that the government is becoming a hindrance to change. It is certainly interested in implementing reform. However, unlike the previous years, the natural monopolies themselves do not resist the government's proposals. Rather, they are eager to lead the process of reform themself.

First, the overall economic and political stabilization allows and necessitates greater attention to the prospects of those sectors' development. To achieve growth, investment is required, and it has become obvious to everyone that the government resources are not to be counted on in the foreseeable future. It should be private investment then, but given their current financial position and organizational status, they are not attractive to big private investors.

Second, the new type (and even generation) of managers have taken over the relevant companies. In the recent years new figures, who are able and willing to work in the logic of the market, have emerged at their helm. This does not only apply to the new type management at UES or Transneft. There has been substantial change in the Railway Ministry's style of management, which is radically different from what it used to be only three years ago. Hence, a conceptually new level of discussions (both political and economic) which the managers of the natural monopolies are having with the government.

Third, the new management is interested in enhancing their control over companies "of their own", being well aware that this is best achieved through restructuring and privatization. If top managers keep information and financial flows under control, they exercise much more efficient control over the situation in their industries, which also strengthens their position in the process of any structural reforms.

It should be added that companies' minority shareholders and/or potential investors in the relevant sectors of the Russian economy have become much more active now. They are also beginning to play a more active game to have such terms of restructuring adopted as would allow them to gain control with the minimum costs. Partly, this is justified by their willingness to invest in the development of particular industries, but, to a considerable degree, this is just speculative capital seeking to take advantage of the share price fluctuations.

The new situation changes the role of the government in implementing reform of the natural monopolies. Today, the main objective of the government is careful appraisal of various interest groups' proposals on reforming these sectors rather than encouragement of reformist steps. Now the government should first of all act as a supreme arbiter in discussions. However, it cannot play this role in a straightforward manner, i.e., discussing the incoming proposals. In the situation of information asymmetry the optimum tactic is encouragement of conflict between various alliances interested in reforming this sector to use the debate between them as a basis for careful and realistic analysis of the recommendations presented.

As specific as individual natural monopolies are, a number of general principles of their reorganization can still be identified. First, it is securing the continuity of their operations, which suggests the responsibility of the management of those sectors for implementing reorganization. Second, this is separation of the state management and business functions (this applies to the Railway Ministry and the Nuclear Energy Ministry). Third, securing financial transparence, which implies the adoption of international accounting standards. Fourth, separation of the monopolistic and potentially competitive businesses. Fifth, securing equal access to the services or products of these sectors.

Financial Markets

Finally, reform of the financial system, banks in the first place, has critical importance. It is this element that is one of the main obstacles to channeling savings into investment. The lack of consensus between the government and the Central Bank on the principles of the banking sector restructuring and improvement of its stability is a serious problem of the current political process. Still, however difficult this problem is, it should not be resolved by crippling the Central Bank's independence. It would be the wrong thing to do because of general theoretical considerations (the Central Bank's independence is one of the most important gains of the first post-Communist decade and is a factor of the monetary system stability). In fact, the main source of the instability of the financial system is not only or not so much its legal framework or organizational structure (however important they are) as the low level of economic agents' confidence in one another, i.e., depositors' confidence in banks and vice versa. This creates the situation where private depositors prefer Sberbank to other banks, while commercial banks prefer to keep funds in the accounts of the Central Bank at a negative real interest rate, or invest them in government securities which have a very low yield compared to commercial loans.

However, the improvement of legislation can alleviate the confidence problem only to a limited degree. A good credit history is much more important here, and this takes time. For this reason, the stability and predictability of the economic and political course is now the primary prerequisite for improving the operation of the financial markets, even though the government, of course, should take serious steps to improve the situation in this sector. Especially steps in such directions as mergers of banks and enhancing their stability, demonopolization of the lending services market (especially retail services), entry of foreign banks.

Factors of Destabilization

At the same time, at the end of 2000, factors, which, if they develop further, might become a source of destabilization of the economic and political situation in Russia, were very clearly discernible.

Growth of real exchange rate is, in principle, a natural phenomenon of a society pulling out of a long period of macroeconomic instability. Undervaluation of the national currency cannot be a constant phenomenon and gradually comes to an end with a sustainable economic recovery. However, it was the low exchange rate that was one of the factors of the economic and political consensus in 1999-2000, which allowed the interests of exporting industries and import substitution to be reconciled. Now the impact of this factor is petering out. It would not be so dangerous in itself if it were occurring against the background of investment growth and especially the inflow of foreign capital. However, investment growth observed in 2000 is still insufficient to compensate for the real exchange rate appreciation, which is reflected in the high level of the banking sector liquidity, with very little of banks' funds channeled to the real economy. The lack of the appropriate conditions has some very unpleasant consequences, which made themselves felt in the fourth quarter of 2000, when growth decelerated substantially and imports started to increase.

The national economy remains extremely dependent on the high world prices for raw materials exported by Russia, especially oil prices. Both too low and too high prices present a serious problem. An adverse impact of low prices (lower than $10 a barrel) on Russia's situation and the government is quite obvious. However, extremely high prices are no less detrimental to the economic and political process in the present-day Russia, and the year 2000, especially the second half of it, provide ample evidence of this. Three negative effects of the developing situation could be highlighted.

First, it creates excessive pressure for the rouble appreciation, with the adverse consequences mentioned above. Second, to keep up economic growth, it would be preferable to retain the low exchange rate, or at least to contain real exchange rate appreciation.

Second, the inflow of foreign currency in the situation of limited investment growth is a factor of inflation acceleration, as, trying to hold back real exchange rate appreciation, the monetary authorities are forced to buy hard currency and issue roubles. In addition, in the specific Russian situation, with the "August syndrome" still persisting, the instruments of the rouble supply sterilization are limited: policymakers, scared by the GKO collapse, are shying away from reestablishing the government securities market. As a result, the Central Bank has to perform a balancing act between inflation and exchange rate appreciation, drawing fire from all the socio-political groups.

Third, the high oil prices are making the government's life even more difficult, as far as the fiscal policy is concerned, than it used to be with low prices. In such a situation it is much harder to pursue a responsible fiscal policy. Additional budget revenues provoke the activity of a variety of lobbies. There are difficulties in all the sectors, and all are demanding money, even those who have got out of the habit of laying claims to the budget in the recent years. In the autumn, the pressure was mounting practically by the week. As a result, the danger of taking the same road as the USSR in the seventies or Russia in the mid-nineties is increasing.

The problem is not confined to pressure from industrial and agricultural lobbies. All the branches of power are facing temptation to gain greater popularity by taking decisions to raise wages, pensions, and all kinds of social payments. Given the current low level of such payments, such decisions are understandable but economically and politically dangerous.

They are dangerous economically because they set the level of the government's commitments which will be impossible to live up to if the conditions of the foreign markets change. In addition, greater consumer demand in the situation of the rouble real appreciation may be largely oriented to imported goods, and thus will not contribute to growth in Russia.

This is where a potentially serious political problem arises of possible divergence between the president's and the government's positions. The president, exposed to the pressure of factors making for political stability and the maintenance of his popularity, may prove to be more inclined to taking populist decisions than the technocratic government. This is what may give rise to the mounting of tensions within the executive branch itself.

In the face of such a development the implementation of deep restructuring of budget spending (which was discussed above), as well as the adoption of a special mechanism of using additional budget revenues raised due to favourable conditions in the foreign markets (in other words, that do not depend on the economic activity within Russia) acquire great importance. This may take the form of a special Stabilization Fund which would allow accumulating resources that would be protected from inefficient use as a result of pressure from all kinds of lobbies.

Dependence of Russia's economic development on the world economic performance is not, however, only related to the movement of prices for the exported primary resources. Russia's post-Communist economy is becoming closely tied to the world economy and will from now on be affected by the world market conditions. Thus, the slowing down of the developed Western countries' growth predicted for 2001, will also have an effect on the performance of the Russian economy. The cyclic development characteristic of the market system in general will gradually start playing its role too. All this has yet to make up an integral system of factors that will affect the performance of the Russian economy and gradually replace the specific features of the post-Communist development. In this particular case we only want to draw attention to the fact that the role of the post-Communist features is gradually receding to the background, while the standard factors of a market economy operation are becoming the main determinants of socio-economic performance.

One of the factors holding back the development of entrepreneurship and economic growth is the weakness of the enforcement system and especially the judiciary. Strengthening of law and contract enforcement mechanisms is a major factor of transaction cost reduction, and thus of sustainable growth. In the current situation, law and contact enforcement is an even more important than the development and approval of new legislation.

Finally, it would be wrong to underestimate the importance of problems related to the level of public support for the government actions. According to the public opinion polls, this level is exceptionally high, and the share of population stating that their position has not deteriorated is on the level of 1997 (with the number of respondents stating that their living standards have actually improved being the highest since 1987). In 2000, however, a trend reemerged towards divergence between the official subsistence level and its appraisal by respondents in public opinion polls (see the diagram). While this divergence should not be overdramatized, the performance of this indicator merits close attention.

Figure 5.1   Subsistence level appraised by public opinion polls respondents versus the official subsistence level

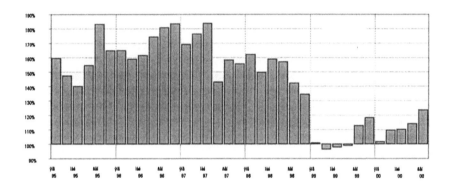

Priorities for 2001

No one doubts that this year's central socio-economic objective is to provide conditions for sustainable economic growth. It can hardly be the sort of growth that is not exposed to any fluctuations of the business conditions, but the government's goal is to reduce the negative effect of these fluctuations and establish the right institutional and structural prerequisites for this.

Prerequisites that are especially important today include: Maintaining the stability of the constitutional system. Understanding of the Constitution as primarily a certain set-up of national life, as stable "rules of the game" is an important source of political as well as economic stability. This is what determines the importance of retaining the 1993 Constitution, currently in force, the renunciation of the idea of amending it, however useful the proposed amendments may seem.

The retention of political liberties is of special importance. In the situation of fundamental transformation of the social system, those liberties, and especially freedom of speech, prove to be an important economic rather than only political phenomenon. Today, the opportunity for free critique of the authorities' economic policy is an important guarantee against mistakes, including populist ones.

Another important factor is maintaining the stability of the budget system, ability of the government and the legislators to secure a balanced budget with both high and low oil prices. The establishment of the Stabilization Fund would be an important step in this direction.

Stabilization of the budget system is directly related to drawing up and implementing the program of budget spending restructuring. This reform involves addressing both macroeconomic and structural problems. Simultaneously, there is interaction of economic and political factors of reform here, as reform of budget expenditures implies determined resistance of all the branches of power to the temptation of taking populist decisions.

One of the key goals for 2001 is implementing a package of deregulation measures (or measures to debureaucratize the national economy) The implementation of this package will demonstrate the government's willingness and ability to secure the sustainability of growth.

It would be of critical importance to launch administrative reform, that is, deep reform of the government, meaning the revision of the functions of the state and its officials, the regulation of these functions to make them consistent with the goal of accelerated growth. Administrative reform should not be confined to raising the government officials' salaries. This reform should be looked upon in the context of and in relation to the measures implemented as part of the deregulation package. It is only as part of this transformation that a wage raise can be considered.

The continuation of the tax reform is one of the priorities of economic policy in 2001. The focus now should be on refining the corporate taxes.

Reform of the banking system is also a priority, for the issue of channelling savings into investment cannot be addressed without it.

Finally, the same economic problem should be addressed through the judiciary reform, which is to be launched in 2001.

The above listed issues make up the outline of the system of institutional and structural reforms, which Russia is to embark upon now. The ability to implement them will become a test of the authorities' efficiency in the short run.

Notes

[1]   For details see Gaidar 1999, *Russian Economy in 1999: Tendencies and Perspectives*, IET, Moscow, pp. 313-319.

[2]   Nevertheless, the fact that the legislators work closely with the executive branch does not mean that their actions are fully coordinated. In 2000 the President used his right of veto 12 times, in each case with respect to a law dealing with social and economic issues.

3   In Marxist economic literature such a regime was defined as Bonapartist. Maneuvering between various political groups to secure the stability of power is regarded as its main feature.

4   There is more than one way of looking upon such pragmatism on the part of the authorities. On the one hand the desire to maintain ideological neutrality is an important prerequisite of political stability and the ability of the authorities to find a common language with various interest groups. On the other hand, there is always a danger that excessive pragmatism may result in accepting proposals that look good at first sight but do not fit into the system of challenges of the modern (post-industrial) world. The existence of ideological priorities and preferences, if they are consistent with a given phase of a society development, allow avoiding swerving and zigzagging, fraught with great shocks. Populist recipes often look very attractive and commonsense outwardly but are very dangerous to stability.

5   For example, the 1992 program was never officially approved. It was severely criticized by most of the political groups. The program was, however, implemented, as it reflected real needs of the Russian economy, even though its implementation took much longer than originally planned.

6   This was pointed out by Gerschenkron, A. (1962), *Economic Backwardness in Historical Perspective*, p. 7, Harvard University Press, Cambridge, Mass.

7   These approaches were most clearly articulated by the Primakov government.

References

Gaidar, E. (1999), *Russian Economy in 1999: Tendencies and Perspectives*, IET, Moscow.
Gerschenkron, A. (1962), *Economic Backwardness in Historical Perspective*, Harvard University Press, Cambridge, Massachusetts.

PART II
TAXATION IN TRANSITION
ECONOMIES

Chapter 6

The Tax System and the Peculiarities of the Russian Economy

Michael V. Alexeev

Introduction

At first glance, Russia's tax system is fairly conventional. It has the same major taxes (corporate and personal income taxes, VAT, excises) as most developed economies and the upper income group of the developing economies. The statutory rates of these taxes in Russia are also well within the international standards. While the tax system may appear conventional, the Russian economy is often viewed as having some peculiar characteristics. The question arises, therefore, whether Russia's tax system adequately reflects the peculiarities of the Russian economy. The list of such major features of the economy that present the greatest challenges to the tax system includes rampant tax evasion, pervasive corruption of tax administration officials, and widespread use of non-monetary means of payment and payment arrears.[1] I will argue that many of the problems of Russia's tax system have been due to its attempts to deal with these peculiar features of the economy. Moreover, the tax provisions aimed at dealing with evasion, corruption, barter and payment arrears have been feeding back to the economy at large, sometimes exacerbating the difficulties these provisions have tried to address. For example, widespread tax evasion affects the tax statutes and tax administration techniques, which in turn impact the taxpayers' behavior well beyond their immediate effect on the extent of tax evasion. This paper will focus on the interaction of the peculiar characteristics of the Russian economy with the functioning of the tax system, emphasizing the tradeoffs produced by the tax system's reaction to these characteristics.

Note that Russia is currently undergoing the most significant tax reforms since the introduction of the current tax system in the early 1990s. At the time of writing of this paper (July 2001), the parts of the new Tax Code relating to tax administration, personal income tax, VAT, and excises have already been enacted and the profit tax chapter of the Code has been in principle adopted by the Duma (the Russian parliament). The discussion below will address mostly the provisions of the new Tax Code. In a few places, however, I will refer to some of the provisions in the pre-Tax Code law.

The next three sections consider the interaction of the tax system with, respectively, tax evasion, corruption within tax administration, and non-monetary means of payments and payment arrears. Section 5 concludes.

Tax Evasion

Russia is notorious for the large extent of tax evasion. According to some estimates, Russian taxpayers evade more tax than they pay. Johnson et al. (1997) put the share of unofficial economy in Russia at over 40 per cent of GDP. Even that estimate appears to be quite conservative as it is based on the assumption that the share of the unofficial economy in Russia in the late 1980s was 12 per cent of GDP. Meanwhile, one of the most detailed study on the subject (Grossman, 1991) put the share of urban household income derived from the unofficial economy in Russia at about 27 per cent in the late 1970s - early 1980s.

The social cost of tax evasion, however, is not equivalent to the government revenue loss caused by the unofficial economic activities. As Slemrod and Yitzhaki (1987) and Mayshar (1991) pointed out, at least part of the revenue loss to the government represents a gain to the taxpayer. Therefore, the rather conventional proposition that tax collection resources directed at reducing tax evasion should be increased up to a point where the marginal dollar of such resources raises one dollar of additional revenues would not maximize social welfare, as long as tax evaders' welfare is taken into account. Incidentally, this consideration also suggests that privatizing tax collections may be counterproductive in terms of social welfare.[2]

In order to determine the best approach to dealing with tax evasion, one needs to understand both the costs of evasion and the costs of anti-evasion policies. One of the most significant costs of tax evasion *per se* may be the effort that the evaders expend to hide their tax liability. Socially, this effort represents a dead-weight loss. Another important cost of tax evasion is due to the extra distortion that it brings into the tax system. Some activities are easier to hide from the tax authorities than others. For example, providers of services usually have greater opportunities for evasion than manufacturers. Given that the statutory rates of major taxes typically are the same for manufacturing and service activities, the effective tax rates on services would then be lower than on manufacturing, leading to efficiency-reducing distortions. The propensity to engage in tax evasion presumably also differs among the individual taxpayers. The possibility of tax evasion then may discriminate against those taxpayers who are less willing to evade, whether due to their moral constraints or to greater risk aversion. This would preclude "honest" and otherwise talented entrepreneurs from entering the activities where tax evasion is widespread. The negative effect on foreign direct investment may be particularly strong.

As mentioned above, the possibility of tax evasion necessitates countervailing efforts on the part of tax administration authorities. The cost of audits is an obvious example of extra administrative costs of tax evasion. The literature on the interaction of tax evasion and tax administration usually emphasizes the administrative costs imposed upon a tax agency. Meanwhile, the role of taxpayer compliance costs due to the provisions in the tax system that are intended to impede tax evasion has been relatively understudied. Such costs include, for example, the requirements to document expenses and the costs that audits impose on the taxpayers. Mayshar (1991) presents a rather general model that reflects these costs, but he does not focus on them. Slemrod (1994) emphasizes the link between tax enforcement and tax avoidance efforts in examining the issue of optimal tax progressivity. Slemrod's model could easily be reformulated with respect to tax evasion. Both models, however, use a representative agent framework that does not account for the fact that compliance costs are imposed both on the evaders and on the honest taxpayers.[3] Nagin (1990) is the only contribution that emphasizes the costs that anti-evasion policies impose on the compliant taxpayers. Meanwhile, the compliance costs of the anti-evasion provisions appear to be particularly prominent in Russia and impose perhaps unusually high costs on all taxpayers, both those who, given the opportunity, engage in evasion and those who do not.

One example of costs generated by the apparent desire to fight tax evasion is the severe limitation on the deductibility of advertising expenditures. According to the current profit tax law in Russia, a taxpayer can deduct advertising expenditures only up to a small fraction of taxable profit. The new Tax Code envisages limiting deductible advertising costs by one per cent of sales. While the deductibility of advertising is limited in many countries, the restrictions in Russia are particularly severe. One reason behind these restrictions is that advertising is too difficult to monitor. For example, a taxpayer can contract with a small fly-by-night firm for it to provide advertising services. The taxpayer would then pay an exorbitant amount for a token advertising effort, and take the deduction for the expense. Meanwhile, the fly-by-night firm secretly returns all or most of the payment to the taxpayer and disappears before even filing a profit tax declaration. This scheme, of course, constitutes fraud and it requires a significant level of cooperation between the fly-by-night firm and the taxpayer. In most countries, such a scheme would be handled under the tax fraud statutes and would not necessitate special treatment of advertising under the tax law. In a country where tax evasion is rampant and the tax administration is either unwilling or unable to prosecute such schemes, however, the government is tempted to impose special limitations on deductibility of certain expenditures - as is the case in Russia. Obviously, these limitations generate economic distortions by raising the after-tax relative prices of non-deductible inputs. The restrictions on the deductibility of advertising impose particularly large costs on start-up firms that do not have established brands and reputations among customers.

Another, perhaps more important example of costs generated by the apparent desire to fight tax evasion is the weakly constrained right of the Russian tax authorities to confiscate funds from the bank accounts of delinquent taxpayers (Art. 46 of the Tax Code). The apparent motivation for this provision was the need to enforce compliance. The instrument has proven to be rather blunt, however. While the confiscation right has probably helped the tax service to collect some funds from would-be evaders, it has likely caused many more honest taxpayers that experienced (or expected to experience) temporary cash flow problems to forgo bank-related transactions. Some of these taxpayers might have left above ground business altogether, while others have resorted to barter and other non-monetary means of payment.[4] Of course, the tax authorities need to be able to confiscate the delinquent taxpayer's property at some point, but it generally should be used as a last resort. The problem with the Russian rule is that it allows such confiscation too early in the collection process, before the difference has been established between a taxpayer whose funds need to be seized and a taxpayer who can be dealt with in alternative ways.

A particularly pure example of a wasteful provision in the Russian tax law that is intended to fight tax evasion but imposes significant costs on all taxpayers is the quarterly (or even monthly) reporting requirement for the profit tax. Apparently, the main purpose of this requirement, which is preserved in the new Tax Code, is to limit the possibilities for fly-by-night firms to be used in tax evasion schemes. Given that in Russia, tax declarations are normally submitted in person and to several different agencies (tax service, statistical agency, and until recently the pension fund) this reporting requirement may be quite onerous not only in terms of extra accounting work, but also due to sheer expenditure of time in the process of submission of tax declarations. Small businesses find this requirement particularly costly, as the declaration submission time is largely independent of the size of the business.

These and many other anti-evasion mechanisms impose costs on the taxpayers but do not represent a transfer to the government, except perhaps in limiting the degree of tax evasion. In particular, this is true with respect to both the extra transaction costs of barter caused by the fear of settling accounts through the banks and the extra accounting efforts and time spent in queues to file tax reports. The argument below shows that while a certain amount of such dead-weight loss may be optimal as a price for reducing tax evasion, the government's misperceptions of the extent of tax evasion could easily lead to suboptimal outcomes. Misperception, of course, often reduces efficiency. The problem with the overestimation of the degree of tax evasion is that there is no reliable feedback mechanism to correct the misperception.

Suppose that in a tax system that raises tax revenue R_0, the tax authorities would like to increase revenue by imposing on the entrepreneurs an administrative requirement A characterized by intensity measured by k, that is intended to raise the cost of tax evasion and that also imposes compliance costs on honest taxpayers. For example, A may represent a requirement to fill out an extra form and k would denote the complexity of the form. Suppose that the amount of effort used by a risk-neutral taxpayer to evade tax is given by $e_i(k)$, and that $e_i' < 0$, $e_i'' > 0$, where $i = 1, ..., N$ is the taxpayer index. This would be a reasonable assumption, for example, if the taxpayer's marginal return to effort in terms of money saved due to evasion declines in k and in effort, while the marginal cost of effort is non-decreasing.[5] Denote the purely administrative compliance cost that A imposes on each taxpayer by $C(k)$, $C'>0$, $C''\geq 0$ (e. g., $C(k)$ may represent the value of extra time necessary to comply with the additional reporting requirements imposed by A). If all taxpayers are identical and if we disregard any change in the labor supply and other economic distortions that result from the changes in effective tax rates due to changes in evasion, the socially optimal value of k would be given by solving:[6]

$$Min_k \{e(k) + C(k)\} \tag{1}$$

The interior solution to this problem is obtained by solving $\partial C/\partial k = -\partial e/\partial k$. Incidentally, the revenue-maximizing government would also want to limit the increase in k, assuming that output declines with an increase in $e(k) + C(k)$. (Output would also presumably decline with an increase in the effective tax rate, but the government can always adjust the effective rate by changing the statutory rate).

This problem becomes more interesting if we consider heterogeneous taxpayers. Suppose that there are two groups of taxpayers. One group consists of intrinsically honest taxpayers (i.e., for $i \in H$, $e_i(k) \equiv 0$ for all k, where H is a set of honest taxpayers) while the other taxpayers are characterized by $e_i(k)=e(k)>0$, $i \notin H$ for all relevant k. Let the honest taxpayers constitute proportion v of all taxpayers. Then the above problem becomes (again, I disregard the changes of distortions caused by changing tax rates):

$$Min_k \{(1-v)e(k) + C(k)\} \tag{2}$$

The first-order conditions for this problem are:

$$\partial C/\partial k = -(1-v) e' \tag{3}$$

So far we have treated v as a parameter. If the government is uncertain about the value of v, however, it makes sense to ask how the solution of (2) would depend on v. Differentiating (3) with respect to v and solving for $\partial k/\partial v$, we obtain:

$$\partial k/\partial v = e'/(C'' + (1-v)e'') < 0 \tag{4}$$

In other words, the optimal value of k is inversely related to the proportion of honest taxpayers, v. This simple argument illustrates that if the government underestimates the proportion of honest taxpayers, it would set the intensity of anti-evasion requirement k higher than is socially optimal.

Note that although an increase in k raises all taxpayers' costs, the overall costs of tax evaders increase faster than those of honest taxpayers. This is because while tax evaders' effort to evade declines in k, their tax payments rise. Given the non-decreasing marginal cost of effort and decreasing return to effort in terms of money saved through evasion, an increase in k causes the evader's tax payment to rise faster than the cost of effort he saves on smaller evasion. This effect of a rise in k may lead to a smaller economic distortion because the effective rates of the evaders and of the honest taxpayers would be closer.

Despite the fact that the effective rates faced by evaders and honest taxpayers become closer, the increase in the intensity of evasion-fighting requirement A, k, can reduce the number of honest entrepreneurs in an open economy, because higher k may raise the honest producers' costs above the world market price of the good. If that is the case, then the government's initial misperception that all entrepreneurs in the economy evade taxes may become a self-fulfilling prophecy.

I have a strong impression that most of the Russian tax policy makers adhere to a view that virtually all entrepreneurs (including potential ones) would evade taxes given the slightest opportunity. The above argument suggests then that if this view is mistaken, the anti-evasion emphasis in Russian tax law and administration is greater than socially optimal.

Not all anti-evasion features impose direct costs on all taxpayers. One of the cornerstones of the current attempt at tax reform is the flattening of the income tax. Effective 1 January 2001 Russia has had a single 13 per cent rate personal income tax. This is not strictly speaking a flat tax, because a number of exemptions and deductions have been preserved, but the new law sharply reduces the statutory marginal tax rates on high income individuals. A major justification for this reform has been the argument that tax evasion and tax avoidance among the rich has been such that the current statutorily progressive income tax has been in fact highly regressive. The effect of this tax reform on the individuals with relatively low incomes depends on the degree to which the flatter tax would reduce the tax evasion among the rich. If this reduction is small, the flattening of the tax would reduce government revenues and necessitate increased collections elsewhere. Given that only a small percentage of the personal income tax revenue has been coming from the top bracket individuals, the expectation is that this particular tax change will be either neutral or revenue enhancing. For the first five months of 2001, personal income tax collections have risen by almost 60 per cent in nominal terms, i.e. more than twice as fast as the rate of inflation. Part of this increase in collections, however, may be due to income shifting by high income individuals from 2000, when they faced high marginal tax rates, to 2001. The true effect of the personal income tax reform will be difficult to ascertain until 2002 collections are known.

Corruption in Tax Administration

By all accounts, corruption and extortion is widespread in most, if not all, branches of the Russian government. It is natural then that the same phenomena would also be common in Russia's tax administration.[7]

Corruption of tax authorities imposes potentially significant costs on the economy. First, corruption usually (but probably not always) makes the tax system less predictable. This additional uncertainty can serve as a powerful disincentive to investment, particularly by the foreign companies (Wei, 1997). Second, corruptibility of the officials necessitates increased amount of costly monitoring of their activities by other officials. Third, corruption makes tax evasion easier. Moreover, evading taxes may be cheaper for those firms that are monitored by corrupt tax officials than for the firms that are monitored by honest officials. This would result in additional distortions to the economy. Notice that corruption may impose costs on honest taxpayers if the corrupt tax officials extort payments from the taxpayers that follow the official rules.

The feedback between corruption and tax evasion may cascade. If corruption increases tax evasion, this may necessitate higher statutory tax rates on whatever tax base can be observed. Given limited penalties, higher tax rates are likely to strengthen the incentives for collusion between the corrupt tax inspectors and taxpayers, resulting in an even greater losses to the state treasury, which leads to higher tax rates, and so on.

As was true in the case of tax evasion, perhaps one of the most significant costs of corruption in tax administration is the cost of the corruption-induced features of the tax system. In Russia, the perception of widespread corruption of tax officials has resulted in a drive to reduce the discretion of the tax service in its interactions with the taxpayers. In some cases, the pro-taxpayer bias appears to be extreme. For example, presumably in an effort to limit the extortion opportunities of the tax inspectors, Article 3 (7) of Part 1 of the current Tax Code states that "all doubts, contradictions, and ambiguities in the tax law that cannot be removed are interpreted to the advantage of the taxpayer" (my translation). Literally understood (and depending on who decides whether the ambiguities can be "removed"), this provision could seriously impede tax collections. Another provision of the same Part 1 of the Tax Code significantly limits the ability of the executive branch, including the tax authorities, to issue instructions that interpret the existing tax statutes (Article 4).

Ironically, the pro-taxpayer bias and constraints on the tax authorities may result in an increased amount of corruption, measured by the total amount of bribes given to the tax officials. The pro-taxpayer bias facilitates tax avoidance and evasion and, given the need to collect a certain amount of tax revenue, leads to higher statutory rates than would have been the case if the rights of the parties were more balanced. The higher tax rates may increase the benefit of concealing the tax base and, therefore, may strengthen the incentives for the taxpayer and inspector to collude.[8] (This applies to the economic activities that are relatively easy to monitor and where there are no "non-removable ambiguities"). As was described in the beginning of the section, this process may in principle lead to a collapse of the tax system because corruption and evasion can snowball.

While in theory such a snowballing effect may result in the collapse of the tax system, this collapse has not happened in Russia. In fact, tax collections have been improving both prior to and after the introduction of the pro-taxpayer provisions mentioned in the beginning of this section. I think that the potential harm of the extreme pro-taxpayer provisions has been diffused by a reasonable interpretation of these provisions. After all, what is or is not an ambiguity in the tax law depends in the end on the court decisions (or on the expectations of the taxpayers and administration regarding the outcome of court decisions) and most courts in Russia have not been known for their pro-taxpayer biases.

Nonetheless, the other costs of corruption are sufficiently serious to warrant the question, how does one alleviate corruption? Åslund (1999) and others have argued that one of the best ways to fight corruption in Russia is to reduce the statutory tax rates. In addition to lowering the incentives to hide the tax base, lower tax rates may facilitate elimination of most exemptions. This would make tax administration simpler and the return to tax avoidance effort would decline as well. Both the rate reductions and the elimination of exemptions would reduce the incentives for collusion between the taxpayer and tax inspector. This "package" approach to tax reform in Russia has been advocated by many others and, in fact, served as an inspiration for the 1997 version of the Russian Tax Code that was defeated in the Duma. The current version of the Tax Code, the most important parts of which have been adopted, is also based on the same principle (e.g., the personal income tax rate reductions mentioned above and the lowering of the profit tax rate from 35 per cent to 24 per cent, with simultaneous elimination of most exemptions). Presumably, however, Åslund (1999) had greater rate reductions in mind than those contained in the new Tax Code.

Revenue-neutral rate reductions combined with a corresponding reduction in the exemptions is a rather non-controversial policy recommendation, particularly if it is accompanied by targeted assistance through non-tax mechanisms to the disadvantaged taxpayers who are currently subsidized by the exemptions. For example, eliminating the exemptions for enterprises that hire the disabled with a simultaneous direct subsidy to the disabled that would keep them at the same income level would not hurt the disabled and would on balance benefit state budget.

It is important, however, that the "lower rates – fewer exemptions" approach does not lead to significant losses of overall state revenues. In 2000, the actually collected revenues by all budget levels in Russia constituted slightly more than 37 per cent of GDP, including payroll taxes and customs fees (Rossiiskaia, 2001). The government economic program drawn up by the new Russian administration proposed to lower the nominal tax burden (i.e. in the absence of tax arrears) on the Russian economy (expressed as a share of GDP) by about 20 per cent during the first stage of tax reform and by an additional 10 per cent during the second stage.[9] While a reduction in the tax burden may indeed stimulate above ground economic activity and reduce corruption, the revenue increases due to these effects may take time to develop. Meanwhile, lower collections in the short run may cause significant damage to the Russian economy.

The above discussion raises an issue of whether Russia collects too much tax revenue. Russia collects less as a share of its measurable GDP than the developed economies, where total tax revenues have averaged well over 40 per cent of GDP. (Note that in the absence of tax arrears, Russia's collections would have been in line with those in a number of developed countries.) The appropriate comparison for Russia, however, would be with the middle to upper income group of developing countries, where tax collections have typically ranged below 30 per cent of GDP.[10] Therefore, Russia's tax collections have been quite a bit greater than in the other developing countries at the same stage of economic development. One may argue, however, that the economic transition from socialism imposes significant additional demands on government expenditures (and hence revenues) justifying a larger public sector than in countries such as Brazil or Mexico. This is due to both the socialist legacy of a large government role in the economy and to the requirements of the transition process, which necessitate an extensive social safety net and large expenditures for restructuring the country's economic and administrative infrastructure. Indeed, according to EBRD (1999), 1998 government budget revenues in Hungary (more than 40 per cent of GDP), the Czech Republic (about 40 per cent) and Poland (more than 40 per cent) significantly exceed those in Russia.[11]

Moreover, all the above percentages are stated in relation to officially measured GDP. Presumably, the Russian underground economy is much larger than those of Hungary, Poland, and the Czech Republic. This means that Russian government collects even less relative to the real size of its economy than do these East European economies in transition. Meanwhile, the underground economic activities rely on many of the public goods produced by the government. For example, trucks carrying untaxed goods drive on the same roads as other trucks, and so on. The underground economy generates public goods as well but the share of its resources allocated to provision of public goods is probably smaller than in the above ground economy.

The fact that an economy in transition such as Russia's may require relatively large public expenditures does not necessarily imply that the state that collects adequate revenues actually spends these revenues in a way that facilitates transition and restructuring. Åslund (1999) argues that the structure of public expenditures is "most harmful" in the countries that have the largest levels of public expenditures in the CIS (Belarus, Ukraine and Russia). He claims that "without even touching social concerns the Russian government could cut eleven percent of GDP in socially harmful expenditures" (p. 15). One may not entirely agree with his calculations, but it is clear that some cuts can be made relatively harmlessly. At the same time, it is also clear that in many areas public expenditures in Russia are clearly inadequate for more or less normal functioning of the economy. For example, the law enforcement agencies appear to be poorly funded, the state employee salaries are low, and much needs to be done to improve the infrastructure of the economy. Åslund's argument is that expenditures cannot be rationalized until they are first sharply reduced. But according to the literature on corruption in general and on corruption in tax administration in particular, the official incomes of the state employees may have to be increased in order to bring corruption to optimal (i.e. presumably lower than current) levels.[12]

Another, more speculative objection to the reduction of nominal tax rates (except personal income tax) has to do with the apparently important role of organized crime in the Russian economy. Alexeev et al (2000) argue that in an economy with sufficiently strong organized crime, it is quite possible that instead of stimulating economic activity, the main effect of lower official tax rates would be a corresponding increase of taxation by organized crime, with no change in the combined tax burden on the businesses.

To sum up, the reduction of statutory tax burden by itself is probably too risky as a corruption-fighting mechanism among the tax authorities in today's Russia. Such reduction would be desirable only if it is accompanied by an increase in collection rates, in order to prevent a significant decline in the effective tax burden. In addition, it may be necessary to raise the tax inspectors' salaries and improve their training. Of course, maintaining the current level of tax collections does not exclude and perhaps even demands various reforms that rationalize the tax structure in general (e.g. elimination of preferential VAT rate for certain commodities, elimination of most exemptions, an increase in the federal share of overall tax revenues, etc).

In light of the above, it would also be beneficial to create a system of specialized tax courts that would speed up tax appeals. Such a system would make corruption more difficult and would create the possibility to improve tax inspectors' incentives by making their bonuses dependent on taxes collected. If it is relatively easy for the taxpayers to appeal the decisions of the tax authorities, the potential abuse from making tax officials' pay dependent on tax collections would be limited. At the same time, such bonuses would normally reduce incentives for corruption.[13] Of course, these bonuses should not represent a large proportion of tax inspectors' compensation due to risk-sharing considerations.

Payment Arrears and Non-Monetary Means of Payment

While rampant tax evasion and corruption characterize several other developing economies (e.g. Brazil, Mexico, Nigeria) Russia is apparently one of very few countries (Ukraine is another example) where payment arrears (PA), both interenterprise and tax, and non-monetary means of payment (NMMP) including barter, play a particularly important role.[14] Both of these phenomena (PA and NMMP) are closely related to the tax system. Presumably one of the main reasons for the non-monetary nature of many transaction is that both PA (this paper will address only the role of interenterprise arrears) and NMMP inhibit monitoring by outsiders, including tax authorities, shareholders, and creditors. And the more difficult it is for the tax authorities to monitor an enterprise, the easier it is for the enterprise to evade taxes.

While the role of NMMP in tax evasion is often mentioned in the literature, the specifics of how barter and other NMMP facilitate evasion are rarely provided. Technically, the non-monetary nature of a transaction should not make any difference. According to the Russian law, non-monetary transactions are accounted for and are taxed in essentially the same way as monetary ones. If anything, the tax statutes treat non-monetary transactions less favorably than monetary ones. Non-monetary transactions, however, are more difficult to monitor, primarily because these transactions are not handled by the banks. When a transaction is performed through the bank, the bank keeps consistent records. In a non-monetary transaction, the parties may keep different records of the same transaction with inconsistent prices, amounts of goods exchanged, and the date of payment. In order to audit such a transaction, the tax authorities would need to compare the records of all trading parties involved, while in a monetary transaction only the firm's bank records would have to be checked. In other words, NMMP facilitate tax evasion because they make fraud easier by hindering auditing.[15] When the transacting parties can represent the same transaction in different ways, the parties' tax incentives would no longer be opposed.[16] This removes or at least hinders an important self-regulating market mechanism that promotes tax compliance.

In addition, there is at least one way in which NMMP facilitates tax avoidance. When the parties use cash method of accounting and the buyer uses a *veksel* (bill of exchange) issued by a third party (e.g., a bank) to pay the seller, the tax law considers the transfer of third party *veksel* as payment. This allows the buyer to deduct the purchase as costs and to take credit for VAT purposes.[17] Meanwhile, the seller does not need to account for the transaction until he realizes the *veksel,* letting the seller postpone his tax liability from the transaction. This mismatch of the dates of accounting for the transaction for tax purposes could be quite beneficial to the taxpayers. As Commander and Mumssen (1998) point out, however, tax avoidance does not appear to be a primary motivating factor in the use of barter in Russia. In fact, according to their survey, most firms claim that inter-firm barter increases their tax liabilities. This is primarily due to the fact that barter prices usually significantly exceed cash ones, while Russia's tax system to some extent taxes gross revenue rather than net values such as profit or value added. The gross revenue taxing features include limitations of the deductibility of certain business expenses, low depreciation rates for tax purposes (at least in the pre-2002 profit tax), and the presence of turnover taxes. Note, however, that the current tax reform will largely eliminate the taxation of gross revenue.

Whether the parties delay payment, use *veksels* to distort the date of the transaction for tax purposes, or resort to outright fraud in a barter transaction to misrepresent the date of payment, all of these techniques to one extent or another rely on the taxpayers using the cash method of tax accounting. A switch to the accrual method, an important element of the current tax reform (although its implementation has been postponed until 2002 at the earliest) would reduce the attractiveness of NMMP and put additional pressure on the sellers to obtain timely payment for their output. More generally, the requirement of accrual accounting for tax purposes would facilitate auditing of taxpayers, because under the accrual method, in order to verify that a transaction has taken place the auditor needs to establish the presence of only one of the three elements: shipment, payment, or issuance of an invoice (for VAT purposes). Under the cash method, the auditor typically needs to establish that both the shipment and payment have been made. Until 2000, the Duma had been unwilling to impose the requirement of accrual accounting on taxpayers.

Ironically, the arguments advanced against the accrual method are precisely the widespread use of NMMP and the frequency of PA.[18] The opponents of the introduction of the accrual method for tax purposes argue that the shift to the accrual method would cause a cash flow problem for and impose additional burden on taxpayers because of the "non-payments crisis" in Russia and due to the pervasive non-monetary transactions. The truth is, however, that the large scale of NMMP in Russia would not impose any more burden on taxpayers under the accrual method than it does under the cash method. If taxes are required to be paid in cash, then in-kind payments for goods or services received by a seller must be converted into cash under both methods. Valuation also presents the same problems under both methods.

The role of PA is somewhat more complicated. It is true that under the accrual method a taxpayer may be liable for tax on sales of goods and services *before* payment is received from the buyer. In addition, as will be elaborated below, the shift to the accrual method from the cash method would result in a one-time increase in the tax liabilities of taxpayers. Nonetheless, there are several responses to the objection that the accrual method causes a cash flow problem for taxpayers in the current environment.

First, it is important to note that in a properly functioning tax system a taxpayer's profit tax liability is only on the difference between his revenue and the cost of his inputs, not the gross revenue. After all, under the accrual method, both revenues and costs are accounted for earlier than under the cash method. Similarly, in the case of the VAT a taxpayer is only liable for his "value added" to the goods and services that he sells, not the total value added (i.e. the selling price). Second, to the extent there are PA in the economy, the accrual method does not necessarily change their total amount, because while it shifts forward tax liability of one enterprise, it also shifts forward the equivalent tax credit (or deduction) of another enterprise.[19] The accrual method simply makes tax liability coincide with the flows of real goods and services, clarifying what portion of the interenterprise arrears is really due to the enterprises and what portion is in essence due to the government. In contrast, under the cash method, a taxpayer's liability for tax on his income or value added is intertwined with the debt owed to the taxpayer by a purchaser of the taxpayer's goods and services until the purchaser pays the taxpayer. Note that the separation between tax arrears and PA brought about by the accrual method implies that the interest on the tax liability portion of the PA owed by purchasers to sellers under the cash method will flow to the benefit of the budget (as it should) rather than to the benefit of the sellers. In addition, as was mentioned above, the scale of the PA problem in Russia apparently has been exaggerated. To the extent that this problem exists, the cash method hides and most likely even promotes PA rather than alleviates them.

A switch to the accrual method does result in a one-time increase (forward shift) of the tax liability. On the day of the switch, the taxpayer becomes liable for the tax on the accrued profit that he otherwise would not have been liable for until later. And, of course, his already accumulated tax liability is preserved. For this reason, a set of transition rules becomes necessary to spread this shifted forward tax liability over a period of time (usually 6-12 months).

Conclusions

Many of the problems and peculiarities of the Russian tax system can be traced to the following three distinguishing features of the Russian economy: tax evasion, corruption within the tax administration, and widespread use of non-monetary means of payment in the economy. At the same time, various features of the tax system affect the degree of tax evasion and corruption and the preferred means of transaction settlement. This paper examined certain aspects of the interactions between the peculiarities of Russia's economy and its tax system. Of course, it would be too ambitious to hope that all of the problems of the Russian tax system could be resolved in the near future. Tax reform currently under way in Russia addresses many of the important issues (e.g. the shift to accrual method for all but small enterprises, significant reduction of various tax exemptions) while other problems remain (e.g., deductibility of advertising expenditures, the statutory bias favoring the taxpayer in his disputes with the tax authorities). Tax reformers in Russia are clearly aware of the three aforementioned features of the Russian economy. Nonetheless, some of the recently adopted laws and reform proposals continue to overestimate Russia's peculiarities, giving them too much weight at the expense of other aspects of the economy. It is particularly true with respect to the tax rules aimed at fighting tax evasion and at minimizing the consequences of corruption in tax administration. I hope that the above discussion helps to clarify the tradeoffs involved in developing a tax system that reflects the country's specificity but does not go too far in that direction.

Notes

[1] Another important feature of the Russian economy closely related to taxation is the federal system of Russia's government. However, the issues raised by the federal structure of the economy are particularly broad and too complex to be included in this relatively short essay.

[2] Privatization of tax collections, however, might improve tax inspector incentives in a model where tax inspectors are corruptible (see for example Vasin and Panova (1999) and Hindriks et al (1999)). For this reason, making tax inspector bonuses depend on the revenue they collect may be beneficial.

[3] Slemrod's model differentiates between rich and poor taxpayers.

[4] This is somewhat similar to Meyendorff's (1998) argument that Russian firms were less likely to apply for bank credit because banks in Russia serve as tax agents of the

government, and opening the firm's books to the bank was almost equivalent to opening them to the tax authorities.

[5] In the simplest terms, let the taxpayer's work time be fixed and let him maximize $\{X(e,k)+L\}$ with respect to evasion effort e, under the constraint $L+e=const$, where $X(e)$ is money saved due to tax evasion, and L is his leisure time. Assuming that $?X/?e>0$, $?^2X/?e^2<0$ and $?^2X/?e?k<0$, we obtain that in the interior optimum $?X/?e*=1$ and $?e*/?k=-(?^2X/?e?k)/(?^2X/?e^2)<0$.

[6] Given statutory tax rates, changes in the evasion efforts would change the effective tax rates. Also, statutory tax rates may have to change because the intensity of evasion efforts affects government revenues. I disregard the influence of such changes on social welfare.

[7] Vasin and Panova (1999) discuss the importance of corruption in Russia's tax administration and model the incentive schemes to alleviate this problem.

[8] In general, the effects of higher tax rates on tax evasion are ambiguous even in relatively simple models of taxpayer behavior. The empirical evidence is also mixed. See Andreoni et al (1998) for a survey of this issue.

[9] An earlier draft of the program suggested a reduction of the nominal tax burden from the current 40-41 per cent to about 37-38 per cent by the end of 2002 and to 35-36 per cent by the end of 2005.

[10] For example, in the mid-1990s consolidated government tax revenues amounted to about 20 per cent of GDP in Argentina, 17 per cent in Bolivia, 28 per cent in Brazil, 21 per cent in South Korea, and 13 per cent of GDP in Mexico (Ter-Minassian, 1997). Shleifer and Treisman (2000) claim that the main problem with respect to tax revenue in Russia is not the total general government tax collections, but that too little of it is collected by the federal government. Russia's federal government does indeed collect a lower share of GDP in taxes than do central governments of the countries listed in this note.

[11] Shleifer and Treisman (2000) have argued that Russia collects adequate tax revenues overall, but that the distribution of tax collections has been too heavily biased in favor of the regional budgets. This may very well be the case, and the current tax reform attempts to correct the situation. The discussion of fiscal federalism issues, however, is outside the scope of this paper.

[12] Acemoglu and Verdier (2000), Vasin and Panova (1999).

[13] Hindriks et al (1999), Vasin and Panova (1999).

[14] See for example Gaddy and Ickes (1998), Commander and Mumssen (1999), and Pinto et al (1999). Note, however, that the role of interenterprise payment arrears in Russia does not appear to be significantly different from that in many other economies in transition or even developed economies. See Schaffer (2000).

[15] Alexeev (1998) discusses some specific examples of tax fraud facilitated by NMMP.

[16] For example, with respect to the profit tax, the buyer is typically interested in inflating his costs for tax purposes, while the seller is interested in understating his revenues.

[17] See MTF Letter of 25 February, 1999, no. 03-4-09/39.

[18] The following arguments for the accrual method are largely based on a 8/14/1997 USAID sponsored Tax Reform Project memorandum co-authored by M. Alexeev, J. McDonald, R. Chewning, and D. Haberly with a substantial input from R. Conrad.

[19] Note, however, that distribution of tax arrears may be very much affected by the shift to accrual. Some caveats to this argument would be needed if we consider transactions between loss-making enterprises and profitable enterprises for the purposes of the profit tax and between exempt and non-exempt taxpayers under VAT.

References

Acemoglu, D. and Verdier T. (2000), 'The Choice Between Market Failures and Corruption', *American Economic Review*, vol. 90, no. 1, pp. 194-211.

Alexeev, M. (1998), 'Nonpayments and Barter in the Russian Economy and the Role of Natural Monopolies', mimeo, Program on Natural Monopolies, IRIS/USAID.

Alexeev, M, Janeba, E. and Osborne, S. (1999), 'Taxation and Evasion in the Presence of Organized Crime', Indiana University, mimeo.

Alexeev, M. and Sinelnikov, S. (eds) (2000), *Problemy nalogovoi sistemy Rossii: teoriia, opyt, reforma*, vol. 1, Institute for the Economy in Transition, Moscow.

Andreoni, J., Erard, B. and Feinstein, J. (1998), 'Tax Compliance', *Journal of Economic Literature*, XXXVI, no. 2, pp. 818-60 (June).

Åslund, A. (1999), 'Why Has Russia's Economic Transformation Been So Arduous?', A paper presented at the World Bank's Annual Bank Conference on Development Economics, Washington D.C (April 28-30).

Commander, S. and Mumssen, C. (1999), 'Understanding Barter in Russia', Working Paper, no. 37, EBRD.

European Bank for Reconstruction and Development (EBRD) (1999), *Transition Report 1999*, EBRD, London.

Gaddy, C. and Ickes, B. (1998), 'Russia's Virtual Economy', *Foreign Affairs*, vol. 77, no. 5, pp. 53-67.

Grossman, G. (1991), 'Wealth Estimates Based on the Berkeley-Duke Émigré Questionnaire: A Statistical Compilation', *Berkeley-Duke Occasional Papers on the Second Economy in the USSR*, no. 27 (May).

Hindriks J, Keen, M. and Muthoo, A. (1999), 'Corruption, Extortion and Evasion', *Journal of Public Economics*, vol. 74, no. 3, pp. 395-430.

Johnson, S, Kaufmann, D. and Shleifer, A. (1997), 'The Unofficial Economy in Transition', *Brookings Papers on Economic Activity*, no. 2, pp. 159-239.

Mayshar, J. (1991), 'Taxation with Costly Administration', *Scandinavian Journal of Economics*, vol. 93, no. 1, pp. 75-88.

Meyendorff, A. (1998), 'Tax Avoidance and the Allocation of Credit in Russia', William Davidson Institute, University of Michigan, Ann Arbor, mimeo.

Nagin, D. (1990), 'Policy Options for Combating Tax Noncompliance', *Journal of Policy Analysis and Management*, vol. 9, no. 1, pp. 7-22.

Pinto, B, Drebentsov V. and Morozov, A. (1999), 'Dismantling Russia's Nonpayments System: Creating Conditions for Growth', Report by the World Bank (September).

Rossiiskaia ekonomika v 2000 godu (Russian Economy in Year 2000) (2001), Institute for the Economy in Transition, Moscow.

Schaffer, M. (2000), 'Discussion: The Non-Cash Economy in CIS: In Quest of Policy Recommendations. Introductory Note: Should We be Worried about the Use of Trade Credit and Non-Monetary Transactions in Transition Economies?', *Economic Systems*, vol. 24, no. 1, pp. 55-61.

Shleifer, A. and Treisman, D. (2000), *Without a Map: Political Tactics and Economic Reform in Russia*, MIT Press, Cambridge, Massachusetts.

Slemrod, J. (1994), 'Fixing the Leak in Okun's Bucket: Optimal Tax Progressivity When Avoidance Can be Controlled', *Journal of Public Economics*, vol. 55, no. 1, pp. 41-51.

Slemrod, J. and Yitzhaki, S. (1987), 'The Optimal Size of a Tax Collection Agency', *Scandinavian Journal of Economics*, vol. 89, no. 2, pp. 183-92.

Treisman, D. (1999), 'Russia's Tax Crisis: Explaining Falling Revenues in a Transitional Economy', *Economics and Politics*, vol. 11, no. 2, pp. 145-69.

Vasin, A. and Panova, E. (2000), 'Tax Optimization under Corruptible Tax Administration', EERC Final Report, Moscow, Russia (December).

Wei, S. (1997), 'Why is Corruption So Much More Taxing than Taxes? Arbitrariness Kills', *NBER Working Paper Series*, Working Paper 6255 (November).

Chapter 7

Soft Budget Constraints and Tax Arrears in Transition Economies

Ruvin Gekker

Abstract

This paper provides an analytical explanation of tax arrears by utilizing simple dynamic models. Paternalistic government in these models is reluctant to enforce the existing tax code and force the failed firms into bankruptcy. It is shown that under certain parameters the weak government will tolerate tax arrears.

Introduction

The early literature on transition from a centrally planned to a market economy was preoccupied by the issues of stabilization, price liberalization and privatization. Institutional reforms were discussed primarily in relation to those issues. Recently increasing number of researchers have adopted Kornai's (1986, 1992) concept of the soft budget constraints (SBC) to provide an institutional account of various problems in transition economies. For example, Berglof and Roland (1997), drawing on the insights provided by the work of Dewatripont and Maskin (1995), explain how the persistence of SBC may coexist with a credit crunch in transition economies. Schaffer (1998) examines a widely observed phenomenon of tax arrears in emerging markets (particularly in the Russian economy). He notes that the tax authorities would typically tolerate the accumulation of tax arrears in the case of financially distressed firms, which means that those firms have the SBC due to paternalism.

This paper attempts to provide an analytical explanation of tax arrears in the Russian economy. Clearly there are some causal relationships between various types of arrears: wage arrears, interenterprise arrears, bank arrears and tax arrears. For instance, in 1993-94 wage arrears have received a lot of attention in the Russian media. As a result of this publicity, Russian firms in oil, gas, electricity and transportation were able to successfully lobby the government to use up to half of their tax arrears balance to settle their wage arrears (a so called "50 – 50" rule). Notice that firms in those sectors have close ties with the government. However, later in 1994 the scheme was extended to all firms in the economy with the restriction that only 30 per cent of tax share could be diverted to paying wages (a so called "30 – 70" rule). Both rules reduced somewhat wage arrears in the Russian economy. At the same time, we can notice a rapid growth of tax arrears in 1994 - 95 (see Table 7.1).

Table 7.1 Schaffer (1998) tax arrears in the Russian economy

Stock (end of Year)	
Date	Total
1993	1.5
1994	4.0
1995	6.5
1996	12.0
1997	11.2

It is interesting to observe a peculiar shift in a pecking order of arrears (see Afanasiev (1998), Alfandari and Schaffer (1996)). In 1992-94 firms first paid their tax debts to the government. Next they paid their debts to the banks. Then they paid their wages to workers and lastly they paid to their suppliers. Starting from 1996, the order has changed. Firms first pay to the banks. Then they settle their debts with suppliers. And finally they pay their tax debts and wages. Commenting on this peculiar shift in a pecking order of arrears, Afanasiev (1998) has proclaimed that "paternalism is dead on the enterprise level". In this paper we claim that paternalism is still well and alive on the state level. It contributes to the spread of the SBC and accounts for an increase in tax arrears in the Russian economy.

Soft Budget Constraints and Tax Arrears

Kornai (1986, 1992) defines the soft budget constraints as a subsidy paid by the state to loss-making enterprises in order to guarantee their survival. It could be a subsidy directly from the state budget or from the state bank. Alternatively, the state could provide a reduction in taxes to a loss-making firm. According to Kornai, paternalistic state is the cause of the SBC. Although Kornai's concept of SBC was introduced in the context of the market socialist system existing in Hungary since 1968, it could be easily modified and applied to the centrally planned economy of the Soviet type.

Another explanation of the SBC was provided recently by Dewatripont and Maskin (1995) (see Maskin (1999) for a recent survey). They view the SBC as a time-inconsistency problem. For example, the state or bank will fund a project in the first period that turned out to be unprofitable (only the firm has information about profitability of project ex ante). However, the prospects for the project in the second period are good, and the state or bank realizes that it would be better to refinance the project rather than terminate it (the first period funding is now simply a sunk cost).

In our modeling we utilize the definition of SBC as ex-post tax subsidies paid by the state to loss-making enterprises. The cause of the SBC is paternalistic preferences of the state.

Managers in the Soviet Union developed a great variety of means to cope with uncertainty and tautness of a planning process. To successfully "storm" at the end of a planning period they required a surplus of labor. They also hoarded valuable strategic materials that later could be useful in acquiring some needed inputs. Managers of the enterprises belonging to the key industries could utilize their connections with the Communist Party authorities. Quite often they themselves were members of obkom, or even members of the Central Committee of the Communist Party. These managers could easily renegotiate their planning obligations with Gosplan or other planning authorities. On the other hand, managers of the enterprises not belonging to the key industries had to rely more on the informal networks that they would create themselves. For example, the barter economy that flourishes now in Russia could certainly be traced back to those early Soviet informal networks. It would be extremely important for the managers relying on the informal networks that the state or planning authorities would have as little information as possible about their informal activities. That would provide them with a better chance to successfully lobby the authorities on a plan reduction. By the way, even the managers of the enterprises belonging to the key industries needed to have some slack in order to successfully cope with a plan. Therefore, they would also have some interest to hide some information from the planning authorities.

From 1995 the Russian government has shifted from a policy of providing explicit subsidies to the firms from the budget to a policy of implicit subsidies in a form of tax arrears, tax offsets and so on. According to Commander and Mumssen (1998) arrears to the enlarged budget ballooned from around 29 billion rubles in 1995 to around 400 billion rubles by mid-1998. They notice, however, that wage arrears during that time remained roughly stable. Further by mid-1998 overdue payables were roughly four times larger than the stock of commercial bank credits to firms. There was a substantial decline over the same period in the share of overdue payables accounted for by suppliers. Therefore, they conclude that "the primary asymmetry at work may not have been the transfer of liquidity across firms, but the transfer of liquidity from the budget and other quasi-fiscal institutions to firms".

Afanasiev (1998), Commander and Mumssen (1998), Gaidar (1999) all point out that large Russian firms reproduce a hierarchical system of bargaining with the state that was typical for a command economy. They consider tax payments as a matter of discretion and bargaining power rather than rules. In most cases bargaining would occur after firms had already accumulated tax arrears. It is interesting to point out that although the government has repeatedly threatened to close down the worst offenders (including such large firms as Avtovaz or KamAz), not a single of the large tax debtors was closed to date. For example, Afanasiev remarks that it is a common knowledge that Avtovaz spent all its tax debts on the 10th model of Zhiguli. Similarly other firms utilize their tax arrears for various investment projects.

Gaidar (1999) emphasizes that in order to successfully lobby for tax breaks, the firm must satisfy several important criteria: a) it must employ surplus labor; b) it must accumulate wage arrears and interenterprise arrears; c) it must have very little or no cash on its account. In fact, formally quite often an enterprise satisfying all these criteria should be bankrupt. However, the bankruptcy law is almost never applied in Russia. Typically, the manager of the firm in Russia controls financial flows within the firm but he is not a sole owner of the firm. Because of unclear property rights in Russia, the manager is trying to use his control over financial resources of the firm. He creates a variety of his own private enterprises that are affiliated with the managed firm and transfers valuable assets to the affiliates. The transfers are facilitated by tax arrears, tax offsets, wage arrears and so on that makes firm's accounting very complex and not transparent. A typical example is Roscoal. The firm accumulated huge wage and tax arrears in 1995-96 losing a lot of money in the process. However, the affiliates made millions on sale's commission that was paid for each ton of coal sold. The general manager of Roscoal was able to purchase properties in the south of France and Spain. In most cases those transfers of financial assets to affiliates are not strictly legal. As a result, most managers are trying to repatriate their profits out of Russia.

Modeling of Tax Arrears

We first model tax arrears in the Russian economy by utilizing a simple sequential game. We assume that nature will determine that some proportion of Russian firms, say α, will succeed in adopting to new market conditions, or, alternatively, that with probability α the firm may succeed in adopting to new market conditions. In this case we assume that the successful firm will pay its taxes T and its management will receive private benefits, B_s ($B_s > 0$). On the other hand, with probability $1 - \alpha$ the firm may fail to adapt to new market conditions in which case it will face the following dilemma. If the firm pays its taxes, then it will go bankrupt (knowing that the liquidation value (L) of the firm is very low, we assume that the management will receive $L = 0$ in this case). However, the firm may refuse to pay its taxes and instead ask the government to provide tax relief. The government may assume a very tough stance towards the firm and force it to pay taxes, in which case the firm will definitely go bankrupt ($L = 0$). Alternatively, the government may tolerate firm's tax arrears, in which case government's tax revenues are equal to 0 (firm's management still receives some private benefits B_f in this case ($B_f > 0$). The following table summarizes payoffs for this sequential game.

Table 7.2 Payoff table game 1

	Successful firm	Failed firm paying tax	Failed firm not paying tax
Firm	B_s	0	B_f
Government	T	T	0

We assume that the government maximizes its tax revenues plus the private benefits of the firm, that is, we assume that the government is paternalistic. Firms on the other hand are maximizing only their private benefits. We say that the firm has a soft budget constraint if its tax arrears are tolerated by the government. The following proposition answers the question about the existence of soft budget constraints in transition economies.

Proposition 1. If $B_f > T$ firms will have soft budget constraints and choose not to pay taxes. The government will tolerate tax arrears if $\alpha > \alpha^* = T - B_f/T + B_s - B_f$.

Proof. If $B_f > T$, then it is optimal for the government to tolerate tax arrears. Since $B_f > 0$, firms naturally will choose not to pay taxes. The expected payoff to the government is $\alpha (T + B_s) + (1 - \alpha) B_f$ which is grater then T as long as $\alpha > \alpha^* = T - B_f/T + B_s - B_f$.

This sequential model provides an explanation of tax arrears in case of distressed or failed firms. Due to a low liquidation value of these firms, a paternalistic government is reluctant to force them into bankruptcy and tolerates nonpayment of taxes provided that $T < B_f$ and α is greater than $T - B_f/T + B_s - B_f$.

Schaffer (1998) believes that in the more rapidly reforming transition economies the distressed firm may generate some positive value added, and therefore the strategy of tolerating tax arrears could be sustainable as long as it is contained within distressed firms and the number of them is not increasing rapidly. The events in Russia (which of course is not a rapidly reforming transition economy) illustrate the danger of tolerating tax arrears. After successful stabilization program in 1995, the number of industrial firms operating at loss in Russia suddenly increased from 26 per cent in 1995 to over 40 per cent in 1996. Particularly huge increases in the number of financially distressed firms were registered in coal industry (58 per cent) and also in nonferrous metallurgy (63 per cent). However, in 1996 many firms in oil, gas and energy sectors also stopped paying their taxes into federal budget even though they did not experienced any serious financial problems. In fact, according to Afanasiev (1998) these nonpayments were used as a source of investment by the firms in oil, gas and energy sectors (it should be pointed out that these sectors accounted for more than 30 per cent of all tax revenues in 1995).

Gaidar points to a presidential election of 1996 as a signal that the Russian government may not enforce tax payments in the near future. Indeed, many firms in different sectors of the Russian industry stopped paying taxes in 1996. This situation can be easily captured by a simple signaling game between the government and a firm. We assume that the government can be either weak (paternalistic) or tough. Both types of the government have the following choice of actions: they can either enforce tax payments or tolerate tax arrears. In turn, firms can choose either to comply with tax payments or not to comply with them. The players have the following preferences. Weak or paternalistic government would prefer to tolerate tax arrears, tough government would prefer to enforce tax payments. Both types would prefer compliance with taxes, and the firm would prefer to comply if the government is tough and not to comply it the government is paternalistic. Assume that there is a high prior probability that the government is weak. Then there is a pooling equilibrium in which this government tolerates nonpayment of taxes and the firm does not comply with tax payments.

Next, we assume that the managerial effort is required in order to restructure the firm and produce new competitive goods. Without such effort, the firm will remain unrestructured and produce old "soft" goods. We also assume that the current tax burden $\overline{T}$ is high and unrestructured firm will make losses (given $\overline{T}$), that is $\pi_u(\overline{T}) \in [-1, 0]$. However, if unrestructured firm will be able to get some tax breaks (tax offsets) limiting its tax burden to $\underline{T}$, than it will make a profit of $\pi_u(\underline{T})$ where $\pi_u(\underline{T}) \in [0,1]$. Finally, we assume that it is worthwhile to restructure and that restructured firm is able to generate a profit of $\pi_r(\overline{T}) > \pi_u(\underline{T}) + 1$.

Suppose that the median voter is interested in provision of public goods, law and order, etc. Therefore, the government reflecting voter's interest would like to collect taxes and minimize tax subsidies to the firm. We assume that the government which collects taxes (and provides public goods) derives some positive political benefits $B_p \in [1,2)$ from its activities. On the other hand, corrupt or paternalistic government can be captured by the industrial lobby.

If management team works hard, they incur disutility e that is uniformly distributed on the unit interval [0,1]. If they shirk they incur no costs. Each management team inherits different amount of relational capital/physical capital (for more information on relational capital see Gaddy and Ickes (1998)). Hence the amount of effort that is needed to successfully restructure the firm will depend on this inheritance. We assume that the firm, which is successful in reducing its tax burden, enjoys some positive rents $R \in [0,2)$. The time sequence of the game is as follows:

- Nature determines the type of the management team.
- The management team either works hard and succeeds in restructuring or it shirks and the firm remains unrestructured.
- If the manager has shirked, he can attempt to lobby the government trying to reduce firm's tax burden.
- The government either capitulates to lobby's pressure and gives tax breaks or holds firm and enforce tax code.
- Payoffs are realized.

Table 7.3 Payoff table game 2

	Restructured firm	Unrestructured firm	Unrestructured firm,
Firm	$\pi_T(\overline{T}) - e$	$\pi_u(\overline{T})$	$\pi_u(\underline{T}) + R$
Government	B_p	B_p	0

If the government is not paternalistic or corrupt, it maximizes its political benefits (or tax revenues). Since $B_p > 0$, nonpaternalistic government provides no tax breaks to the firm. The management team then works hard to restructure the firm receiving the payoff of $\pi_r(T)$ – e. On the other hand, paternalistic government maximizes its political benefits plus the benefits of the firm. Since $\pi_u(\underline{T})$ is a reported profit we can assume that the manager will make it sufficiently close to 0. Hence the decision to grant tax subsidies will depend on the size of political benefits and personal rents. If R > B_p, then the government will provide tax subsidies to the firm, that is, $\pi_u(\underline{T})$ + R > $\pi_u(\overline{T})$ + B_p.

Proposition 2. If R > B_p, the government will provide tax subsidies to the firm. The firm will choose not to restructure provided that R - $\pi_r(\overline{T})$ > B_p - $\pi_u(\underline{T})$.

In his recent survey Pirttila (1999) emphasizes that the inherited structure of taxation from socialism is characterized by a strong reliance on enterprise taxation. In the case of slow reforming economies, such as the Russian economy, numerous tax exemptions and incentives included in the tax code actually soften budget constraints for the firms and present them with the opportunity of not restructuring. Pirttila notes that "while Western tax experts may regard the Russian tax system as incomprehensible, and even irrational, the system may well reflect an overall slow reform policy within the administration".

Concluding Remarks

In this paper we have provided an analytical explanation of tax arrears by utilizing simple dynamic models. Essentially, paternalistic government in these models is reluctant to enforce the existing tax code and force the distressed firms into bankruptcy. As a result, it tolerates tax arrears under certain parameters.

Alternatively, it is possible to explain the persistence of tax arrears by employing the mechanism similar to Brainard and Verdier (1994). In their model, the introduction of tax benefits in the current period will create an increased demand for more tax benefits in future periods. Hence a government susceptible to lobbying will provide such benefits. By incorporating election in their model, it is possible to account for a persistent political failure in Russia with respect to tax collection.

References

Afanasiev, M. (1998), 'Liberalization and Stabilization: Five Years After', Moscow IET.
Alfandari. G. and Schaffer. M. (1996). '"Arrears" in the Russian Enterprise Sector', in S. Commander, Q. Fan and M. Schaffer (eds), *Enterprise Restructuring and Economic Policy in Russia*, EDI/World Bank, pp. 87-139.
Berglof, E. and Roland, G. (1997), 'Soft Budget Constraints and Credit Crunches in Financial Transition', European Economic Review, vol. 41, no. 3, pp. 807-817.
Brainard, S. and Verdier, T. (1994), 'Lobbying and Adjustment in Declining Industries,' European Economic Review, vol. 38, no. 3-4, pp. 586- 95.
Commander, S. and Mumssen, C. (1998), 'Understanding Barter in Russia', EBRD working paper no. 37.

Dewatripont, M. and Maskin, E. (1995), 'Credit and Efficiency in Centralized and Decentralized Economies', *Review of Economic Studies*, vol. 62, no. 4, pp. 541-55.

Gaddy, C. and Ickes, B. (1998), 'To Restructure or not to Restructure: Informal Activities and Enterprise Behavior in Transition', WDI Working Paper no. 14.

Gaidar, E. (1999), 'Lessons of the Russian Crisis for Transition Economies,' *Finance and Development*, vol. 36, no. 2, pp. 6-9.

Kornai, J. (1986), 'The Soft Budget Constraint', *Kyklos*, vol. 39, no. 1, pp. 3-30.

Kornai, J. (1992), *The Socialist System: The Political Economy of Communism*, Princeton University Press, Princeton, New Jersey.

Maskin, E. (1999), 'Recent Theoretical Work on the Soft Budget Constraint,' *American Economic Review*, vol. 89, no. 2, pp. 421-26.

Pirttila, J. (1999), 'Tax Evasion and Economies in Transition: Lessons from Tax Theory', BOFIT Discussion Paper no. 2.

Schaffer, M. (1998), 'Do Firms in Transition Economies Have Soft Budget Constraint? A Reconsideration of Concepts and Evidence', *Journal of Comparative Economics*, vol. 26, no. 1, pp. 80-103.

Chapter 8

Effective versus Statutory Taxation: Measuring Effective Tax Administration in Transition Economies

Mark E. Schaffer and Gerard Turley

Abstract

Wide differences between effective or realised average tax rates and tax yields that would result if statutory tax rates were strictly applied indicate tax compliance and collection problems. Due to the greater politicisation of tax systems in transition economies (TEs), we would expect the shortfalls in effective tax yields for TEs to be larger than a benchmark for the mature market economies where tax systems are well established, the administrative capacity is stronger and tax arrears are tolerated less frequently. The methodology involves calculating an effective/statutory (E/S) tax ratio. Initial results indicate that the leading TEs have E/S ratios similar to the EU average. There appears to be a positive correlation between progress in transition and effectiveness of tax collection, as measured by our E/S ratio. For slow reformers, the effectiveness of tax collection appears to vary with the extent of state control. Those TEs that have maintained the apparatus of the state have done well in tax collection compared to those countries where there is evidence of state decay. This raises a number of broad policy issues relating to the speed of transition, the interaction of politics and economic reforms, the capacity of the state to govern and the need for market institutions to develop.

Introduction

This paper attempts to measure the effectiveness of tax administration in transition economies (TEs) and how it compares to a benchmark from the mature market economies. We measure the administrative efficiency of tax collection by comparing statutory tax rates with effective tax yields. This method of measuring the administrative capacity of tax systems has been alluded to in the taxation literature but not systematically pursued in cross-country comparisons. Alex Radian, in his inquiry into tax administration in poor countries, noted that effective tax rates are lower than legal tax rates (Radian, 1980). David Newbery raised the issue of differences between statutory and effective tax rates, again in the context of developing countries, when he stressed the importance of examining the effective tax system rather than the legally defined tax system (Newbery and Stern, 1987). In the same World Bank publication, Vito Tanzi suggested that the gap between the statutory tax system and the effective tax system might be large in developing countries (Newbery and Stern, 1987). Elsewhere, Burgess and Stern (1993) argued that the wedge between the statutory and effective tax systems can be reduced by improvements in administrative capabilities. In this paper, we take a methodology previously used for measuring fiscal or revenue capacity in federal states (ACIR, 1962) and adapt it to enable inter-country comparisons of effective vs. statutory taxation. We then use actual fiscal and national accounts data from 25 TEs and, as a benchmark, the average for the 15 member countries of the European Union, to measure the effectiveness of tax administration.

Tax exemptions, deferrals, write-offs and arrears that firms receive or extract from the state are widespread, not only in transition economies but in market economies as well. In a broader sense, these tax concessions are often manifestations of a tax system that is politicised. One possible result of this bargaining and general politicisation of the tax system is a low level of tax compliance combined with a high incidence of tax avoidance.[1] Measuring the extent of this financial aid using firm-level information is difficult and faces obvious data difficulties, e.g. these concessions may not be widely known or may not show up in the government's budget. By measuring the difference between effective and statutory taxation at the aggregate level, our methodology enables us to obtain aggregate measures of the degree of effectiveness of tax collection that can be compared across countries, for different taxes, and over time. In this paper we develop indicators that allow us to measure how broadly and strictly valued added tax, payroll tax, and corporate income tax are implemented and complied with in TEs. We use the average of the EU-15 countries as an appropriate benchmark for comparison. Our focus is on comparisons for the most recent year available; comparisons over time will be pursued in future work.

The Tax System in TEs

The tax system that existed under the socialist command economy was different from a Western-style tax system. There was no corporate income tax system, in the usual sense of the term. State enterprises were subservient to the various ministries and any 'profits' made were expropriated by the state. Likewise, losses were made good by arbitrary pricing and subsidies. Often, tax rates were numerous and non-parametric, tax structures were complex and differentiated, and tax liabilities were discretionary and negotiable. The main sources of tax revenue were typically enterprise profit tax, turnover tax (with highly differentiated, product-specific rates) and payroll taxes; direct taxes on individuals were unimportant. Although taxation as a percentage of GDP was high in socialist countries, administrative costs were low and tax collection was straightforward as firms tended to be large and closely monitored. In the Soviet system, 'taxes' were collected from the enterprise, with the State Bank acting as the fiscal agent of the state. Once the socialist system collapsed, TEs, some lacking an explicit tax system (or culture), had to build a market-oriented, rule-based tax system (including a market-type tax administration) from scratch. The creation of a new tax system involved the introduction of a corporate income tax system. Not only did this involve changes in how enterprises were treated by the state in terms of taxation, but it was also introduced in conjunction with other policies, such as price liberalisation, demonopolisation and privatisation. A VAT system to replace the turnover tax was introduced in the early years of transition and was in place in most TEs by 1994. Tax on individuals accounted for a small proportion of the total tax take in socialist countries: the transition to a market economy meant that a personal income tax system as operates in market economies was also to be introduced.

In the context of TEs and taxation, we are interested in the hardening of budget constraints of firms. Hence, the firm is the unit of analysis in this paper. As for the different taxes paid by the firm, corporate income or profit tax, value-added tax and social security taxes are mostly linear, flat-rate taxes.[2] Neither sales taxes (because they are levied at one stage only) nor excise taxes (because they are product-specific) are considered in our study. We do, however, treat social security contributions as a payroll tax.

As mentioned above, we will concentrate on three taxes paid by the firm: corporate income tax (CIT), value-added tax (VAT) and social security tax (SST). Although VAT is essentially a tax charged on final purchasers, it is imposed at different stages of production at the firm level. For these three taxes, we estimate the difference between effective average tax rates and tax yields that would result if statutory tax rates were strictly applied. The methodology is explained below.

Methodology

Our methodology is based on one commonly used in measuring tax or fiscal capacity in federal states. The ACIR Representative Tax System (RTS) method was initially proposed in the early 1960s and has been modified on several occasions since then (see ACIR 1962; 1971; 1982). Essentially, by applying national average or representative tax rates to member-state tax bases, the RTS method shows the amount of revenue that could be collected by the individual member states of a federal country, i.e. their fiscal capacity. With some modifications, we apply this methodology to sovereign states (and transition countries, in particular) rather than to states within a federal system.

We begin with some definitions. Statutory tax rates are the rates that taxpayers are required to pay by law. Effective tax rates are the realised average tax rates. These are the same average tax rates as employed by Whalley (1975), Lucas (1990) and Mendoza et al. (1994).[3]

Let Y be the *gross* tax base and T be actual tax payments; hence income net of tax is Y-T. We denote by t the statutory tax rate applied to *gross* income. The effective tax rate e, also defined on a gross basis, is calculated by dividing actual tax payments T by the appropriate gross tax base, or:

$$e \equiv \frac{T}{Y} \tag{1}$$

Using the statutory and effective tax rates thus defined, we calculate two indicators that measure the administrative efficiency of tax collection. The first indicator is the ratio of effective tax to statutory tax. The *effective/statutory (E/S) ratio* is defined as follows:

$$\textit{Effective / statutory ratio} \equiv \frac{e}{t} \equiv \frac{T}{tY} \tag{2}$$

This indicator measures the extent of the wedge between the statutory tax rate and the realised average tax rate. A ratio close to 1 indicates that the effective tax rate is close to the statutory tax rate. A ratio below 1 indicates that the effective tax yield is falling short of what application of the statutory tax rate would yield. Differences across countries in the extent of this shortfall in revenue may be accounted for by tax breaks, tax arrears and tax avoidance measures.[4]

As approximations of the gross tax base Y, we use national accounts measures of income: for VAT, total national income (GDP); for SST, income from labour; and for CIT, income from capital. These are, of course, only rough approximations of the actual statutory tax bases. For example: even in market economies, large portions of the economy are exempt from VAT (e.g., public administration and education); corporate income tax applies only to corporations and the usual tax base is net of depreciation and interest; for all three taxes, entities must usually be over a certain size threshold before becoming liable for taxation. Furthermore, the national accounts statistics of transition countries are generally regarded as less reliable than those of developed market economies, including their statistics on the division of GDP into labour and capital income. National accounts measures of income do, however, have the important advantages of being both readily available and, in principle, readily comparable across countries. Moreover, our focus is not on levels of effective taxation *in* countries but on comparisons of levels *across* countries, and as noted the reasons for these deviations between income measures and statutory tax bases are found in all countries.

Our second indicator entirely avoids these possible problems with national accounts measures of income by simply not attempting to match tax payments to the appropriate tax base. The *normalised tax yield* (NTY) instead relates tax payments adjusted for cross-country differences in statutory rates to GDP, and is defined as follows:

$$Normalised\ tax\ yield\ \equiv\ \frac{T}{GDP}\frac{b}{t} \tag{3}$$

where t is the statutory tax rate and b is a benchmark rate. Put simply, the normalised tax yield tells us what the tax yield (for a particular tax) would be for a specific country if the statutory tax rate were the same for all countries.

In the definitions above, we have used the convention of a tax base that is gross of tax. In practice, statutory tax rates are sometimes defined relative to a tax base that is inclusive of tax and tax liabilities are paid out of gross income; and sometimes statutory rates are defined relative to a tax base that is net of tax. Corporate income tax (like personal income tax) is an example of the former; tax liability is calculated by applying the corporate tax rate to gross profit. VAT and SST are examples of the latter. Firms calculate their gross VAT liability by "adding on" VAT as a percentage of the pre-tax price, and SST is typically calculated as a percentage of wages and salaries paid. We use the former convention – the tax base is *gross* of tax – for our calculations for all three taxes considered. This requires adjustments to the statutory tax rate for both VAT and SST.[5]

Denote by t^N the tax rate applied to *net* income $Y(1-t)$ that would yield the identical tax revenue as the tax rate t applied to *gross* income Y. We then have, by definition:

$$tY\ \equiv\ t^N\left[Y(1-t)\right] \tag{4}$$

Rearranging equation (4) yields:

$$t\ \equiv\ \frac{t^N}{1+t^N} \tag{5}$$

Equation (5) is used to convert a tax rate defined by statute as applying to net income into the equivalent tax rate on gross income.

We illustrate this adjustment by reporting the benchmark rates used to calculate our normalised tax yield indicator. We denote by b^N the benchmark net tax rate equivalent to the gross rate b. We take as our benchmark rates the approximate (rounded to the nearest five or ten per cent) average statutory tax rates in use in the 15 member states of the European Union: $b^N=20\%$ for VAT, $b^N=40\%$ for SST, and b=35% for CIT. The following table reports the equivalent gross and net rates for these benchmarks; the figures in bold are the statutory rates as legally defined by statute.

Table 8.1 Benchmark tax rates, gross and net equivalents rates defined by statute in bold

	b	b^N
VAT	16.7%	**20%**
SST	28.6%	**40%**
CIT	**35%**	53.8%

Data Coverage and Sources

Our primary interest is in examining the administrative efficiency of tax collection in TEs and how it compares to levels in well-established market economies. We use the mean of the EU-15 countries as a benchmark, taking 1996 as the benchmark year.

There are 25 ex-socialist countries in our study; the TEs that are not included are those where tax data are difficult to obtain (Mongolia, Vietnam), where the tax system is highly complicated (China) or where war has occurred (Serbia-Montenegro, Bosnia-Herzegovina). Ten of our 25 countries are CEE countries (Albania, Bulgaria, Croatia, Czech Republic, FYR Macedonia, Hungary, Poland, Romania, Slovak Republic and Slovenia) for which we use data primarily for the period 1991 – 1997. The remaining 15 are all FSU countries (Armenia, Azerbaijan, Belarus, Estonia, Georgia, Kazakhstan, Kyrgyzstan, Latvia, Lithuania, Moldova, Russia, Tajikistan, Turkmenistan, Ukraine and Uzbekistan) for which the relevant period is 1992 – 1997.[6] All these countries have a corporate income tax system, of sorts. All 25 countries with the exception of Croatia, FYR Macedonia and Slovenia had a VAT system in place by 1996. All TEs in our study have a social security tax system mostly financed by payroll taxes, with contributions being made by employers and/or employees. For all countries in our study, tax coverage is for general government, comprising of central *and* state, regional or provincial units of government *and* local government.

An exercise in calculating statutory versus effective taxation depends on data pertaining to tax rates, tax takes and tax bases. As for statutory taxation, the basic tax rates are taken primarily from international tax handbooks. In particular, we used the IBFD's *European Tax Handbook,* Coopers & Lybrand's *International Tax Summaries* and Ernst & Young's *Worldwide Tax Guides.* We also used various EBRD *Transition Reports.* Tax payments were obtained from the governments' fiscal accounts where taxes are reported on a cash basis, i.e., counting actual receipts rather than accrued liabilities. Where possible, tax payments data are from the IMF's *Government Finance Statistics Yearbook* (*GFSY*) or the CIS *Statistical Yearbook.* Other publications used include the OECD's *Revenue Statistics,* the IMF's Staff Country Reports and statistical yearbooks for various countries.

As already mentioned, the tax bases for the three types of taxes are taken from the national accounts. For VAT, we use GDP as a proxy for the VAT base.

Although in all VAT systems there are some goods and services that are exempt from VAT, the most important of these exemptions are quite standard (e.g., public administration, education) and hence GDP is a reasonable proxy. For CIT, we use gross operating surplus as a proxy for the tax base on corporate capital income. Operating surplus corresponds to value added after deducting the compensation of employees and net taxes on production; it is the balancing item in the national accounts. Due to the difficulties in acquiring reliable estimates for the operating surplus of corporations for 25 countries, we instead use the operating surplus of the economy.[7] For SST, we use compensation of employees as a proxy for the tax base. Compensation of employees is the sum of gross wages and salaries plus employers' social contributions.

Although imperfect, these are reasonably good approximations given the omissions in the national accounts, the dubious nature of some transition countries' data and the cross-country nature of the exercise. The main publications used for national accounts data are the IMF's *International Financial Statistics Yearbook*, the OECD's *National Accounts Main Aggregates*, the CIS *Statistical Yearbook* and statistical yearbooks for various countries.

The data sources used for all 25 countries are listed in Table 8.5, in the Appendix.

The statutory tax rates and the actual tax/GDP ratios for each of the 3 taxes, for our 25 countries are reported in Table 8.2.

As we can see from Table 8.2, many of the 25 transition countries in our study have the same statutory tax rates. This is particularly true for value-added tax where 11 of the FSU countries have a VAT rate of 20 per cent. Yet, the actual tax/GDP ratios across countries differ quite substantially. Assuming tax bases are not too dissimilar across countries, one interpretation of differences in tax ratios is the quality of tax administration across countries. The methodology outlined in section three allows us to investigate this further.

Results and Analysis

Table 8.3 is a cross-country comparison showing the two indicators for the three different taxes for the 25 transition countries. We report estimates for the TEs for 1997 as the 1998 data for some FSU countries is distorted by the August 1998 Russian crisis. The benchmark is the 1996 average of the EU-15 countries. Our estimates are highly approximate and precise values should be treated accordingly. Nevertheless, they do provide a measure of effective tax administration and, in the case of some TEs, point to poor tax collection and weak tax administration.[8]

Table 8.2   Statutory tax rates and tax/GDP ratios for 25 TEs, 1997

Country	VAT		SST		CIT	
	Statutory tax rate	VAT/ GDP	Statutory tax rate	SST/ GDP	Statutory tax rate	CIT/ GDP
CEE Countries						
Albania	12.5	4.6	42.5	3.9	30	0.7
Bulgaria	22	6.2	44	6.9	36	6.4
Croatia	--	--	43.4	14.4	35	2.0
Czech Republic	22	7.1	47.5	15.2	39	3.4
FYR Macedonia	--	--	30.1	12.3	15	0.7
Hungary	25	7.9	57	13.1	18	1.9
Poland	22	8.3	48.2	11.0	38	3.1
Romania	18	4.7	34	7.1	38	4.3
Slovak Republic	23	8.4	50	14.4	40	3.7
Slovenia	--	--	38	13.8	25	1.2
FSU Countries						
Armenia[1]	20	3.3	38	2.9	30	2.5
Azerbaijan	20	3.8	39	2.5	32	2.8
Belarus	20	9.4	37	10.1	30	4.7
Estonia	18	10.4	33	10.7	26	1.9
Georgia	20	3.2	34	2.2	20	0.6
Kazakhstan	20	3.5	32	6.2	30	2.4
Kyrgyzstan	20	5.6	37	5.9	30	1.1
Latvia	18	8.8	37	10.5	25	2.4
Lithuania	18	8.7	31	7.0	29	1.6
Moldova	20	9.4	40	7.2	32	2.4
Russia	20	7.2	39.5	9.9	35	4.2
Tajikistan	20	1.5	38	1.6	40	1.2
Turkmenistan	20	7.2	31	4.5	25	5.2
Ukraine	20	8.1	40	11.1	30	6.1
Uzbekistan[1]	17	6.1	43	6.7	37	7.9

Sources: IBFD, 1998; IMF 1999.

[1]   The figures for Armenia and Uzbekistan are for 1996.
--:   not applicable.

Table 8.3 Statutory and effective taxation, 1997
E/S = effective/statutory ratio; NTY = normalised tax yield

Country	VAT		SST		CIT		EBRD Transition Indicator
	E/S	NTY	E/S	NTY	E/S	NTY	
CEE Countries							
Albania	0.42	7.0	n.a.	3.7	n.a.	0.8	2.58
Bulgaria	0.34	5.7	0.61	6.5	0.31	6.3	2.75
Croatia	--	--	n.a.	13.6	n.a.	2.0	3.00
Czech Republic	0.40	6.6	0.94	13.5	0.23	3.0	3.46
FYR Macedonia	--	--	n.a.	15.2	n.a.	1.6	2.63
Hungary	0.40	6.6	0.80	10.3	0.26	3.7	3.67
Poland	0.46	7.7	0.76	9.7	0.20	2.9	3.42
Romania	0.31	5.1	0.83	8.0	0.21	4.0	2.67
Slovak Republic	0.45	7.5	0.93	12.3	0.22	3.3	3.25
Slovenia	--	--	0.94	14.3	0.15	1.6	3.21
FSU Countries							
Armenia[1]	0.20	3.3	0.27	3.0	0.16	3.0	2.38
Azerbaijan	0.23	3.8	0.46	2.6	0.12	3.1	2.04
Belarus	0.57	9.4	0.87	10.7	0.39	5.4	1.63
Estonia	0.68	11.4	0.83	12.3	0.22	2.6	3.42
Georgia	0.19	3.2	0.38	2.5	0.04	1.1	2.71
Kazakhstan	0.21	3.5	0.68	7.3	0.15	2.8	2.71
Kyrgyzstan	0.34	5.6	0.68	6.2	0.06	1.3	2.83
Latvia	0.58	9.6	0.76	11.1	0.23	3.4	3.08
Lithuania	0.57	9.6	0.71	8.4	0.13	2.0	3.04
Moldova	0.56	9.4	0.60	7.2	0.18	2.6	2.63
Russia	0.43	7.3	0.71	10.0	0.33	4.2	3.00
Tajikistan	0.09	1.5	0.31	1.6	0.04	1.0	1.58
Turkmenistan	0.43	7.2	n.a.	5.5	n.a.	7.3	1.46
Ukraine	0.49	8.2	0.80	11.1	0.63	7.1	2.46
Uzbekistan[1]	0.42	7.0	0.61	6.4	0.47	7.5	2.38
EU-15 Mean	0.45	7.4	0.88	12.5	0.24	3.0	

[1]   The estimates for Armenia and Uzbekistan are for 1996.
--:   not applicable.
n.a.: not available.
EBRD Transition Indicator: average indicator for 1997.

As we can see from the table, the (unweighted) means of the E/S ratios in the EU-15 for VAT, SST and CIT are 0.45, 0.88 and 0.24 respectively. When we normalise the EU-15 VAT, SST and CIT yields at our benchmark rates of 20 per cent (b=16.7%), 40 per cent (b=28.6%) and 35 per cent respectively, we get normalised tax yields of 7.4, 12.5 and 3.0 per cent of GDP respectively. How do the rates for TEs compare with these levels for the EU?

The results indicate that the 25 transition countries on average are not as effective in tax collection or enforcement compared to the average for EU countries. The (unweighted) means of the E/S ratio for the TEs for VAT, SST and CIT are 0.40, 0.69 and 0.23 respectively. Moreover, the variations from the mean are large for the TEs, compared to the EU countries. For the EU-15 countries, the standard deviations of the E/S ratio for the three tax categories are 0.06, 0.18 and 0.12 respectively. This compares to 0.15, 0.20 and 0.14 respectively for the TEs.

For many transition countries, revenue erosion has become a serious obstacle in their attempts to embrace effective fiscal policy.[9] Pre-transition, many ex-socialist economies had high government revenue shares of GDP. With most of economic activity taking place in the state sector, tax collection was a straightforward task. In contrast, for a market economy, the private sector dominates and confrontation between taxpayers and tax collectors is not uncommon. Thus, in the transition from a centrally planned to a market economy, a fall in revenue was not unexpected. Yet, for some transition economies, the fall in revenue has been excessive, with tax/GDP ratios currently at levels below what is considered normal in many market economies. Of course, for many TEs with income per capita levels below $1,000 per annum, tax capacity is low (see Tait, Gratz, and Eichengreen, 1979). Our research indicates that, in addition to having a low tax capacity, TEs have relatively low tax effectiveness rates i.e. the efficiency with which taxes are collected is lower on average in TEs than in market economies.

We now turn our attention to factors related to effective tax administration in transition countries. We begin by investigating the relationship between the effectiveness of tax collection and progress in transition. *A priori*, we might expect to find a positive relationship between progress in transition and effective tax administration.

We take as our measure of progress in transition the average of the EBRD transition indicators for 1997;[10] these are reported in Table 8.3 for all 25 TEs in our study. We present the relationship between progress in transition and the effectiveness of tax administration by means of a scatterplot in which the average EBRD transition indicator is plotted on the X-axis and the E/S ratio is plotted on the Y-axis. This exercise is carried out separately for the three categories of taxes covered in our study.[11] The horizontal line in each of the scatterplots is the relevant EU mean, plotted to provide a benchmark for comparison. All three scatterplots are depicted in Figure 8.1. Our second indicator, the normalised tax yield (NTY) is plotted against the average EBRD transition indicator in Figure 8.2. As the E/S ratio and the NTY measure are highly correlated, the scatterplots in Figures 8.1 and 8.2 are similar.

The relationship between progress in transition and effectiveness of tax administration comes out quite clearly in two of the three taxes we are examining, namely VAT and SST. The largest difference is between the so-called leading reformers (Poland, Hungary, Slovenia, Czech and Slovak Republics, the Baltic States) and the laggard reformers (the Balkans and most of the CIS countries), but there are other differences of interest between the TEs. One interesting comparison is between the Ukraine and Russia. Although Russia has made more progress in transition (as judged by the EBRD transition indicators) than the Ukraine, it fares worse in terms of tax collection (as measured by our E/S ratio). Russia's poor relative performance as regards to tax collection may have something to do with the nature of its federal tax system.[12] In particular, perverse incentives arising from divided property rights between different levels of government exasperate the tax collection problems in Russia. It is not uncommon for enterprises and regional governments to collude against the federal government and the tax collection agency, the STS (State Tax Service). Likewise, any improvements in tax collection at subnational levels are likely to be penalised or "taxed away" by reductions in transfers (see Shleifer and Treisman, 2000).[13]

We examine the three categories of taxes separately. In the discussion that follows, we only refer to one set of scatterplots, namely Figure 8.1.

- *Value-Added Tax*

There is a strong positive correlation between progress in transition and the effectiveness of VAT collection. All the leading reformers that have a VAT system have E/S ratios that are close to the EU benchmark of 0.45. These advanced reformers are all clustered in the top right-hand corner of 8.1(1a). In contrast, the majority of the laggard reformers are clustered in the bottom left-hand quadrant: the slow reformers have E/S ratios below the EU benchmark. The interesting feature is captured in the top left-hand quadrant where a small number of slow reformers (Moldova, Belarus, Turkmenistan and Ukraine) have high E/S ratios. Slow reformers with relatively high E/S ratios and normalised VAT yields may be accounted for by the observation that these TEs have maintained a functioning state, a feature that may have prevented the revenue erosion that is prevalent in most of the slow reforming Tes.[14]

- *Social Security Tax*

As in the case of VAT, there appears to be a positive correlation between progress in transition and the effectiveness of SST collection. All the leading reformers occupy the top right-hand quadrant of 8.1(1b). This group of TEs has E/S ratios similar to the EU benchmark of 0.88. This is in sharp contrast to the bulk of the slow reformers that have E/S ratios and normalised tax yields below the EU benchmark. Among this group, the lowest E/S ratios are concentrated in TEs that have suffered internal conflicts (Armenia, Azerbaijan and Tajikistan) or that have witnessed a collapse of the state (Georgia, for example). Again, we see that there are a small number of so-called slow reformers that have managed to maintain tax discipline, in this case with respect to payroll taxes. Belarus and the Ukraine both have E/S ratios close to the EU benchmark. As with VAT collection, strong presidential leadership (Lukashenka and Kuchma, respectively) combined with functioning state institutions, albeit in need of reform, may explain these high E/S ratios and normalised tax yields.

• *Corporate Income Tax*

The mean of the E/S ratio in the EU-15 for corporate income tax is 0.24. The normalised tax yield is 3 per cent of GDP. Again, we see from 8.1(1c) that the leading TEs are all tightly clustered around the EU benchmark. This contrasts sharply with the laggard reformers, some with E/S ratios *above* the EU level. One possible explanation for why some of the slow reformers have high normalised CIT yields is the upward inflation bias in profits arising from historical cost accounting. High inflation rates prevalent in TEs would generate large profits and high tax yields. This may explain why the leading TEs, in general, experience a *fall* in the E/S ratio for CIT during the transition period. The average E/S ratio in 1991, at the beginning of transition, for Hungary, Poland and Czechoslovakia was 0.42. By 1997 the average E/S ratio for these (now four) advanced reformers had fallen to 0.23.

To summarise, leading reformers (advanced CEE countries and the Baltic States) and countries that have maintained a functioning state (Belarus, Ukraine and Uzbekistan) have higher levels of tax compliance and collection than either slow reformers (Romania, Bulgaria),[15] countries with decaying or corrupt states (Russia, Georgia) or countries that have suffered internal conflicts (Armenia, Azerbaijan, Tajikistan). A somewhat similar result emerged from the EBRD/WB Business Environment and Enterprise Performance Survey (BEEPS) section on progress in economic reform, quality of governance and state intervention (see text below). Whereas countries that have adopted partial reforms score badly in terms of the quality of governance, it is the most advanced *and* the least advanced countries that score well in terms of governance. Likewise, the survey results indicate that "progress in transition is not necessarily synonymous with a reduction in state intervention in enterprises" (EBRD, 1999, p.122). Again, high levels of state intervention are evident in many of the leading transition countries *and* in the least advanced transition countries. These results raise serious issues, including the need to rethink, in the context of the transition experience and often in a political and institutional vacuum, the state's capacity to govern and the need for market institutions to develop.

The EBRD's transition indicators summarise overall "progress in transition". We now briefly explore one possible specific contributor to the ineffectiveness of tax administration, namely corruption and bribery. It is not uncommon for enterprises in TEs (and in market economies, although presumably less so) to pay bribes to government officials in return for various services or favours. As these payments are direct private benefits to public officials, they do not turn up in the government fiscal accounts. Yet, in all other respects, they can be viewed as unofficial taxes that add to the tax burden of enterprises. Is it possible that TEs that report low 'official' tax revenue shares as a percentage of GDP have high 'unofficial' taxes, in the form of bribes?

In Table 8.4 we reproduce a measure of the extent to which firms pay bribes to government officials. The measure was constructed from the BEEPS, conducted by the EBRD and the World Bank in over 3,000 firms in 20 countries and reported in EBRD (1999). To estimate a measure of bribes, firms were asked what percentage of annual revenues were made by 'firms like yours' in 'unofficial payments' to public officials. In the countries surveyed, the average bribe tax ranges from a low of 2.1 per cent of annual revenues in Croatia to a high of 8.1 per cent in Georgia. For comparison, Transparency International's Corruption Perceptions Index (CPI), the most recognised measure of corruption, is also reported.[16]

Table 8.4 Bribe tax and corruption for TEs

Country	Ave. Bribe Tax	CPI	Country	Ave. Bribe Tax	CPI
CEE Countries			Azerbaijan	6.6	8.3
Albania	na	7.7	Belarus	3.1	6.6
Bulgaria	3.5	6.7	Estonia	2.8	4.3
Croatia	2.1	7.3	Georgia	8.1	7.7
Czech Republic	4.5	5.4	Kazakhstan	4.7	7.7
FYR Macedonia	na	6.7	Kyrgyzstan	5.5	7.8
Hungary	3.5	4.8	Latvia	na	6.6
Poland	2.5	5.8	Lithuania	4.2	6.2
Romania	4.0	6.7	Moldova	6.1	7.4
Slovak Republic	3.7	6.3	Russia	4.1	7.6
Slovenia	3.4	4.0	Tajikistan	na	na
			Turkmenistan	na	na
FSU Countries			Ukraine	6.5	7.4
Armenia	6.8	7.5	Uzbekistan	5.7	8.2

Sources: EBRD *Transition Report 1999*; Transparency International's website: www.transparency.de/

Figures 8.3(3a) and 8.3(3b) plot our E/S ratio measure for VAT and SST against the average bribe tax as a percentage of annual firm revenues, for 18 and 19 transition countries respectively.[17] Countries that have a high measure of tax collection efficiency (Estonia, Poland and Belarus, for example) also have a relatively low average tax bribe. In contrast, countries with ineffective tax administration (Armenia, Azerbaijan and Georgia, for example) have a relatively high average tax bribe. The correlation coefficients are –0.54 and –0.74 respectively. As we did before, we plot the normalised tax yield (NTY) in Figure 8.4. Again, as we expect, the scatterplots in Figures 8.3 and 8.4 are similar.

If we use Transparency International's CPI as the measure of corruption, we get similar results. Although interesting, more evidence needs to be gathered before any strong conclusions can be drawn.

Conclusions and Further Research

In this paper we adopted an existing methodology to measure the effectiveness of tax administration. Comparing effective with statutory taxation allows us to get a handle on the administrative capacity of tax systems. The results indicate that, on average, the 25 TEs are not as effective in tax collection as compared to the average of the EU countries. A more surprising result is the differences between TEs: in particular, the ability of some slow reformers to maintain high tax collection rates.

As for policy implications, tax administration reforms have lagged behind general tax reforms since transition began, often because administrative reforms (and consequently the benefits) take time. Market-oriented fiscal institutions (tax administration, treasury) do not develop overnight. Administrative reforms involve changes in incentives and in the behaviour of taxpayers and public officials. In general, TEs with tax collection problems need to widen the tax base by subjecting previously exempt income to taxation, reduce exemptions and allowances and, where possible, implement lower (to discourage tax avoidance and evasion) and single (to avoid the rent-seeking activities of producers) tax rates. Ending the tradition of bargaining and negotiating between the authorities and the taxpayer might prove more difficult given the political constraints in TEs. For federal systems (Russia, for example), intergovernmental fiscal relations need to be rule-based and transparent. Specific tax administration measures for TEs might include strengthening the tax administration (assessment, collection, enforcement) agencies in terms of organisation and personnel (as well as the legal and accounting professions), codification of the various tax laws, greater efforts at improving the data on taxpayers, simplifying the registering, reporting and filing requirements, greater penalties (monetary and otherwise) for non-compliance and/or positive encouragement for compliance and educating taxpayers about their obligations. In the implementation of these reforms, it is important that the constraints (and the traditional values and practices) of TEs are recognised.[18]

As for future work, we would like to extend our data coverage to a larger set of countries. In particular, we would like to include non-EU OECD countries and, where possible, developing countries. Inclusion of non-EU OECD countries would provide us with an alternate and possibly more suitable benchmark to the EU-15. The more interesting possibility would be to apply our methodology to tax data for a range of developing countries in Latin America, Asia and Africa and for the Newly Industrialised Countries of South East Asia. This would allow us to compare ex-socialist transition countries with countries that closely resemble TEs either in terms of initial conditions or in terms of a 'transition' experience. For example, a more suitable comparison for the fast growing countries like Poland,

Estonia and Hungary might be the Tiger countries of South East Asia. Likewise, the FSU countries of Central Asia and the Caucasus states more resemble, in terms of GDP per capita and sectoral composition, developing countries than EU countries. One implication of this would be a need to extend the tax classifications to include foreign trade taxes. Although revenue from duties on international trade is tiny for EU countries, it is a major source of revenue for developing countries and for some transition countries. By extending the coverage to developing countries, it would also allow us to make more meaningful policy prescriptions as regards tax reform for transition countries. This is the next step in our research. Alternately and in the context of EU enlargement, tax harmonisation and fiscal convergence, our effective tax rates can be used to examine the overall tax burden and the distribution of the tax burden across different tax bases in EU countries and in the transition accession countries. We will pursue this work at a later stage.

In this paper, we briefly examined some factors that might impinge on tax administration and collection in transition countries. In particular, we explored the significance of two factors, namely progress in transition and corruption. We would like to extend this line of research. Other possible explanatory factors may include the shadow economy and tax evasion, the initial conditions, political constraints and the distribution of power, GDP per capita and levels of development. Some of these factors are not unique to TEs, applying to developing and developed countries alike.

With respect to fiscal and tax reform, the first decade of transition has focused primarily on tax design. If further revenue erosion is to be avoided, the next decade must concentrate on administrative reform. In the *Transition Report 1994*, the EBRD called for a strengthening of tax administration, an issue that "lies at the core of fiscal reform".[19] For many TEs, this policy recommendation is as relevant today as it was in the early years of transition.

Notes

[1]   This paper deals with tax avoidance as distinct from tax evasion. Tax avoidance is defined as the use of the tax system to minimise tax liabilities or obligations. It is a legal activity as distinct from the illegal (and acutely difficult to measure) activity of tax evasion. One way that enterprises can reduce their tax burden is by transferring their tax liabilities abroad. Transfer pricing is common in market economies where multinational corporations use their foreign subsidiaries that operate in low tax jurisdictions to reduce their overall tax burden. A well-known case is that of Rupert Murdoch's News Corporation, a company that made £1.4 billion in profits in Britain but reportedly paid no corporation tax there (*The Economist*, 29/1/00).

[2]   A linear tax is a tax whose marginal rate is constant.

[3]   These are aggregate average tax rates as distinct from the effective marginal tax rates that are commonly used in studies of household income, income distribution and taxation. Aggregate tax rates are normally used in macroeconomic modeling and in the taxation, economic growth and supply-side economics debate. For the problems associated with measuring effective tax rates, see Fullerton (1984).

4   Accounting for tax evasion will depend on whether the national accounts adjust for the hidden economy. If there is an evasion adjustment in the calculation of GDP, tax evasion is captured by our measure; how fully will depend on the accuracy of the adjustment.

5   We are therefore using gross income only and adjusting statutory rates as necessary. The alternative approach would be to use statutory rates in conjunction with gross or net income, as appropriate. This approach, however, encounters data availability problems with net income. As noted above, we use national accounts measures of gross income that are only approximations of the actual tax base. Calculating net income from these approximations and the actual tax yield introduces further measurement error into the tax base approximations. By contrast, our tax rate adjustment in equation (5) is an identity and introduces no such measurement error.

6   The USSR was disbanded in December 1991 and was replaced by fifteen independent republics.

7   Likewise, we use gross rather than net operating surplus because the treatment of depreciation varies from one jurisdiction to another. Aside from depreciation provisions, corporate tax systems differ from country to country, in respect of treatment of interest payments, stock appreciation provisions and integration with the personal income tax system. Accordingly, computations arising from cross-country comparisons of corporate tax systems should be treated with caution. This is particularly true when the cross-country comparisons include the likes of Russia whose accounting rules are different to international standards.

8   Treisman (1999) uses a 'tax accounting' method to measure the effectiveness of tax collection, in Russia. In his paper, the unexplained parts of the fall in tax revenues are attributed to the poor quality of tax administration, i.e. ineffective tax collection.

9   The primary objective of taxation is to raise revenues, as efficiently and equitably as possible, in order to finance government spending. It was the great French financier Jean-Baptiste Colbert (1619-83) who once said, "The art of taxation consists in so plucking the goose as to obtain the largest possible amount of feathers with the smallest possible amount of hissing." In many of the FSU countries, the government's revenue problem is further exasperated by the realisation that a portion of revenue is in non-cash form.

10 The EBRD transition indicators are a set of numerical indicators across a range of dimensions, under the headings – enterprises, financial institutions and markets and trade. The purpose is to measure the progress of economic reforms. A more detailed explanation can be found in any of the EBRD *Transition Reports*.

11 As we can see from Table 8.3, the results for CIT are different to those for either VAT or SST. This observation applies to the two groups of countries in our study, namely EU countries and transition countries. Accordingly, in any analysis of our calculations, we treat the three categories of taxes separately.

12 Recently described as a 'country that has moderate statutory tax rates but a corrupt system of tax administration' (see Friedman *et al*, 1999).

13 According to various sources, tax collection (and, in particular, federal tax) improved in Russia throughout 1999.

14 The ability of some slow reforming TEs to collect tax (Ukraine and Belarus, in particular) has been alluded to in the transition literature, in Murrell (1996), EBRD (1994, 1999) and elsewhere. Johnson, Kaufmann and Shleifer (1997) argue that it is the repressive nature of states (Belarus, possibly Uzbekistan and Turkmenistan) and their willingness to suppress the unofficial economy that explains high collection rates. The case of Moldova is less clear. It is true that VAT collection has improved, due to

the recent elimination of many exemptions. Nonetheless, its total tax/GDP ratio, at close to 30 per cent in 1997, seems very high for a country with a GDP per capita of less than $600. One possible explanation is that the GDP figure may be an underestimate, failing to adequately account for the unofficial economy.

[15] After the 1996/97 financial crisis in Bulgaria, the authorities introduced various reform measures, including changes to the tax administration system. These and other tax reform measures contributed to an improvement in tax collection in 1998, reflected in higher E/S ratios for both VAT and SST.

[16] The organisation Transparency International ranks countries, on the basis of surveys, in terms of the degree to which corruption is *perceived* to exist among public officials and politicians. The CPI score ranges from 0 (highly corrupt) to 10 (virtually corrupt free). To allow for comparisons with the BEEPS bribery tax, we have adjusted the CPI scores, e.g. Bulgaria's CPI score of 3.3 is adjusted to 6.7. The CPI scores recorded in Table 6.4 are for 1999; scores for previous years are unavailable for many of the TEs.

[17] From the 20 countries in the EBRD/WB survey, we exclude Croatia and Slovenia from Figure 8.3(3a) as neither country had a VAT system in place in 1997. Figure Figure 8.3(3b) does not include Croatia as there is no E/S ratio available.

[18] Many of the TEs are poor with very low incomes per capita. In 1997, the Caucasus states of Armenia, Azerbaijan and Georgia had an (unweighted) average GDP per capita of US$640 approx. The five Central Asian states (Kazakhstan, Kyrgyzstan, Tajikistan. Turkmenistan and Uzbekistan) had an average GDP per capita of approx. US$615 (EBRD, *Transition Report 1999*).

[19] EBRD, 1994, p. 88.

References

Advisory Commission on Intergovernmental Relations (ACIR) (1962), *Measures of State and Local Fiscal Capacity and Tax Effort, M-16*, Washington DC.

Burgess, R. and Stern, N. (1993), 'Taxation and Development', *Journal of Economic Literature*, vol. 31, pp. 762 – 830.

Ebrill, L. and Havrylyshyn, O. (eds) (1999), 'Tax Reform in the Baltics, Russia, and other Countries of the Former Soviet Union', *IMF Occasional Paper*, no. 182, International Monetary Fund, Washington D.C.

European Bank for Reconstruction and Development (1994), *Transition Report 1994*, EBRD, London.

European Bank for Reconstruction and Development (1999), *Transition Report 1999: Ten Years of Transition*, EBRD, London.

Friedman, E., Johnson, S., Kaufmann, D. and Zoido-Lobaton, P. (1999), 'Dodging the Grabbing Hand: The Determinants of Unofficial Activity in 69 Countries', paper presented at the Fifth Nobel Symposium in Economics: The Economics of Transition, Stockholm.

Fullerton, D. (1984), 'Which Effective Tax Rates?', *National Tax Journal*, vol. 37, pp. 23–41.

162 *Institutional Change in Transition Economies*

Holzman, F.D. (1962), *Soviet Taxation: The Fiscal and Monetary Problems of a Planned Economy*, Harvard University Press, Cambridge.

International Bureau of Fiscal Documentation (1998), *European Tax Handbook*, IBFD, Amsterdam.

International Monetary Fund (1999), *Government Finance Statistics Yearbook 1999*, IMF, Washington D.C.

International Monetary Fund (1999), *International Financial Statistics Yearbook 1999*, IMF, Washington D.C.

Interstate Statistical Committee of the Commonwealth of Independent States (1999), *Commonwealth of Independent States in 1998: Statistical Yearbook*, Statistical Committee of the CIS, Moscow.

Johnson, S, Kaufmann, D. and Shleifer, A. (1997), 'The Unofficial Economy in Transition', *Brookings Papers on Economic Activity*, vol. 2, pp. 159 – 221.

Lopez-Claros, A. and Alexashenko, S.V. (1998), 'Fiscal Policy Issues during the Transition in Russia', IMF Occasional Paper, no. 155, IMF, Washington D.C.

Lucas, R.E, Jr. (1990), 'Supply-Side Economics: An Analytical Review,' *Oxford Economic Papers*, vol. 42, no. 2, pp. 293 – 316.

Mendoza, E.G, Razin, A. and Tesar, L.L. (1994), 'Effective Tax Rates in Macroeconomics: Cross-Country Estimates of Tax Rates on Factor Incomes and Consumption', *Journal of Monetary Economics*, vol. 34, no. 3, pp. 297 – 323.

Murrell, P. (1996), 'How Far Has the Transition Progressed?', *Journal of Economic Perspectives*, vol. 10, no. 2, pp. 25 – 44.

Newbery, D. (1987), 'Taxation and Development', in D. Newbery and N. Stern, (eds), *The Theory of Taxation for Developing Countries*, Oxford University Press for the World Bank, Washington D.C, pp. 165 – 204.

Newbery, D. (ed) (1995), *Tax and Benefit Reform in Central and Eastern Europe*, Centre for Economic Policy Research, London.

Organisation for Economic Co-operation and Development (1999), *OECD National Accounts Main Aggregates 1960 – 1997*, OECD, Paris.

Organisation for Economic Co-operation and Development (1999), *OECD Revenue Statistics 1965-1998*, OECD, Paris.

Radian, A. (1980), *Resource Mobilization in Poor Countries: Implementing Tax Policies*, Transaction Books, New Brunswick, New Jersey.

Schaffer, M.E. and Ambrus-Lakatos, L. (eds) (1997), *Fiscal Policy in Transition*, Forum Report of the Economic Policy Initiative, no.3, Centre for Economic Policy Research, London; Institute for East-West Studies, Warsaw and New York.

Shleifer, A. and Treisman, D. (2000), *Without a Map: Political Tactics and Economic Reform in Russia*, MIT Press, Cambridge, Massachusetts.

Slemrod, J. (ed) (1992), *Why People Pay Taxes: Tax Compliance and Enforcement*, University of Michigan Press, Ann Arbor, Michigan.

Surrey, S. (1964), 'Tax Administration in Underdeveloped Countries', in R. Bird and O. Oldman, (eds), *Readings on Taxation in Underdeveloped Countries*, John Hopkins Press, Baltimore, Maryland. pp. 503 – 33.

Tait, A.A, Gratz, W.L.M. and Eichengreen, B.J. (1979), 'International Comparisons of Taxation for Selected Developing Countries 1972 – 1976', *IMF Staff Papers*, vol. 26, no. 1, pp. 123 – 56.

Tanzi, V. (1987), 'Quantitative Characteristics of the Tax Systems of Developing Countries', in D. Newbery and N.Stern (eds), *The Theory of Taxation for Developing Countries*, Oxford University Press for the World Bank, Washington D.C., pp. 205 – 41.

Tanzi, V. (ed) (1993), *Transition to Market: Studies in Fiscal Reform*, IMF, Washington D.C.

Treisman, D. (1999), 'Russia's Tax Crisis: Explaining Falling Revenues in a Transitional Economy', *Economics and Politics*, vol. 11, no. 2, pp. 145 – 69.

Whalley, J. (1975), 'Distortionary Factor Taxation - A Calculation of Effective Tax Rates in the UK 1968-70', *The Manchester School*, vol. 43, pp. 1 – 30.

Appendix

Table 8.5 Data sources for the 25 TEs

Country	Tax Rates	Tax Payments	GDP	Capital and Labour Income
Albania	IBFD; EBRD	IMF1	IMF2	NA
Bulgaria	IBFD; EBRD	IMF1	IMF2	NSO
Croatia	IBFD; ERBD	IMF1	IMF2	NA
Czech Republic	IBFD; EBRD	IMF1	IMF2	NSO
FYR Macedonia	IBFD; EBRD	IMF1	IMF2	NA
Hungary	IBFD; EBRD	IMF1	IMF2	NSO
Poland	IBFD: EBRD	IMF1	IMF2	NSO
Romania	IBFD; EBRD	IMF1	IMF2	NSO
Slovak Republic	IBFD; EBRD	IMF1	IMF2	NSO
Slovenia	IBFD; EBRD	IMF1	IMF2	NSO
Armenia	IBFD; EBRD	IMF1; CIS	IMF2; CIS	CIS
Azerbaijan	IBFD; EBRD	IMF1; CIS	IMF2; CIS	CIS
Belarus	IBFD; EBRD	IMF1; CIS	IMF2; CIS	CIS
Estonia	IBFD; EBRD	IMF1	IMF2	NSO
Georgia	IBFD; EBRD	IMF1: CIS	IMF2; CIS	CIS
Kazakhstan	IBFD; EBRD	IMF1; CIS	IMF2; CIS	CIS
Kyrgyzstan	IBFD; EBRD	IMF1; CIS	IMF2; CIS	CIS
Latvia	IBFD; EBRD	IMF1	IMF2	NSO
Lithuania	IBFD; EBRD	IMF1	IMF2	NSO
Moldova	IBFD; EBRD	IMF1; CIS	IMF2; CIS	CIS
Russia	IBFD; EBRD	IMF1; CIS	IMF2; CIS	CIS
Tajikistan	IBFD; EBRD	IMF1; CIS	IMF2; CIS	CIS
Turkmenistan	IBFD; EBRD	IMF1; CIS	IMF2; CIS	NA
Ukraine	IBFD; EBRD	IMF1; CIS	IMF2: CIS	CIS
Uzbekistan	IBFD; EBRD	IMF1; CIS	IMF2; CIS	CIS

Notes: IBFD: International Bureau of Fiscal Documentation's *European Tax Handbook*
        EBRD: European Bank for Reconstruction and Development's *Transition Reports*
        IMF1:   International Monetary Fund's *Government Finance Statistics Yearbook*
                (*GFSY*)*
        CIS: Statistical Committee of the Commonwealth of Independent States
                *Statistical Yearbook**
        IMF2 : International Monetary Fund's *International Financial Statistics*
                *Yearbook**
        NSO: various National Statistics Offices' *Statistical Bulletin*
        NA: Not Available

* An alternate source used is the International Monetary Fund's *Staff Country Reports / Recent Economic Developments* for the various countries

Figure 8.1 Effective tax administration and progress in transition

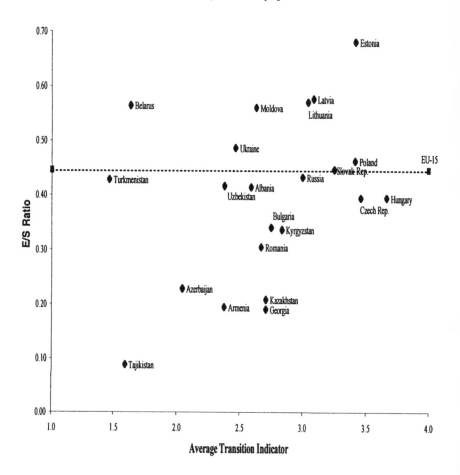

8.1a VAT effective/statutory ratio 1997 vs. progress in transition

8.1b SST effective/statutory ratio 1997 vs. progress in transition

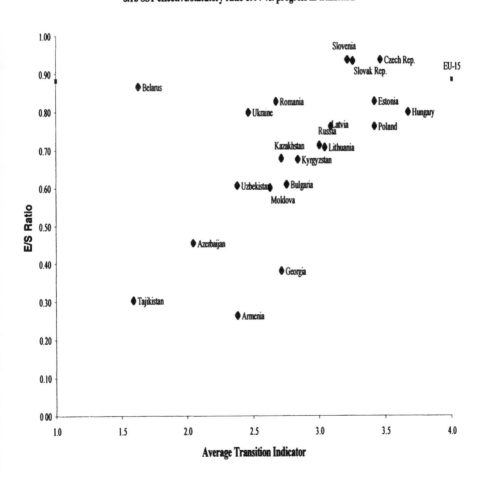

8.1c CIT effective/statutory ratio 1997 vs. progress in transition

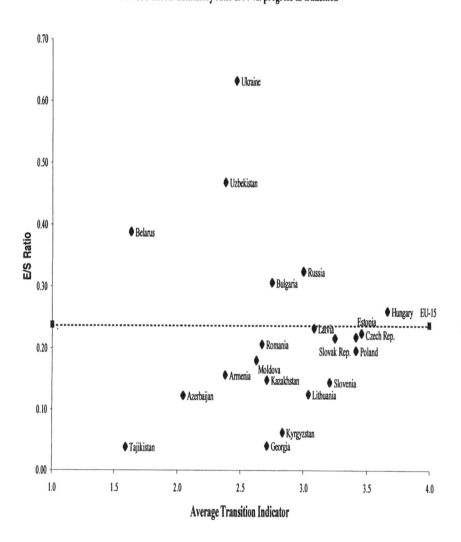

Figure 8.2 Effective tax administration and progress in transition

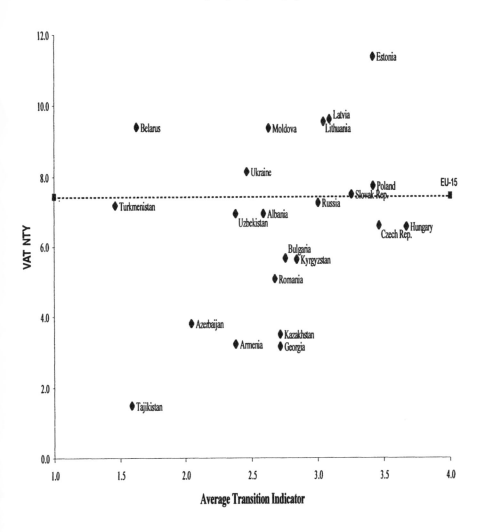

8.2a VAT normalised tax yield (NTY) 1997 vs. progress in transition

8.2b SST normalised tax tield (NTY) 1997 vs. progress in transition

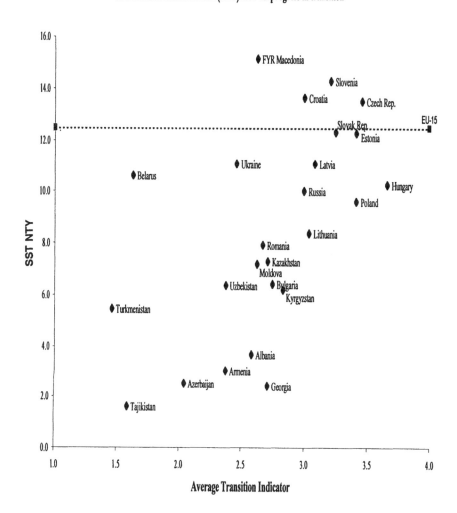

8.2c CIT normalised tax yield (NTY) 1997 vs. progress in transition

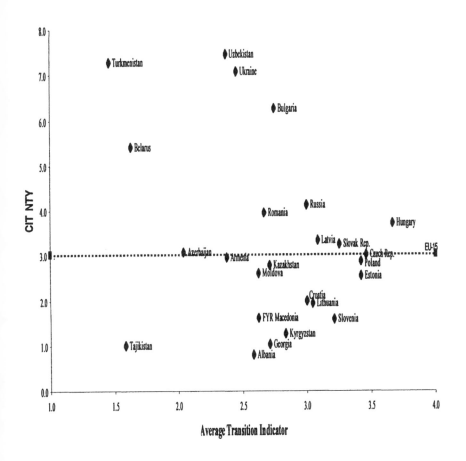

Figure 8.3   Effective tax administration and bribery

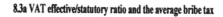

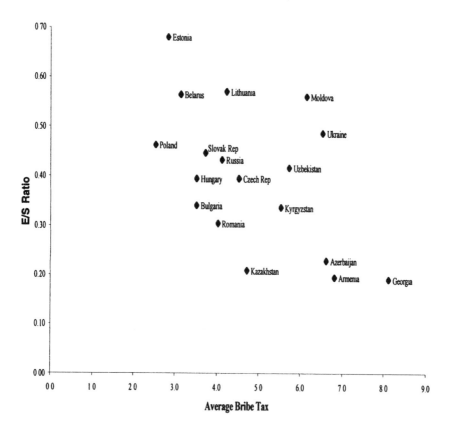

8.3a VAT effective/statutory ratio and the average bribe tax

8.3b SST effective/statutory ratio and the average bribe tax

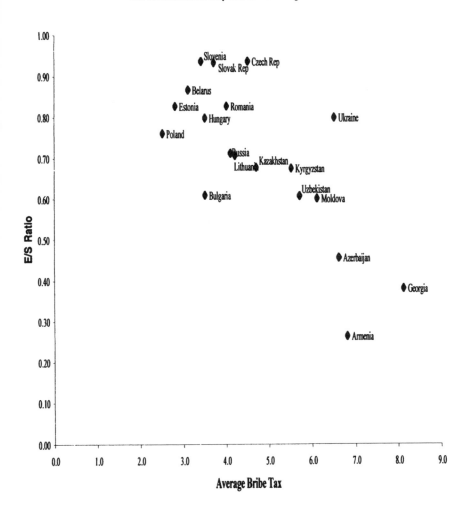

Figure 8.4   Effective tax administration and bribery

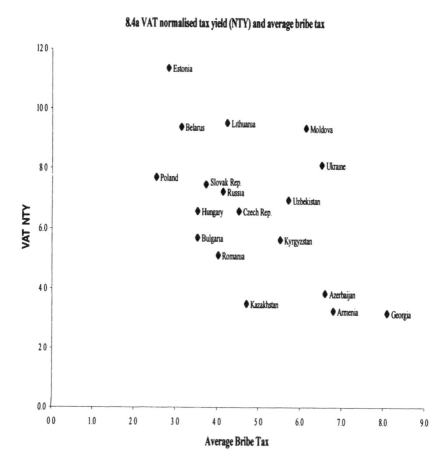

8.4a VAT normalised tax yield (NTY) and average bribe tax

8.4b SST normalised tax yield (NTY) and average bribe tax

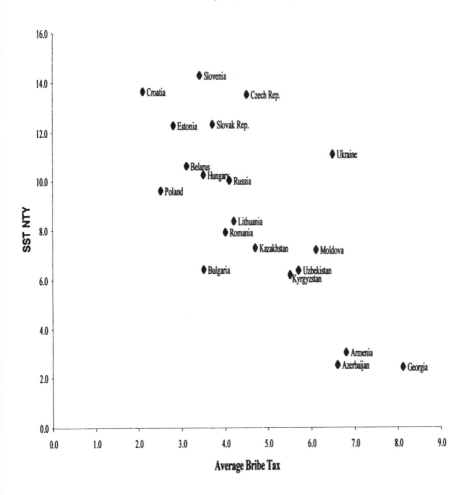

PART III
REGIONAL DEVELOPMENTS AND
INSTITUTIONAL REFORMS

Chapter 9

Regional Disparities and Transfer Policies in Russia: Theory and Evidence

Era Dabla-Norris and Shlomo Weber

Abstract

In this paper we examine economic disparities across regions in Russia and offer a theoretical treatment of various transfer rules between different regions. We argue for a consistent application of the principle of *partial equalization*, which implies that the more depressed regions should be subsidized by the more advantageous regions, but, the burden on more prosperous regions should not be excessive. Although, in contrary to the partial equalization principle, the gaps between donors and recipients have widened since the transition, there are some signs that this trend could be reversed.

Introduction

Russia inherited from the Soviet Union an economic structure that was highly geographically unbalanced. Capital accumulation and industrial location were a result of a concerted government policy to locate key industries in a small number of regions. But even after the collapse of the Soviet Union, the gap between more prosperous regions, including Moscow and St. Petersburg, and less developed ones, has not been reduced. Actually, the gap has widened during the last decade of transition.

The imbalances in economic conditions across Russia's 89 regions have naturally produced a variety of very distinct fiscal situations and policies.[1] Moreover, disparities in per capita revenue collections have increased steadily during the transition. In facing a complicated web of rising horizontal imbalances, all regions in Russia have been broadly divided into two groups: a small group of "donor" regions that make a positive net contribution to the center, and the rest of transfer or subsidy recipients, the more economically depressed regions.[2] In order to deal with disparities among regions, those *horizontal imbalances* became a focus of the transfer policies initiated by the central government.

There are many instances where transfers are explicitly or implicitly targeted to deter regional imbalances. As Ahmad and Craig (1997) note " ... national governments may wish to ensure that citizens in different regions and localities have access to a certain modicum of publicly provided services." The horizontal imbalances in fiscal capacity can be addressed by equalization transfers from the center (as in Australia, Canada and Denmark) or between regions (as in Germany). In all these countries, explicit inter-regional transfers rules are largely motivated by equity and solidarity considerations.

In this paper we offer a theoretical treatment of various transfer rules between different regions and outline the principle of *partial equalization*. This principle implies that, on one hand, the more depressed regions should be subsidized by more advantageous regions. However, the burden on more prosperous regions should not be excessive. Thus, one may aim to reduce the gap between donors and subsidy recipients but the gap should not be eliminated or even made too small, in part, due to political economy considerations.[3]

Le Breton and Weber (2000) analyze different compensation schemes that prevent a threat of secession by different regions in a country. They show that under certain conditions, there exist secession-proof compensation schemes which entail a degree of partial equalization. In this paper, we do not explicitly model the threat of secession by different regions in a country. Instead, we focus on different types of transfers schemes that meet the government's objectives of reducing horizontal balances while implicitly taking into account political economy considerations.

The paper is organized as follows. In the next section we provide a brief description of regional disparities in Russia. In Section III we focus on horizontal imbalances among Russian regions. Section IV is devoted to the theoretical analysis of general transfer rules. In Section V we examine the practical aspects of the federal transfers' policy in Russia and to what extent they adhere to the theoretical rules examined in the previous section. In Section VI we briefly discuss an impact of political factors on transfer policies of the central government. We conclude the paper with some final remarks.

Russia: The Story of Regional Disparities

The economic structure of the Soviet Union was characterized by a very high degree of geographical concentration. Capital accumulation and industrial location were a result of a concerted government policy to locate key industries - such as steel and energy-intensive heavy machine building - in a handful of regions. Such patterns of regional concentration appear to have increased during the 1990s in the Russian Federation. For instance, in 1995, 75 per cent of metals and 74 per cent of fuels were produced in just ten regions.[4] Oil and gas come mostly from the two Siberian regions of Khanti-Mansiiskiy Autonomous Okrug (AO) and Yamalo-Nenetskiy AO, that jointly produce four-fifths of Russia's oil (Freinkmen et al (1999). More than 50 per cent of machinery was also produced in the top ten regions. As a result, most of the country's GDP is produced in a minority of regions. It was estimated that in 1995, the top ten regions produced about 44 per cent of the country's total GDP, with Moscow city alone accounting for 13.1 per cent.

At the same time, a number of regions are small, underdeveloped, often located in remote parts of the country, and have a long history of dependence on federal assistance. The absence of a diversified industrial structure in many regions and the resultant dependence on a single sector of economic activity has left them particularly vulnerable to the liberalization of prices and trade following the transition to a market economy.

Many of the industrial-location decisions made in Soviet Union were non-sustainable in a market competitive environment and the collapse of the military-industrial complex also contributed to the sharp variation in industrial contraction across regions. For example, if average regional output contracted by over 57 per cent in real terms between 1990 and 1996, the drop in individual regions ranged from 87 per cent in Aginskiy-Buryatskiy Autonomous Okrug to just 15 per cent in Yamalo-Nenets (Freinkmen et al (1999)). The dramatic variation in the proportion of loss-making enterprises across regions and the pattern of investment flows to regions have also accentuated the pattern of differentiation.

This variation in economic performance and specialization translated into sharp interregional differences in the standards of living, with unemployment levels and income inequality varying significantly across regions. Table 9.1 shows that the coefficient of variation for per capita regional GRP increased over the 1992-1997 period. By individual regions, the City of Moscow received 20 per cent of all income in 1995, but it represented only seven per cent of the population (Martinez-Vazquez (2000)). The incidence of poverty has also been regionally concentrated, with three quarters of the residents of Tuva Republic classified as poor, as compared to only 19 per cent in Moscow.

In summary, Russia's 89 regions exhibit dramatic variation in economic structure and performance - a pattern that appears to have been exacerbated in the post communist period. Economic activity, wealth, and tax burdens are increasingly concentrated in a handful of regions (notably Moscow), while many regions remain economically depressed, with high unemployment, unprofitable enterprises, and a growing reliance on federal transfers. These interregional differences, rooted in geographical variation and inherited economic structures, have led to a diversity of regional economic and political interests and posed a significant challenge to the evolving system of intergovernmental relations.

Table 9.1   Regional economic disparities, 1992-1997
(Per Capita GRP in Roubles)

Year	Mean	Coefficient of Variation	Minimum	Maximum
1992	123.5	0.875	19.4	786.0
1994	3,712.3	0.746	618.1	20,909.6
1995	9,487.9	0.836	1,881.9	59,004.5
1996	13,554.6	1.039	2,628.0	108,443.5
1997	13,887.9	0,976	2,608.6	102,262.1

Source: Dable-Norris, Martinez-Vasquez and Norregaard (2001).

Horizontal Fiscal Imbalances

Naturally, variations in regional economic conditions have translated into a divergence in their fiscal situations and policies. Russia's regions during the early years of transition were broadly divided into two groups: a minority of "donor" regions that contribute more to the center than they got back, including Moscow, St. Petersburg and eight other well-off regions; and the remainder subsidy recipients regions – that were largely economically depressed, ran large deficits and were heavily dependent on federal aid.[5]

Disparities in per capita revenue collections have increased steadily during the transition. As shown in Table 9.2, the coefficient of variation for revenue collections across regions (inclusive of the federal share of all revenues) increased from 0.68 per cent in 1993 to over 1.2 per cent in 1998, with the five highest collection regions accounting for over 40 per cent of all revenue collections in 1998. With respect to own revenues (exclusive of the federal share), the twenty highest revenue collection regions represented over 66 per cent of all subnational revenue collections in 1998 (Table 9.3). As expected, the high collection regions were also the richest regions, although many of them also accounted for the largest share of arrears to the federal budget and were the main holders of extrabudgetary funds that do not have to be shared. In fact, while all the main taxes have to be shared between the regions and the federal government in fixed proportions dictated by law, as will be discussed below, regions varied greatly in the share of taxes left with their budgets.

Regional budget spending in Russia also shows a marked variation. For instance, the best-off region in 1993 spent close to 12 times more in per capita expenditures than the worst-off region, with the gap widening to over 24 times in 1998, as shown in Table 9.4. The coefficient of variation for expenditures per capita across the regions increased by 46 percent over this period. Regions also vary in their allocation of resources across different categories of spending, with some regions spending significantly higher proportions of their budgets on subsidies. Recent studies of the determinants of subsidies across regions have found that even controlling for fiscal resources, economically depressed regions tended to spend less on subsidies than the wealthier regions.

The issue of regional disparities and horizontal imbalances in fiscal capacity is addressed by the central government through revenue sharing and transfer policies, the theoretical aspects of which we study in the next section.

Table 9.2 **Measures of regional fiscal disparities: per capita regional revenue collections, 1993-1998**
(in thousands of Roubles)

Year	Mean	CV	Minimum	Maximum
1993	149.71	0.68	0.01	566.24
1994	573.75	0.89	33.77	2,993.17
1995	1,296.44	0.86	88.45	7,201.64
1996	1,879.43	1.13	132.71	14,871.69
1997	2,509.32	1.42	162.52	28,200.82
1998	2,284.52	1.21	294.89	21,167.24

Source: Dabla-Norris, Martinez-Vasquez and Norregaard (2001).

Table 9.3 **Concentration of total revenue collections among oblast: share of total revenues collected by selected regions, 1993-1998**

	1993	1994	1995	1996	1997	1998	POP98 (millions)
5 highest collection regions	27.9	30.5	30.8	31.4	33.9	32.5	20.0
10 highest collection regions	43.0	44.7	45.2	46.0	48.9	47.8	33.5
20 highest collection regions	62.6	64.5	64.3	65.1	66.5	66.2	52.9
Coef. Of Variation, Per Capita Revenue Collections	0.68	0.89	0.86	1.13	1.42	1.21	

Source: Dabla-Norris, Martinez-Vasquez and Norregaard (2001).

Table 9.4   **Measures of horizontal fiscal imbalance: per capita regional expenditures, 1993-1998**
(Roubles)

Year	Mean	Coefficient of Variation	Minimum	Maximum
1993	219.7	0.775	100.6	1189.2
1994	959.7	1.191	359.8	8000.7
1995	1904.9	1.023	720.2	13004.3
1996	2835.7	1.067	1050.3	16521.1
1997	3730.1	1.187	1336.7	30543.5
1998	3184.4	1.022	1121.5	22559.8

Source: Dabla-Norris, Martinez-Vasquez and Norregaard (2001).

Model

A.   Environment

We examine a model with one country that consists of K heterogeneous regions.[6] The regions differ on a variety of characteristics, such as capital accumulation, economic performance, industrial base, wealth of mineral resources, that determine the revenue base of each region. We denote the revenue base of region k by R_k and its expenditure needs by E_k, where $k = 1,2,\ldots,K$.[7] The difference between R_k and E_k, the net revenue, is denoted by α_k:

$$\alpha_k = R_k - E_k$$

The gap in net revenues represent *horizontal imbalances* between different regions, with a higher value of α indicating a more advantageous region. A net revenue gap may be positive (denoting a surplus) or negative (denoting a deficit). Regions with deficits experience a greater fiscal pressure which is assumed to at least, partially be relieved by the central government. For simplicity of presentation we assume that surpluses are ordered such that:

$$\alpha_1 > \alpha_2 > \ldots > \alpha_k$$

That is, the surplus of regions is descending from region 1 to K. We assume that no region has a zero surplus (or deficit) and let k^* be the region with the smallest surplus. It would immediately follow that the region k^*+1 has the smallest fiscal deficit:

$$\alpha_1 > \ldots > \alpha_{k^*} > 0\ \alpha_{k^*+1} > \ldots \alpha_K$$

Now let us turn to the role of the central government. We assume that the central government assigns a special budget B to address disparities and horizontal imbalances across regions. For simplicity, we do not discuss how the value of B is determined and assume that it is given.[8] In order to address existing fiscal imbalances across regions, the central government determines a two-step policy: first, it determines which regions are donors and which are to be the recipients of federal aid. Second, the central government determines the size of donors' contributions and the value of federal transfers for each of the aid recipients. The budget is assumed to be balanced in the sense that the total sum of the special budget B and all donors' contributions equals the total value of aid provided to the recipient regions.

Note that the ordering the regions from the wealthiest to the poorest substantially simplifies the first part of the government policy of identifying donors and recipients. In effect, the government simply determines a cut-off index l, where $1 \leq l < K$, such that all regions k with $k \leq l$ are donors whereas all regions with a deficit are recipients. It is natural to assume that only regions with surpluses can be considered as donors. Therefore, l does not exceed the cut-off value k^*, i.e. $l \leq k^*$. However, since we do not require that every region with a surplus to be a donor, it follows that regions with small surpluses can be exempt from participation in the transfer program. Given the set of l donors, the central government determines a uniform rule that specifically identifies a share t_k such that every donor $k \leq l$ contributes a share $t_k \alpha_k$ of its surplus. The regions with a deficit (those with $k^* < k \leq K$ receive a transfer payment of $-t_k \alpha_k > 0$.

The balance budget condition for the central government requires:

$$\sum_{k=1}^{l} t_k \alpha_k + B + \sum_{k^*+1}^{K} t_k \alpha_k = 0 \qquad (1)$$

We assume that, as is the case in many developing countries, regions face an aggregate deficit and that the total special budget, B, does not cover the total deficit D, i.e.,

$$D = \sum_{k=1}^{K} \alpha_k < -B < 0 \qquad (2)$$

B.   *The Uniform Transfer Rule*

Consider first the case where the central government designates all k^* regions with a surplus as donors and uses a *uniform transfer rule*, such that all regions contribute the same shares, i.e., $t_k = t$. Equation (1) can then be written as:

$$t\sum_{k=1}^{K}\alpha_k + B = tD + B = 0 \tag{3}$$

The value of the redistributive parameter $t(k^*)$ is then given by:

$$t(k^*) = -\frac{B}{D} \tag{4}$$

Equation (2) implies that t is a positive number between 0 and 1. This conclusion yields the important principle of *partial equalization*. It states that, on one hand, poorer regions should be subsidized (indeed, the rate t is positive and some equalization does take place). On the other hand, the fact that the value of t is less than 1 guarantees that fiscal gaps between regions are not completely eliminated. That is, if a region k has a higher surplus than region m, i.e., $\alpha_k > \alpha_m$, then even after the transfer, the fiscal gap still persists as $(1-t)\,\alpha_k > (1-t)\,\alpha_m$. To summarize, this principle suggests that gaps between regions should be reduced but not completely eliminated. It is also important to note that for any two regions k and m, with $k < m$ we have:

$$\alpha_k(1-t(k^*)) > \alpha_m(1-t(m))$$

The uniform rule with k^* donors, therefore, satisfies the condition of *ranking invariance* in the sense that the ranking of the regions surpluses and deficits is not altered by the transfer policy. If region k has a higher surplus than region m, the net surplus of region k would still be higher than that of region m. Income invariance seems to be a reasonable and quite modest requirement on transfer policy. Indeed, it would be very difficult for the central government to convince a region k, that has a greater surplus than region m, to be engaged in transfer policy that would reverse the order of the net surpluses between these two regions.

C.   The $\overline{\alpha}$ – Transfer Rule

Consider now a government transfer policy that designates regions with small surplus neither as donors nor as transfer recipients. In other words, in addition to donors and recipients, the government introduces a third *intermediate* class of regions that do not belong to either of two groups. The government, thus, determines a threshold value, $\overline{\alpha}$, such that all the regions that satisfy

$$0 < \alpha_k < \overline{\alpha} \tag{5}$$

are exempt from their contribution to the transfer program. Let $l < k^*$ be such that:

$$\alpha_{l+1} > \overline{\alpha} \geq \alpha_l$$

Then regions 1, 2 ,...,l are designated as donors, whereas regions k^*, k^*+1, ... ,K are the transfer recipients. In this case, the balanced budget condition can be written as:

$$t\sum_{k=1}^{l}\alpha_k + t\sum_{k^*+1}^{K}\alpha_k + B = 0 \qquad (6)$$

The value of the parameter $t = t(\overline{\alpha})$ is given by:

$$t(\overline{\alpha}) = -\frac{B}{D - \sum_{k=l+t}^{k^*}\alpha_k} \qquad (7)$$

Since D < - B, the value of $t(1)$ is again positive but is lower than 1. It is worth pointing out that the function $t(\overline{\alpha})$ is decreasing in $\overline{\alpha}$. Indeed, the higher the cut-off value $\overline{\alpha}$, the smaller the number of donors. A smaller number of donors would, in turn, reduce the size of transfers payments.

Since $0 < t(\overline{\alpha}) < 1$, the principle of partial equalization holds in this case as well. The disadvantageous regions receive transfers while advantageous regions keep a part of their surpluses.

Let us now turn to the ranking invariance of surpluses and deficits. Obviously, this is preserved within each of three groups: donors, recipients as well as the intermediate regions. Since all recipients have a net deficit even after transfers, the only possibility for the ranking to be reversed is when the donor with the lowest surplus has a lower net surplus than one of the intermediate regions. This situation can not occur when the following inequality is satisfied:

$$\alpha_l(1 - t(\overline{\alpha})) > \alpha_{l+1}$$

By substituting the expression for $t(\overline{\alpha})$ from (7), we obtain:

$$\alpha_l(1 + \frac{B}{D - \sum_{k=l+1}^{k^*}\alpha_k}) > \alpha_{l+1}$$

or

$$0 < B < (1 - \frac{\alpha_{l+1}}{\alpha_l})(\sum_{k=l+1}^{k^*} \alpha_k - D) \tag{8}$$

The intuition behind this result is quite simple. There is not a possibility of ranking reversal if the special budget is sufficiently small. In this case, transfers are not sufficiently large to alter the ranking of regions surpluses. However, if the special budget is relatively large, then the implementation of the uniform proportional policy could be problematic in light of potential political economy considerations. Let us turn therefore to the case where the central government may abandon the uniform transfer rule.

Note that, the uniform transfer rule examined in the previous subsection, is in fact, a special case of the $\overline{\alpha}$-rule for $\overline{\alpha} = 0$. Indeed, if $\overline{\alpha}$ is equal to zero, all regions with a positive surplus will be designated as donors.

D.   General Transfer Rule

Consider now a transfer rule that assigns different rates to different regions. As in the previous section, the government determines the threshold value, $\overline{\alpha}$, such that all regions with a positive surplus below $\overline{\alpha}$ would not be required to participate in the transfer program. Let l again denote the region with the smallest surplus among the designated donors. The government then establishes a transfer rate for donors, $t_1,...,t_l$ and for recipients $t_{k^*+1}, \ldots , t_K$. We impose a *progressivity* condition both for donors:

$t_1 > t_2 > \ldots > t_l$

and for recipients:

$t_{k^*+1} < t_{k^*+2} < \ldots < t_K$

From the balanced budget condition (1) we obtain:

$$\sum_{k=1}^{l} t_k \alpha_k + \sum_{k+k^*+1}^{K} t_k \alpha_k + B = 0 \tag{9}$$

To examine the restrictions that the principle of partial equalization and ranking invariance impose on the values of ranking shares, note first that all values t_k would be chosen between 0 and 1. In addition, the condition of ranking invariance for donors implies that:

$$\alpha_1(1-t_1) > \alpha_2(1-t_2) > \ldots > \alpha_l(1-t_l),$$

or the series of inequalities:

$$t_1 < 1 - \frac{\alpha_2}{\alpha_1}(1-t_2), t_2 < 1 - \frac{\alpha_3}{\alpha_2}(1-t_3),...,$$

$$t_{l-1} < 1 - \frac{\alpha_l}{\alpha_{l-1}}(1-t_l) \qquad (10)$$

Similar conditions for recipients imply:

$$\alpha_{k^*+1}(1-t_{k^*+1}) > \alpha_{k^*+2}(1-t_{k^*+2}) > ... > \alpha_K(1-t_K),$$

or

$$t_{k^*+1} > 1 - \frac{\alpha_{k^*+2}}{\alpha_{k^*+1}}(1-t_{k^*+2}), t_{k^*+2} > 1 - \frac{\alpha_{k^*+3}}{\alpha_k^*2}(1-t_{k^*+3}),...,$$

$$t_{K-1} > 1 - \frac{\alpha_K}{\alpha_{K-1}}(1-t_K) \qquad (11)$$

Finally, order invariance implies that:

$$\alpha_l(1-t_l) > \alpha_{l+1}$$

or

$$t_l < 1 - \frac{\alpha_{l+1}}{\alpha_l} \qquad (12)$$

The inequalities (9)-(12) determine the set of values for transfer shares under a general transfer rule.

Federal Government Responses to Regional Diversity and Disbursement Pattern of Federal Transfers

Since the beginning of the transition, the federal government has attempted to accommodate the extreme economic and fiscal differentiation of regions discussed above using a combination of policies, including tax assignments (tα for donors) and intergovernmental transfers (B + tα for aid recipients).[9] In this section we examine the disbursement pattern of federal transfers and revenue sharing arrangements in relation to some of the theoretical principles outlined in the previous section.

The initial phase of transition (prior to 1994) was characterized by ever-changing and individually customized revenue assignments for each regional government in the annual budget (non uniform tα). The basic rule adopted was to use different combinations of the main federal taxes (the VAT, personal income tax, enterprise profits tax and excises) to "regulate" the revenues of regional governments. Sharing rates were customized so that individual subnational governments had just enough revenues to finance their "minimum" expenditure budget.[10] A forecast of subnational government own revenues were subtracted from the minimum expenditure budgets to arrive at the gap to be financed with revenue sharing. For poorer regions with modest tax bases, and where the retention of 100 per cent of taxes collected within their territory was insufficient to finance the minimum expenditure budget, the remaining gap was financed through "subventions" or lump-sum transfers from the center (B in our model).

The practice of setting differential rates for regional deductions from federal taxes represented a deviation from the uniform transfer rule described above. For instance, in 1993, the share of federal axes transferred to consolidated regional budgets varied from 100 per cent for Tartarstan, 54.6 per cent for the wealthy cities of Moscow and St. Petersburg to 45 per cent for other regions (Table 9.5).[11] In essence, while the wealthier regions were allowed to retain a larger share of federal taxes collected within their territory, revenue sharing arrangements varied greatly even among the subset of wealthy regions.

At the same time, the share of federal aid in total revenues also showed a marked variation (Table 9.5). Financial aid to regions was provided through a variety of mechanisms: equalization transfers, mutual settlements, subsidies and grants, and budget loans. Between the years 1992 – 1994, federal budget transfers to regions, increased from 1.7 to 3.8 per cent of GDP or 20 per cent of regional revenues. More importantly, non-transparent transfers, such as mutual settlements and subsidies to Moscow accounted for over 80 percent of all federal financial aid to regions. While the overall size of federal equalization transfers remained quite small, they represented a significant source of revenues for many of the economically depressed regions.[12] For instance, for the 20 least developed regions in Russia, federal transfers accounted for 50 - 60 per cent of subnational revenues in 1999 (OECD, 2000).

Reforms undertaken since 1994 have brought about greater uniformity to revenue sharing and expenditure arrangements between the federal government and the regions. A new system of *formula-based equalization transfers* the Fund for Financial Support of Subjects of the Russian Federation (FFSR) was introduced (see Figure 9.1).

Table 9.5 Indicators of asymmetry in fiscal federalist relations

	Share of federal aid in total regional revenues (%)		Share of taxes transferred to consolidated regional budgets (% of total tax collections)	
	1993	1998	1993	1998
Regional Average	18.1	13.15	62.9	62.9
Tartarstan, Bashkortostan and Sakha	0	17.2	100.0	84.3
Other Republics	47.0	35.6	65.6	70.5
Oblasts and krays	17.6	14.4	62.2	68.1
Cities of Moscow and St. Petersburg	10.6	1.0	54.6	45.3
Autonomous oblast and okrugs, of which oil and gas-producing	5.2	3.4	49.1	68.7
Other	79.4	45.1	67.3	79.1

Source: OECD (2000).

For instance, Lavrov et al (2001) note that by 1996-98, the number of donor regions, for which the amount of taxes collected in their territory and credited to the federal budget exceeded the amount of financial transfers received, increased to 30 (out of 89 subjects of the federation).[13]

The explicit economic rationale for a majority of center-region transfers since 1994 has been to reduce horizontal imbalances of regions. Empirical analysis of the effectiveness of equalization transfers by La Houerou and Rutkowski (1996) and Martinez-Vazquez and Boex (1997), however, suggests that federal transfers, for the most part have not been equalizing. This is particularly true in the case of non-FFSR transfers, which represented over 90 per cent of all financial aid to regions in 1993.

Figure 9.1   Russia's transfer system, 1992-1998

During 1992-1994, the bulk of all transfers were negotiated "subventions" to those regions for which own revenues and shared revenues were insufficient to fund their minimum expenditure budget. In 1994, the Russian government introduced a new system of equalization transfers, the *Fund for Financial Support of the Regions (FFSR)*. This had two "windows". The first window, called "Regions in Need of Financial Assistance", was designed to equalize revenue availability across regions. The second window, called "Regions in Need of Additional Financial Assistance", was designed to provide additional funding to regions with expenditure needs not covered by other financing sources, including the first window.

In the early years of transition, total funding for the FFSR was not fixed but determined annually in the budget and divided between the two windows. For 1994, total funding for the FFSR was 22 per cent of the federal share of VAT collections; for 1995, 27 per cent of federal VAT collections; for 1996 and 1997, 15 per cent of all federal tax collections except for tariff revenues; and for 1998, this was lowered to 14 per cent (Dabla-Norris, Martinez-Vazquez, and Norregaard (2000).

The first window of the FFSR equalized revenues across regions by comparing actual revenues per capita for the most recent year for which data were available in each region, to the average revenues per capita in one of three groups of regions (the Northern territories, the Far East and the rest of the country) based on similarities in the cost of living. Regions with per capita revenues below some percent of the group average were entitled to an equalization transfer. The transfer actually received was an apportionment of the available funds among all the regions entitled to transfers. The second window of the FFSR estimated expenditure needs for each region by adjusting expenditures (actual disbursed expenditures and not a measure of expenditure needs) in a base year for all changes in legislation in the intervening years. Those regions with expenditures exceeding revenues plus transfers from the first window were entitled to a transfer and the available funds apportioned among all the regions entitled to a transfer.

While the FFSR system represented a significant improvement over the previous system, it had several shortcomings. First, its limited and variable funding reduced the ability for equalization and generated budgetary uncertainty for subnational governments. Second, its outcomes were to subject to political negotiations. Third, its formula (the manner in which variables were computed) was changed frequently, contributing to revenue unpredictability for regional governments. Finally, the methodology employed past achieved levels of revenue and expenditures as primary criteria for allocation of transfers, thereby, undermining incentives to improve fiscal performance at the subnational levels (OECD 2000).

In general, empirical analysis suggests that while federal transfers exacerbated regional revenue inequality in 1994, they appear to have somewhat reduced it in 1996 and 1997 (Freinkmen et al (1999) and Dabla-Norris, Martinez-Vazquez and Norregaard (2000)) and, thus, at least partially, reestablished the principle of partial equalization. In addition, while the impact of FFSR and other transfers in reducing per capita expenditure disparities across regions has been limited (suggesting a small B), there is some evidence to suggest that transfers have been increasingly equalizing tax capacity and expenditure needs across regions (Table 9.6).

If partial equalization is not the only determinant of the patterns of redistribution, what explains why some regions obtained larger amounts of federal aid than others? Recent empirical analysis suggests that while equity considerations have played an increasingly important role, the major motives in the past have been political in nature.

Treisman (1996 and 1998) and others have remarked on the important role that separatist demands have played in the actual flow of fiscal resources between the center and the regions in Russia. He found that regions that demonstrated the capacity and resolve to threaten economic or constitutional order were rewarded with larger fiscal transfers and tax benefits.

Table 9.6 Disparity of per capita revenues across regions, 1999

	Before equalization	After equalization
Richest to poorest ratio	90	20
Gini index of inequality	0.39	0.33

Political Factors in Decentralization

The process of the reform of the system of intergovernmental relations in Russia has been foremost a political process. The relevance of politics in the Russian federation is undoubtedly related to its vast territory, significant regional disparities in industrial development and resource endowments, and its ethnolinguistic diversity. These factors exerted strong centrifugal forces on the country.

The Russian federation was essentially created out of a process of disintegration of the Soviet Union when Russia and other former Soviet republics refused to remit tax revenues to the Soviet government in Moscow, proclaimed that their laws took precedence over Soviet laws and ultimately declared themselves independent. This process set a precedent for many of the autonomous republics in Russia also to declare their independence or to assert high degrees of autonomy (Teague, 1996). The assertiveness of the regions, especially the ethnic republics, to ensure a measure of autonomy for themselves intensified during 1992-1993, with up to 30 regions withholding their contribution to the federal budget and demanding special tax regimes or federal subsidies (Wallich, 1994).[14] These negative centrifugal forces gained momentum, often leading to separatist demands and open opposition to federal government policies, at a time when the federal government attempted to unilaterally shift expenditure responsibilities and mandates to regional governments, without providing adequate funding.

In response to regional opposition and centrifugal forces, the federal government appears to systematically have offered greater advantages and privileges to the "difficult" regions.[15] The federal government, empowered by the 1993 constitution, entered into a series of bilateral, "special-channel" arrangements with the regions in an attempt to balance regional objectives that conflicted with national interests.

Figure 9.2 Bilateral arrangements

The basis for distinction between the 89 regions in Russia was the 1978 Constitution which adopted a nationality-based logic for distinguishing between units, with the ethnic republics enjoying the greatest autonomy from the federal government, followed by the other forms of republics, oblasts, metropolitan cities, oblasts, and autonomous okrugs.[16]

With the collapse of the Soviet Union, the status of regional-federal relations was embodied in the Federation Treaty of 1992, which attempted to institutionalize some of the informal bargaining that took place between the center and regions during this period. The Federation Treaty provided for greater regional administrative autonomy and participation in federal law-making for the republics, but krais and oblasts were denied this privilege. This asymmetry was eliminated in the 1993 Constitution which declared all subjects of the Federation equal with all entities receiving the right to develop their own legal systems, but granted the ethnic republics special rights such as the passing of their own constitutions and electing their own heads of government. However, ambiguity in Articles 71 and 72 of the Constitution concerning the division of powers between the federal government and regions, as well as provisions in the Constitution have allowed the federal authorities to enter into bilateral arrangements with separate regions.

Special arrangements. such as those granting exclusive rights over natural resources to the republics of Tatarstan and Bashkortostan signed in 1994, have often reflected political realities and compromises in face of strong regional opposition and centrifugal forces. These treaties, however, set a precedent that was picked up by other constituent units of the Russian Federation. Pressure from non-republic units opened the treaty process to oblasts and krais as well, resulting in a proliferation of treaties in the 1994 - 1998 period. In general, regional positions on federation issues and federal policies have been dominated by the "donor" versus "transfer recipients" divide. By 1997, 32 of the 89 subjects of the federation had signed such treaties, and by 1998 the total had reached 45 (OECD (2000)). The expanded use of bilateral treaties has resulted in a complex bargaining game, in which all regions have an incentive to deviate from federal laws and obligations in order to extract concessions from the center. Differences in the bargaining power and relative credibility of the participants, however, have served to reinforce the pattern of asymmetric federalism that has emerged since independence.

The regions, first based on ethnic claims, and later simply on threats and demands, bargained for and obtained preferential fiscal treatments (see Box 2). At the same time, demands from poorer regions emerged for increased regional redistribution and the federal government was pressed to continue to fund a wide array of goods and services that it had earlier sought to offload on the regions. This type of response created an asymmetric federalism (Wallich, 1994), and explains the use of non-uniform transfers between the center and regions during the early years of transition.

Concluding Remarks

In this paper we examined the issue of increasing regional disparities and widening horizontal imbalances among the regions in the Russian Federation. The state planning policies of the former Soviet Union created a very uneven economic structure that produced a great variance in terms of capital accumulation, industrial and revenue base across the regions. The gap between more prosperous and less developed regions actually increased over the last decade.

During the early years of transition, federal transfers failed to achieve a degree of partial equalization equalizing and were largely non-uniform in nature. This was in large part due to political factors including the pervasiveness of bilateral negotiated arrangements between the federal and regional governments. In recent years, the move towards more uniform tax sharing arrangements and increasing reliance on formula based equalization transfers suggests that there has been a move to achieve a measure of partial equalization.

Notes

[1]   The Russian federation is made up of 89 regions consisting of 21 ethnically defined republics, 49 oblasts (provinces), the Jewish Autonomous Oblast, 6 krais (territories), 10 autonomous okrugs (areas), and 2 metropolitan cities (Moscow and St. Petersburg) that are collectively referred to as 89 "subjects of the federation".

[2]   Lavrov et al. (2001) argue that federal funds are distributed to regions not only in the forms of transfers but also as direct expenditures (in the form of wage payments to federal employees, funding of federal programs, etc.), which are at least as important as other forms of financial aid provided to regions. Accounting for federal budgetary expenditures can often obfuscate the distinction between donor and subsidy regions. In this paper, however, we abstract from federal budgetary expenditures in regions.

[3]   It is interesting to note that due to the heavy economic burden if unification of East and West Germany. the transfer system used there exhibited a degree of over-equalization. Spahn and Fottinger (1997) note that while the fiscal capacity of poorer former East German provinces increased after the transfers, the contribution paid by rich former West German states reduced their fiscal capacity below the average.

[4]   Russia Economic Trends (1997).

[5]   In 1996, the most heavily subsidized regions were Chechnya (where transfers financed 93 per cent of expenditures), Dagestan (61 per cent), and Tuva (51 per cent) (OECD (2000)). Some natural resource rich regions that are remote from the

European hinterland, such as Sakha, also continue to rely excessively on federal subsidies to provide food, energy, and other supplies.

[6]   A similar model in a different framework has been considered by Dr'eze (1993).

[7]   The revenue base of each region can be regarded as the "own revenues" of that region.

[8]   In reality, the size of B may depend upon existing tax sharing arrangements between the center and regions. For instance, if B is funded through shared federal taxes, a smaller number of donors could imply a smaller pool of funding for equalization transfers.

[9]   Intergovernmental transfers in Russia can be divided into two general categories: equalization transfers (since 1994, the Fund for Financial Support of regions (FFSR)) and other transfers. The size of these other transfers in Russia during the 1994-98 period in some years exceeded the funding of the FFSR. A large share of the other transfers took the form of "mutual settlements", which included negotiated injections of funds, compensation for central government programs and mandated emergency grants, and other forms of non-budgeted support.

[10]   See Dabla-Norris, Martinez Vasquez and Norregaard (2001) for details.

[11]   In addition, actual revenue sharing between the federal government and regions has often differed significantly from the statutory rates stated in the law.

[12]   In 1998, they represented close to 2 per cent of GDP and less than 14 per cent of total subnational revenues.

[13]   The remaining 59 regions were either recipients over the entire period or were donors in some years.

[14]   The regions that stopped or greatly reduced remittances to the federal government early in 1992 included the ethnic republics of Tatarstan, Chechnya, Sakha (Yakutia) and Bashkortostan.

[15]   Shleifer and Treisman (2000) note that, "In essence, the federal government appeased regions that threatened political or economic stability-by declaring sovereignty, staging strikes, or voting for the opposition in elections-by allocating them larger transfers or tolerating their tax withholding".

[16]   The territory of administrative units formed by the republics, oblasts, and autonomous okrugs covers 53 per cent of the territorial area of Russia and includes 20 per cent of the total population.

References

Ahmad, E. and Craig, J. (1997), 'Intergovernmental Transfers', in T. Ter-Minassian (ed), *Fiscal Federalism in Theory and Practice*, International Monetary Fund, Washington, D.C.

Dabla-Norris, E., Martinez-Vasquez, J. and Norregaard, J. (2001), *Fiscal Decentralization and Macroeconomic Performance: The Case of Russia, Ukraine, and Kazakhstan*, IMF Forthcoming.

Dr'eze, J. (1993), 'Regions of Europe: A Feasible Status, to be Discussed', *Economic Policy*, vol. 11, pp. 265-301.

Freinkmen, L., Treisman, D. and Titov, S. (1999), 'Subnational Budgeting in Russia: Preempting a Potential Crises', World Bank Technical Paper, no. 452.

La Houerou, P. and Rutkowski, M. (1995), 'Federal transfers in Russia: Their Impact on Regional Revenues and Income', *Comparative Economic Studies*, vol. 38, pp 21-44.

Lavrov, A. and Makushkin, A. (2001), *The Fiscal Structure of the Russian Federation: Financial Flows Between the Center and Regions*, East West Institute.

Le Breton, M. and Weber, S. (2000), 'The Art of Making Everybody Happy: How to Prevent a Secession?', IMF Discussion Paper.

Martinez-Vazquez, J. and Boex, J. (1998), 'A Methodology for Implementing Transfers to Depressed Regions in the Russian Federation', US Government Technical Assistance Team, Moscow.

Martinez-Vazquez, J. and Boex, J. (2000), 'Fiscal Decentralization in the Russian Federation: Main Trends and Issues', The World Bank.

OECD (2000), *Russian Federation*, OECD Economic Survey.

Polishchuk (1999), 'Legal Initiatives in Russian Regions: Determinants and Effects, IRIS Working Paper', University of Maryland, College Park.

Shleifer, A. and Treisman, D. (2000), *Without a Map: Political Tactics and Economic Reform in Russia*, MIT Press, Cambridge.

Spahn, P. and Fottinger, W. (1997), 'Germany' in *Fiscal Federalism in Theory and Practice*, International Monetary Fund, Washington, DC.

Teague, E. (1996), 'Russia and the Regions: the Use of Ambiguity', in J. Gibson and P. Hanson (eds), *Transformation from Below: Local Power and the Political Economy of Post-Communist Transitions* , Edward Elgar, Cheltenham, U.K.

Treisman, D. (1996), 'The Political Economy of Intergovernmental Transfers in Post-Soviet Russia', *British Journal of Political Science*, pp. 299-335.

Treisman, D. (1999), 'Russia's Tax Crises: Falling Revenues in a Transitional Economy', *Economics and Politics*, vol. 11, pp. 145-70.

Wallich, C. (1994), *Russia and the Challenge of Fiscal Federalism*, The World Bank.

Chapter 10

Regional Development Theory and Policy: an Example for Russia?

Michael P. Cuddy and Sarah Callanan

Introduction

National economic development has always taken precedence over regional development both in the evolution of economic theory and in the formulation and implementation of economic policy. This is probably not too surprising since the advance of the nation state is, invariably, a priority of national governments. In addition, the economic success of the nation is a necessary condition to the implementation of regional policy - if you do not have the finances to engage in regional policy, there is little point in pursuing such a strategy. It is also likely that the imperative of national development has had a significant influence on relegating the evolution of regional development theory and implied policies to a secondary role.

Nevertheless, regional development theory has evolved as a recognised branch of the economics discipline. It recognises that within any broadly defined geographic space, and especially within the nation state, smaller geographic areas are at differing stages of economic development and experience unequal rates of growth. The theory most generally engaged in explaining differential regional growth rates is that which is used to explain national economic growth. The dominant theory over the past 50 years has been the neo-classical growth model. However, regional economists and economic geographers, arising from their experience and research in the field, generally did not share the dominant view. Their alternative view of regional development emphasised regional specific factors, which influenced the rate of economic growth. Indeed, the basis for the alternative view predates the 20th century and this basis has been articulated in different ways and elaborated over time. At the close of the 20th century mainstream economists have been climbing on board the alternative view, which deviates very significantly from the neo-classical growth viewpoint. Indeed, the neo-classical growth model as an explanatory tool of national growth is itself being abandoned for the more realistic endogenous growth models. This brings the understanding of national and regional growth closer together.

Despite the predominance of the neo-classical theory, which essentially prescribes a laissez faire approach to policy intervention, regional economic policies have been implemented to address problems of unequal levels of regional development and regional economic growth rates. These interventions are justified both by those who subscribe to neo-classical theory, on the basis of market failure, and by adherents to the alternative theories, which accept that factors outside of the neo-classical model framework effect regional economic performance. Economic theories, and implied policy interventions, which seem to have yielded positive results, have become more sophisticated over time. Interventions, which have become more refined, increasingly presume the presence of certain preconditions in the regional economy.

Intervention in support of regional development is increasingly challenged in the context of sustainability. It is clear that intervention in the market process can give visible temporary advantage and contribute to raising the economic growth rate in a region, in the short to medium term. However, the question posed, particularly by the subscribers to neo-classical growth theory, relates to the durability of these intervention impacts, that is will the higher growth rate continue in the long term?

Russia has had a unique experience in the 20th century in the context of regional development. It was special, in the first instance, in that for most of the century the economy was centrally planned and, therefore, regional policy was dominated by political rather than economic considerations. This gave rise to an economic landscape, which is highly unlikely to have evolved under, primarily, market forces. Second, now that the market has been embraced as the mediator of spatial resource allocation, regions are feeling the pressure, to varying degrees, depending on the strength or weakness of attributes, which are already recognised factors influencing development in regions of the traditional market economies. Indeed, as pointed out by Dabla-Norris and Weber (see previous chapter), Russia is faced with extreme divergences in levels of regional development and access to social services. The problem then facing the Federal government and the regions of the Federation is how to address and promote regional economic development. The question is to what extent can regional economic theory and the policies, which have been successfully implemented in the industrialised market economies, inform intervention measures to assist in this task?

In the context of market liberation in Russia and the emergence of a single market and currency area, it may be of interest to note that the impact of economic and monetary integration on regional economic development has exercised the minds of economists in the developed industrialised economies. This is particularly relevant in the context of European economic integration and North American integration. The European Union has already established a Single European Market and is in the process of establishing a Single Currency Area. What is the impact on the European regions of this integration? If the EU is not an optimal economic or monetary area for economic policy, then what will be the effect on regional growth rates? This question has previously been asked in respect to the United States, which has essentially been a unitary market since the Union was formed - is it an optimal region for common economic policy measures; in particular, is it an optimal single currency area? These issues are equally pertinent to Russia today.

This chapter reviews the theories of regional development, and the policy initiatives, which have flowed from these theories, aimed at promoting regional development. It also asks what lessons can be learned from the debate on optimum economic areas and regional policy in the context of economic and monetary integration. Finally, it looks at the Russian experience and the current political and economic situation there and the appropriateness of conventional regional policy in addressing the regions' problems. It concludes that explicit regional policy, à la the industrialised market economies, provides a useful framework for analysing current regional economic issues. However, the policy measures, which emanate from these theories are predicated on the existence of the fundamental aspects of a functioning market economy. Conceiving and applying such regional policy measures in the absence of the fundamental requirements of the market will give rather poor value for money.

Theoretical Perspectives

It is difficult to classify theories explaining regional development, the differing stages of economic development, rates of growth and levels of GDP per capita. They have diverse origins, and not all of them fit easily into the central body of economic theory or are not easily subject to empirical testing. Also, although having different origins, sometimes they address similar factors influencing regional development. However, since the purpose here is to try to identify policy measures emanating from theory, a working classification is presented (Table 1). Basically, there is the neo-classical model and the alternative models of regional development. The alternative models are then sub-divided.

Neo-Classical Model

The neo-classical growth model has been the basic explanatory model of economic growth up until the 1990s, with capital and labour as the two main contributing factors, and the level of technology as a third but exogenous factor.[1] It fitted into the general neo-classical theory. However, even in its hey-day, this growth model had a rather poor explanatory power when empirically applied. The two principal problems were the measurement of the two endogenous variables, capital and labour, and the meaning and stability of the exogenous factor, technology. Probably more unsatisfactory from a policy point of view was the sheer implausibility of the implications of this model in the context of real world experience, arising from the extremely restrictive and unrealistic assumptions underlying the model, neglecting time, space and distance.[2]

The neo-classical model predicts complete convergence in factor prices and growth rates across regions. If there is capital accumulation in one region for whatever reason, given the assumption of identical production functions, the price of capital will decrease and wages will increase. Labour will flow in from low wage to high wage regions and capital will flow in the opposite direction. Flows will continue until all differences in factor prices and growth rates have disappeared. Exogenously determined growth rates are reached and regional economies will converge towards the long-run steady state position, while differences in productivity among regions are transitory. The neo-classical growth model is closely associated with the theory of comparative advantage and specialisation in production based on the abundance of the factors. This gives an additional flexibility to the model, whereby factor returns are equalised across regions through specialisation and trade.

Table 10.1 Theories of regional development and associated policy measures

Theories →	Neo-classical	Alternative theories		
		Location	Agglomeration	Endogenous/ Indigenous
Policy measures ↓	Market intervention 1. Labour market 2. Capital market 3. Technology	1. Transport 2.Communications 3. Public service infrastructure 4. Industry with low transport cost 5. Trade barriers	1. Growth poles 2. Development corridors	Institutional factors effecting entrepreneurship (i) Political (ii) Social & cultural (iii) Clustering (iv) Networks (v) Information

The reality is that the neo-classical growth model has not, however, been very good at explaining economic growth, and the predicted equalisation of factor prices and GDP per capita between regions has not materialised. The explanation for this apparently poor performance of the model has been found in "market failure", where certain assumptions of the theoretical model have been violated. Following decisions taken by the individual economic actors in the demanding and supplying factors of production, market failure exists when markets fail to clear, or where they clear at prices and quantities, which do not match social preferences (Bristow, 1996). This can come about due to obstacles to factor mobility, barriers to entry into the market or through positive or negative externalities. The upshot is that national or regional welfare falls short of what it would be if markets cleared in an efficient manner.

More recent developments, building on the neo-classical growth models, have endogenised technological change (Romer, 1990). Technological change then depends on certain factors, which are themselves location dependent. This, of course, moves the neo-classical model closer to the alternative models in explaining regional growth and its associated variables.

Alternative Models

All the alternative theories of regional development emphasise regional characteristics, which make them different from other regions and which explain the differential rates of economic growth.

(i)   Location factors
Location and distance from markets has entered into the literature over the past two centuries emphasising different aspects of the spatial dimension and their impact on cost and prices (Chisolm, 1990; Glasson, 1974). Von Thunen emphasised the impact of distance from the central market location and the declining land rents directly reflected in this distance. Weber reflected on the location decision of the firm in minimising transport and labour costs and taking advantage of agglomeration effects. Christaller develops the concept of the spatial pattern of distribution of places into an interdependent network of "central" place and "lesser" central places. He calls the integrated settlements a regional functional system. Losch extends this theory to a spatial production system with locational specialisation and trade between centres, both upwards and downwards in the settlement network.

(ii)   Agglomeration factors
The impact of concentration or agglomeration on economic growth and development has a number of strands to its evolution in regional development theory. Marshall, in his *Principles of Economics* (1890), identified external economies, which lower production costs to the firm, adding to its competitiveness and by extension lowering the location or regional production costs leading to competitive advantage and growth. Schumpeter postulated that certain sectors are innovative, flowing from technical progress, investments take place and growth ensues; on the contrary others weaken and decline. This leads to unbalanced growth across sectors. Perroux built on this concept with his theory of sectoral growth poles, where "motor" units are poles to "functional reference systems", which are established through linkages. Hirschman links the sectoral growth idea to growth centres due to the agglomeration economies and consequently the evolution of the spatial growth pole or the polarisation concept.

Myrdal in his *An American Dilemma* (1944), articulates the principle of Cumulative Causation which may evolve from agglomeration or locational factors.

He shows how increasing returns can be realised through specialisation and economies of scale and how initially small advantages can grow and be magnified. This was further elaborated into a theory of regional development in his *Economic Theory and Underdeveloped Regions* (1957). He shows how advantages of development locations or growth poles can become cumulative leading to expanding growth and development, while the backward location can become increasingly disadvantaged (virtuous and vicious circles). Focusing on the contrast between developed and underdeveloped countries, he concludes that the former have achieved major advances in science, technology and industrial production and thus have become locked into a path of cumulative development, while the latter are condemned to stagnation and declining per capita incomes. This is in strict opposition to the neo-classical theory, which propounds the idea of diminishing returns, competition, mobility of factors, sharing of gains and general equilibrium (harmony).

(iii)   Endogenous factors

Different strands of economic and social organisation theory have contributed to the focus on local conditions, which are hospitable to business development, the creation of value added and the enhancement of the productivity of factors of production. The focus is primarily local indigenous development. Entrepreneurship is at the heart of local indigenous development. Higgins and Savoie (1995) define entrepreneurship as "the capacity to introduce new technologies and new products, to develop new resources, to improve business organisation and management; the ability to bring to life innovations of all kinds; and to bring together the required land, labour and management in an efficient and dynamic enterprise to make innovations succeed". But why do some places generate their own prosperity while others fail as markets and technologies change? The answer lies in the local "innovation millieu" or "munificent environment", which spawns innovation and entrepreneurial activity (Maillat, 1993; Sweeney, 1996).

These favourable local conditions include political stability, efficiency of public administrations and governmental and non-governmental support systems. They also comprise the evolution of efficient institutional structures. These institutional structures comprise both the decision-making actors like households, business, trade unions and government and the institutional framework (culture, tradition, social norms of behaviour and legal and fiscal systems) within which these decisions are taken (Figure 1). Emerging from these different local attributes is the concept of social capital, referring to those features of social organisation (trust, norms, co-operation and networks) which improve the efficiency or lowers the cost of transactions between various public and private actors (Putnam, 1993).

Networking is central to Porter's (1998) concept of "clusters". Enterprises with similar labour, service and public support requirements are spatially grouped together, both through the impulse of market forces and through public sector intervention, to generate certain externalities in Perroux type economic space, which leads to greater efficiency of firms and the competitiveness of regions. The deepening of this efficiency over time through the conscious action of the actors, particularly the public actors, building on their experience with previous cycles of actions or programmes has led to the concept of the "learning" region, which is central to sustaining the virtuous circle, à la Myrdal.

One of the criticisms from neo-classical economists of the alternative model of regional economic development is the lack of rigour and the fact that it hasn't been mathematically formulated for econometric estimation and the testing of the embodied hypotheses. Krugman's contributions in the 1990s were less to do with new insights into the alternative theory and more to do with an attempt to apply rigour in the theoretical formulation (Krugman, 1991, 1993 and 1996). Unfortunately, the analysis of regional economic development cannot be contained within the framework of strict economic parameters but rather spills over into other disciplines, in particular political science and sociology.

Figure 10.1   Institutional factors and regional economic development

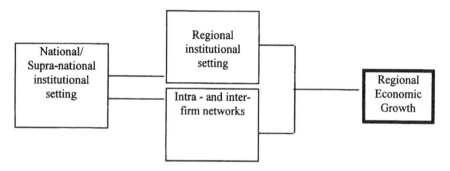

Regional Development Policy Measures

Regional policy has two principal objectives:

(i)   To increase national output through the efficient use of regional economic resources; and

(ii)   To ensure comparable (equal) life chances and living standards to the citizens of all regions.

The principal focus here is raising output and income per capita in the regions and thereby contributing to national economic output. To the extent that the second objective is not realised, net transfer payments are made from central funds to the lagging regions. However, these are primarily to bring social services towards the national norm and have limited impact on personal incomes.

National regional development policy, in combination with policy initiatives of regional or local government, is normally an integral part of national economic policy. These two sets of measures are complementary to each other and are worked out within a planning framework. They are sometime loosely referred to as top-down and bottom-up policies, respectively, although such a classification is rather arbitrary. However, with respect to these various policy measures, it is relatively easy to associate them with different regional development theories, although it is not always clear which has come first, has practice followed theory or theory followed practice?

Neo-Classical Model

Market failure comes about due to the fact that certain assumptions of the model do not obtain in the real world. This justifies intervention by government in order to maximise economic efficiency and social welfare.

Labour market: The labour market may be in equilibrium but at a sub optimal level due to obstacles to an outward shift in the demand or supply of labour. The demand for labour may be shifted outward by removing bottlenecks in the creation or the expansion of enterprise. These may include institutional constraints, such as legislation, stigma associated with certain aspects of entrepreneurial activity or the availability of credit. The labour demand may also be shifted out by un-blocking information flows, which deny access to market opportunities or to labour itself. The supply of labour may be constrained due to mobility constraints, in moving between enterprises or moving from one region to another. It may also be constrained due to the lack of appropriate skills. Policy measures can be devised to address all these failures in the labour market.

Capital market: The capital market may also be in equilibrium at a sub-optimal level due to mobility and other constraints. The non-availability of credit for investment in small and medium enterprises, particularly in less populated areas is a common phenomenon. This restricts investment demand, which can be overcome if part of the credit suppliers' risk cost, for which no market exists, is absorbed by the state. This idea can be extended to large investment opportunities, which are not availed of due to unknown risk or lack of managerial skills. This requires a set of measures to attract foreign direct investment, which brings the necessary finances and the managerial skills. These measures can include the provision of information, which is necessary for the investors' decision making, the subsidisation of factors costs, which militate against investment decisions, or underwriting the risks. Foreign direct investment also addresses the problem where local savings are inadequate to fund desirable investment for economic development and where local entrepreneurs are incapable of raising the finances for and managing large investment projects. It is also a powerful factor in the spread of technology and best practice, which has a cumulative impact on investment.

Technology: Technology whether embodied in labour and capital or exogenous in management, information, networks, etc., has both a private and public good dimension. That which is embodied in capital and labour has an externality effect on other businesses with which it does business and to which labour can flow. It

206

Institutional Change in Transition Economies

also adds to the competitiveness of the "cluster" to which it belongs. Upgrading the skills of labour or replacing technologically obsolete equipment implies a cost to which the enterprise does not reap full benefit. There is thus an argument to subsidise the upgrading of human and physical technology. Information systems and networks are even more in the domain of public goods and consequently must be invested in by the public authorities in order to maximise social benefit.

External economies and diseconomies: External economies are associated with the concentration of economic activity and external diseconomies are associated with over-concentration and dispersed activity. Following from individual decisions of economic actors to locate, there is a collective result which may lead to a sub-optimum concentration (over or under-concentration) where external economies (dis-economies) are not maximised (minimised) due to the divergence of private and social costs. Normally the policy action takes the form of encouraging secondary growth poles, which restricts the over concentration in the primary poles and at the same time increases the external economies in the secondary growth centres. This also addresses the associated problem of non-existent markets in areas of dispersed activity – a certain threshold of economic activity is required to induce the emergence of certain markets, which in turn generate their own external economies.

Alternative Models

(i)   Location

Distance from final markets or from the source of inputs, and the costs of this distance and its impact on profits and firm viability, is the central focus. Reducing the impact of distance on economic activity is the target of policy measures. Most obvious are the transport infrastructure and efficient transport systems. One of the principal challenges is to develop an integrated transport system, which draws on the optimum combination of different modes of transport. Another is the optimum combination of a public and private transport service. Transport is a public good and the market does not deliver the socially optimum amount, consequently the public sector must intervene.

Similarly, telecommunications, which is associated with accessing markets, is an important factor in reducing the cost of distance. It has become increasingly important with digitisation and the information age, particularly in the context of globalised markets. Speed of access to information in a global context is at the heart of competitiveness. Developing and upgrading the telecommunications infrastructure and installing high-speed lines are an essential part of the strategy of regional development. Indeed, public service infrastructure, in general, is a prerequisite for regional development. This includes, in addition to transport and telecommunications, energy, healthcare, and education.

In regions, which are distant from major centres, the market is likely to favour those industries. which have low transport costs. At the limit are those services, which can be delivered through the internet. Regional policy measures support and promote these developments. It also supports the abolition of any barriers to trade, where specialisation and trade is at the heart of regional development.

Location related infrastructure is primarily top-down driven and funded by national governments.

(ii) Agglomeration factors

The external economies generated by concentration or agglomeration of economic activity and the lack of external economies associated with dispersed activity, are well known to spatial planners. Although receiving less attention in the theoretical literature, there are, also, external diseconomies generated by over concentration, such as traffic congestion, pollution, anti-social behaviour. Throughout the second half of the 20th century, when national and regional planning was a thriving activity across western economies, recommendations to capture concentration external economies and to limit the external dis-economies were very much in vogue. The principal tool proposed is the growth poles concept. The idea is to divert some of the market driven economic activity away from the major city (cities) to secondary centres, located spatially in a strategic fashion, so that they would eventually grow in a self-sustaining way within the market framework. Infrastructure support and a battery of incentives and dis-incentives are used to attract industry to the designated secondary (and tertiary) growth poles and away from the major growth poles which are driven by market forces. The concept is extended to the creation of growth corridors, linking smaller cities along a high-speed transport route, with development nodes along the way. Small towns or cities can also be grouped together to form a loose growth centre. More recently the concept of "gateways" has emerged, where lower level centres are developed, which link into the main and secondary growth poles, forming a development network.

The principal obstacle to the growth pole policy is political. All politicians wish to have their constituency associated with a growth pole and, therefore, economic development. This sort of pressure can descend to the absurdity of every town and village being designated a growth pole, which, of course, defeats the whole purpose of the policy. This policy measure may be classified as top-down, since it is more likely to be successful when limited to a small number of centres, and only the central government can effectively implement such a policy.

(iii) Endogenous factors

The emphasis here is on local or indigenous enterprises whose development is influenced by factors endogenous to the locale. In particular, the idea is to have a local environment which is favourable to entrepreneurial activity and the full exploitation of local economic resources. This environment is influenced, primarily, by institutional factors, both informal and formal. The informal factors are the product of many impulses, including politics, social values, history, cultural heritage and links to the wider society. These evolve over time and can respond only slowly to formal policy initiatives. The formal institutions (Figure 1), however, can be developed through policy initiatives. These include internal organisation of enterprises to exploit new technologies and systems, clustering of enterprises to generate external economies associated with critical mass of specialised labour and services, networks between enterprises and support agencies, global access to information and the continuing upgrading of the local knowledge base.

Particularly critical at the local level is the efficient operation of the capital and labour markets, where failure is most likely to occur. Policy initiatives included under the neo-classical model are of vital importance at the local level.

Regional Development Plans and Agencies

Most governments prepare national and regional development plans, and implement regional development programmes consisting of policy measures. Regional plans and programmes fit into the national plan framework. Although plans and programmes are intended to meet certain objectives, they are primarily of an indicative nature and are voluntarily responded to by the socio-economic actors. They consist of a battery of incentives and disincentives intended to direct economic development along a certain desired track. Plans are normally drawn up by technical experts, under the direction of the regional authority or regional development agency, and with a wide level of consultation among various socio-economic actors and representative groups. Typically, a plan will start with an analysis of the present socio-economic situation, which includes a statement of the region's strengths, weaknesses, opportunities and threats. A vision statement will set out the broad objectives and the strategic plan will set the basis for the actions to be taken. A regional development programme evolves from the strategic plans and articulates regional priorities, the policy measures to achieve objectives, implementation administration and mechanisms, and the financial means and sources. It normally signals the role of the private and public sectors in achieving the programme goals.

Agencies, which are subject to or directed by government ministries but established and operating outside the bureaucracy of ministry administrations, are a well established vehicle for implementing government policy. Regional development agencies are, similarly, a well-established implementing apparatus of regional development policy initiatives. Since all development happens at the local level, the need for decentralisation of power in relation to regional development is well recognised. The local institutions are in the primary position to identify potential development areas, and potential threats to development, at the local level.

These agencies normally have a corporate structure, which incorporates a coalition of interests, including the local authority(ies), relevant ministries and national development bodies, and representations from a broad spectrum of local socio-economic interests, including business, trade unions, professional bodies, educational institutions, social groups. They normally have significant level of autonomy. They play a quite a significant role in regional planning and programming, in co-ordinating policy measures and implementing agencies of national ministries, in creating the local environment for economic development and promoting the region nationally and internationally.

Policy Initiatives and their Impact on Regional Development: Some Western Experience

It would be interesting to know the success of regional policies in meeting the two objectives set out in Section 3, above. However, studies normally focus on the second objective, namely, convergence of income or output per capita across regions. The contribution to national growth is normally not addressed, primarily because of the difficulty of separating out the effects of regional policies from other policies and natural or induced circumstances.

Regional Development Policy Initiatives

United States and Canada: Regional policy in the US has been informal or implicit, consisting of federal industrial policy led by military expenditure on production and on R&D, and the efforts of state governments in inter-state competition, with the corresponding response from the private sector. Federal government has privileged a number of large cities as distinct from the "primate" city. Also, military spending has been distributed among the states through political intercession. The States have engaged in providing the local environment to facilitate and encourage start-ups and to attract investment. The principal approach in the 1960s and 70s was amelioration of the infrastructure. The 1980s and 90s have seen a move to support softer interventions. These extend from (mainly indirect) subsidisation of capital and labour, through various incentives related to industrial location and training support, to institutional strengthening, networking and the general augmentation of social capital. These state initiatives are funded primarily from local funds.

There are quite conflicting views on the impact of regional policy on the spatial distribution of economic activity in the US. The complementary actions of top-down type of industrial policy and the bottom-up type of regional policy pursued in the US has had the effect of flattening the urban hierarchy and, in general, getting a better spatial spread of economic activity (Markusen, 1996). The more recent explosion of IT activity has concentrated primarily in urban agglomerations, which is offsetting past gains in spatial redistribution. However, earlier work by Blanchard and Katz (Martin and Tyler, 2000) shows significant divergent and cumulative employment growth rate differences across the states of the US. Despite economic shocks (positive or negative) the "natural" underlying rate of employment growth emerges.

The latest evidence form Canada suggests that there has been a convergence of income per capita between provinces (Coulombe, 2000). This is due primarily to different relative rates of urbanisation.

European Union: All of the current EU member states have practised regional policy to varying degrees for decades, with top-down regionally differentiated national sectoral policies as the primary instruments. These were combined, more recently, with more radical regional policies administered at the local level, from the bottom-up. Regional policy was very much an internal national instrument until the EU introduced the so-called "structural funds" from the late 1980s, following on the "single market" and with the objective of bringing about "social cohesion". Prior to that, EU regional policy consisted almost exclusively of the Regional Fund supported by the European Investment Bank and it was primarily directed at building regional infrastructure. The "structural funds" were quite significant in financial terms and were targeted at the poorest regions, declining industrial regions and rural regions, comprising 35 per cent of the geographical territory of the EU. These funds combining the social fund, the regional fund and the structures component of the agricultural fund, were applied in an integrated, multi-annual way, based on worked out regional plans and implementation programmes. The third in a sequence of consecutive five-year plans, covering the period 2000-2006, have commenced. The measures encompass infrastructure development, training and re-training, innovation and technology transfer and increasingly sophisticated partnership and networking programmes.

Those member states, which were not covered by the structural funds, have been implementing their own regional policies.

Just as in the US, the results of policy actions in the EU have been ambiguous and contradictory. According to Hart (1998), the broad core-periphery structural characteristics of EU in the 1990s differed little from those of 25 years earlier. Armstrong (1995) finds general convergence at the EU level but continuing wide disparities in economic and social wellbeing at the national level. Boldrin and Casanova (Martin and Tyler, 2000) find evidence of convergence among EU member states in GDP per capita, particularly in the 1990s. Martin and Tyler (2000) find significant divergence in employment growth rates at this same national level. The latter find regional employment path divergences internally in all countries, even in those which exhibit above EU average growth rates. This general divergence, which was quite manifest in the 1980s, has slowed somewhat in the 1990s, perhaps reflecting the impact of the more significant structural funds. Maurseth (2001) finds that convergence has speeded up from the end of the 1980s, although it was "noisy", that is, there was considerable "leap-frogging" between regions. In general, Martin and Tyler conclude that the evolution of regional employment over a 25-year period in the EU has not been dissimilar from that experienced in the US.

Economic Integration

Although economic integration is not a regional development policy, its impact on regional economic development has stimulated significant interest. The United States is an example of a large and varied spatial entity where economic and monetary union has effectively existed throughout its history as a state. The

European Union has been undergoing economic and monetary integration with the continuing evolution of the Union. The need for and the effectiveness of regional development policy in the context of integration, particularly where regional policy is considered to be politically and economically important, is worth a brief glance.

The United States: The US has had a long history as an effective single market and single monetary area, despite certain inter-state restrictions in trade and banking. There has been essentially free mobility of goods, services, labour and capital and, despite inter-state variations, a fairly uniform tax area, which has, therefore, created a highly competitive environment. The impact of the unitary market on such a large geographic area and the extent to which less developed regions could compete in this unitary market has been the focus of attention from time to time. If one takes the neo-classical viewpoint then growth rates will equalise in the long term and, therefore, intervention is not necessary (as long as market failures are not present). However, the Federal support for large infrastructure projects, like the Tennessee Valley project, suggests that this viewpoint was questioned. The issue of optimum currency zones is addressed by Mundell (1968) in the context of large differentiated geographic space, like the US. Different currencies in strong and weak regions would allow the weaker region to compete more painlessly through a devaluation of its currency in the face of adverse shocks to the economic system. The alternative is highly flexible prices, in particular wages, with labour absorbing most of the shock. Otherwise resources, including labour, will move away from the depressed area. The very high mobility of labour in the US suggests that this is the option which was generally exercised in periods of regional economic depression. Clearly, the idea of different currencies was not considered as a practical option, given the ease of transactions facilitated by a single currency.

European Union: The Single European Act, which came into law in 1985 and was gradually implemented throughout the late 1980s, allowed the EU to gradually move towards a single market with free movement of factors and products. Whereas goods and services have been allowed to pass relatively freely across international frontiers, the movement of labour has been less mobile, due to language barriers and the non-uniformity of qualifications across countries. Initially there was a certain amount of apprehension, particularly in the less developed regions. It was feared that the enhanced competition would lead to the elimination of the smaller and less competitive local enterprises which depended on local markets. It was also feared that access to investment finance would be more restricted to projects at the low end of the returns spectrum. However, although there has been a restructuring of capital markets following the legal establishing of the Single Market, the market is as yet far from being unified. The introduction of a Single Currency zone has been much more contentious. The principal economic argument in favour is the lowering of transaction costs due to the common currency. The principal argument against it is the elimination of a policy instrument, namely monetary policy and the corresponding devaluation or revaluation instrument, in the face of local recession or demand led inflation.

It is clear that the existence or the creation of a single market for products and factors leads to more intense competition across the comprised geographic space. This is further facilitated and intensified by a common currency. So, what effect does this have on regional development? The neo-classical model suggests that the equilibrium situation of equalised factor prices and growth rates would be more quickly recovered following a dis-equilibrating shock to regions or sectors in the system if a single market exists. However, the alternative model would contend that, in the absence of intervention, the more developed regions will become richer and the less developed regions will become more disadvantaged. This later point of view is argued forcibly and is given theoretical underpinnings by Krugman (1999). It is given empirical support in the work of Martin and Tyler drawing on their own work in the EU and the work of Blanchard and Katz in the US.

Krugman begins from the classic (Marshallian) idea of externalities created by a concentration of economic activity. The competitive imperative springing from integrated markets induces regional specialisation (and associated clustering) in production and increased trade, which further enhances the external economies and gives rise to increasing returns. However this specialisation leaves the region vulnerable to economic shocks. Consequently when shocks do occur there is an economic downturn and, due to the mobility of factors of production, factors are engaged elsewhere. The greater the degree of economic and monetary integration, the greater the ease of mobility. Although the region will return to its natural rate of growth, it will do so at a lower level of economic activity. The more integrated markets in the US versus the EU and the greater level of regional specialisation explain the greater regional variation in the rate of employment creation in the US compared to the EU.

Market integration is not yet complete in the EU and, in particular, labour mobility is sluggish. Furthermore monetary integration is just commencing. If Krugman is correct, then the enhanced integration in the EU will lead to more uneven growth of employment creation, with regional divergence rather than convergence being the eventual outcome. Clearly, given the ambiguity of outcome with respect to regional policy to date, with increasing integration a more effective regional policy is called for in the future if convergence remains a policy objective.

Russia and the Relevance of Regional Policy

Russian Regions

The Russian economic landscape, which emerged from the soviet period, was a vast territory with widely scattered pockets of development, centred around cities but with a very weak urban hierarchy. This was primarily the result of sectoral policies implemented by ministries whose main objective was increased output and the exploitation of natural resources. These decisions were based on political argument rather than costs. Consequently, location, distance and environmental costs were of limited relevance. These inherited attributes are critical to the future development of many regions.

Disregarding the institutional structures, which will dominate future economic development in Russia, market forces will have a profound effect on the current spatial allocation of resources. It is difficult to predict what that new landscape will look like in the absence of a full understanding of the market viability of industries and enterprises in the different locations, and the extent to which the market will be allowed to dictate the pace of change. One can only imagine that in 10-15 years time it will be markedly different from today. Already, in the soviet period, output per capita varied greatly across regions, both as a result of productivity differences and industrial mix. As market prices began to replace administered prices, these differences became evident. Significant regional differences have emerged and even more significant intra-regional differences, with cities and their multi-dimensional attributes playing a critical role (see Nabla-Norris and Weber in previous chapter). Public service provision, based on tax revenue per capita, even after transfers from central government, was vastly different across regions. The most recent data from the All-Russian Centre for Living Standards (2001) show that the ratio of monetary income per capita between the richest and poorest region in March 2001 is 20. It shows that of the 88 regions in the Russian Federation, 21 had above the average for all regions, while 67 were below the average. Indeed, 16 regions had less than half the average. The consumption per capita across the regions shows an even more diverse picture, where the ratio of the highest to lowest is 28. These differences are likely to intensify as the present restrictions on the mobility of factors (for example, social ties of labour to enterprises, registration requirements), in a theoretically unified market and monetary area, are removed. These differences may decline over time through labour outflow from the poorer to the richer regions. However, this is likely to intensify the problems of social service provision and social structures in these poorer regions.

The Market Environment

The creation of value added through entrepreneurial activity is the lynchpin of economic development in a market driven economy and so it is for regional development in Russia. The pre-condition for entrepreneurial activity is a hospitable market environment where risk is minimised. This demands in the first instance a stable, strong and effective government structure extending from central to local level. Going along with power of government is responsibility to its citizens. Unfortunately, in Russia this side of the democratic process is not yet very mature.   A considerable evolution of civil society is required, including representative or pressure groups who can negotiate with government and insist that it lives up to its promises and injects transparency into government transactions. Simple, unambiguous legislation underpinning property rights and market transactions must be effectively policed and enforced. The present situation, where laws are open to local interpretation and where they are exploited by the local elites supported by organised crime for "rent seeking" activity, kills all but the most courageous or the most privileged entrepreneurs.

In all developed market economies, there is a plethora of support structures, systems and networks within which market transactions and entrepreneurial activity takes place. These institutional structures reduce transaction costs and lead to competitiveness. These structures are not very advanced in Russia today. Also, the informal institutions, including norms, values, attitudes, etc. among private citizens and public administrations and their implementing arms are not positively disposed to or supportive of private entrepreneurial activity.

The future of Russian economic development and the Russian regions will depend primarily on home grown business enterprises. However, in the context of globalisation, world trade, competition and specialisation, regional development will also depend on the capacity to attract and grow internationally competitive and sustainable enterprises. Both for indigenous enterprises and international business, institutional structures and support systems are essential to their development.

The foregoing are minimalist requisites for the growth of entrepreneurial activity and value added in Russia today. Unless these essential elements are in place, there is little merit in pursuing regional development policies, indeed, it is simply a waste of money and effort. Additional critical issues must also be addressed within a national strategy in order for a market led regional development strategy to be successful. These include sectoral strategies, the role of government and the private sector in implementing sectoral strategies and development strategies for different corporate structures. They also include supports for minimum living conditions for all members of society (anti-poverty programmes); and provision of social services (health, education, etc.) for long term development of the economy and the general welfare of society.

Regional Development Policies

Neo-classical model: Policy intervention emanating from the neo-classical model addresses market failure. The problems facing Russia today are more to do with "market emergence" in moving from a centrally planned to a market driven economy than "market failure". Policy measures should address three areas, the labour market, capital market and technology. The challenge in the labour market is to respond to the market impulses in re-configuring the industrial and service production mix in order to reflect consumer, capital, government and export preferences (see Pavlov in previous chapter). Labour must be re-deployed both from old to new uses within existing enterprises which are likely to survive in a restructured form, and away from bankrupt or otherwise defunct enterprises to newly emerging sectors and enterprises. On the supply side, the two broad issues are training/retraining and mobility. Training is required to meet the needs of new occupations and new functions in commercial enterprises. The present restrictions on mobility must be addressed. These include the worker interest in the social assets of old enterprises. These assets, which include housing and access to other social services, must be commercialised and become tradable. In addition, the residential restrictions on labour, through requirements of local registration and associated entitlements and sanctions when violated, must disappear.

The present constraints on labour demand relate to the creation and expansion of enterprise. The current multiplicity of bureaucratic exigencies to be fulfilled in establishing and running an enterprise must be streamlined. The entrepreneur must be protected from public and private racketeers through enforceable property rights and business transaction legislation. Finally, the availability of investment and working capital credit at reasonable interest rates, is essential to enterprise development and thus the expansion of labour demand. Although there are many successful micro-credit schemes in operation in Russia, there is no systematic real credit facility available. The credit activities of Sperbank (Savings Bank) seem to be tied too closely to the interests of the local elites. Public authorities at the local level must seriously engage the credit issue if enterprise is to expand in response to market opportunities. Foreign direct investment is not going to engage seriously in investment opportunities in the Russian regions until those issues, which currently have a negative impact on local enterprise development, are addressed.

Critical to the clearance of the labour market is information on both the demand and supply side. The Federal Employment Offices in the regions have been addressing this issue for some time now. It is the objective of the Ministry of Labour and Social Affairs to create a federation wide multi-layered information system on labour demand and supply in all regions in the federation.

Investment or capital demand is constrained by the availability of credit, as discussed above, in the context of labour demand. The supply of investment funds in developed industrialised countries comes from own funds, the banking system and from the stock market. The stock market is normally available only to well established business or where the risks are fairly readily assessed. In Russia, there is only very limited access to the stock market and the banking system issues very limited funds for investment. Consequently, own-funds is the predominant source. However, in an economy like Russia, where economic activity is so sluggish, it is difficult to accumulate own funds and consequently, in the absence of intervention, investment will be limited and economic growth will be slow. Intervention in the credit and capital market can take many forms. The state can work closely with the banking sector, identify why it is so difficult to extend investment credit and take appropriate steps to unblock the system. It can, for example, assist in providing training programmes for bank employees in investment and risk assessment. It can also limit the risk to banks by providing bank guarantees. The state may also engage directly in banking for specific purposes, as happened, post World War II, in many European countries, for example for housing, industrial sectors, small and medium enterprises or agriculture. The state may also wish to substitute for the absence of the stock market, through taking shareholding in specific enterprises. Again there are adequate precedents in western economies for such initiatives.

Upgrading of technology levels is another area of market failure, or where the market on its own is unable to realise the optimum level of technology. Most industrial enterprises, which have survived the transition, are operating with internationally outmoded technology. This has a depressing effect on competitiveness, with respect to product type and quality, both in the individual enterprises and in industry as a whole. The continuing obsolescence of technology is closely linked to the tightness of the credit market. The state therefore has a role to play in upgrading the capital stock, through grant aiding capital investment or encouraging joint ventures which upgrades the technology level. Normally, the upgrading of technology must be accompanied by skill upgrades. This ties in with the general necessity to re-skill labour and the need for state intervention in this activity.

Alternative Models

(i)   Location factors
Russia and its regions are well served by the basic transport infrastructure of road, rail, air and water (internally), with a high level of integration of these various modes. However, this infrastructure was put in place to meet a level of economic activity comparable to the present level. As the economy expands the infrastructure will be inadequate to meet the new needs. Also, there has been a very significant deterioration of all transport infrastructure due to lack of investment and basic maintenance. Given the geographic size of Russia, it is unlikely that the access transport infrastructure of regions, which are sparsely populated and are large distances from centres of concentration, will keep pace with need. Since new investment will not be commercially justifiable and since the opportunity cost of state investment may be higher in other spheres, regional policy will dictate the exploitation of resources to meet local market demands and/or the production of goods which have low transport costs.

The telecommunications' system requires considerable investment to meet modern market requirements, particularly in the context of the digital age. Although local mobile telephone networks have developed very rapidly in all of the larger cities, they will not meet the need for distance communication and digital traffic. Although the market will eventually correct these shortcomings, the real problem relates to the smaller centres, where policy initiatives must be directed if they are not to remain permanent economic backwaters.

Where trade barriers exist, removing them promotes regional development. The biggest obstacle in the Russian regions has been restrictions on trade imposed by local authorities in order to extract a rent for public or personal purposes. These restrictions related mainly to inter-regional trade in Russia or with the former CIS countries. Since little international trade, apart from natural resources, has developed and is unlikely to develop to any significant level in the short to medium term, joining the WTO is unlikely to have great significance for regional development. It will only be relevant when industrial structures and technology can allow firms to provide a quality of product and consistency of supply to cross the international competitive threshold.

(ii)   Agglomeration factors

Policies focussing on generating external economies associated with centres of concentration and the "thickness" of the market are difficult to implement in reality. First, there is the political difficulties of choosing a limited number of growth centres as against the alternatives. Secondly, there is the problem of how these selected growth centres or developmental corridors are to be developed. Russia's geographic space is very far flung and is characterised by basically a two tier urban structure, large cities, on the one hand and towns and villages, on the other. The existing large centres have the capacity to be self-sustaining once a hospitable market environment has been created. Once the local demand is created, the support services to underpin competitive advantage and reinforce economic growth will follow.

The principal challenge to Russian regional policy makers will be those regions which have large areas of dispersed population - extensive rural areas with little potential external economies. Although very significant surplus labour exists in agriculture and the rural areas, there is no location within which to concentrate non-agricultural activity enterprises and the necessary support services. This may be addressed to some extent by clustering small towns and villages in order to create a threshold of concentration to generate external economies. However, given the institutional and organisational requirement to realise such a policy initiative, it may be premature to contemplate in Russia at this stage.

(iii)   Endogenous factors

Local factors, which influence the emergence and development of enterprises, are the main focus here. These factors are primarily institutional in nature, but which have a capacity to respond to local need and adapt to changing circumstances. They include informal institutions like norms of interrelations and transactions including trust, reciprocity, mutual help or support networks and the general ethos of private enterprise, in the current transition context, among the general population and formal institutions. These are closely associated with history, religion and cultural attributes and are not very much in tune with, or supportive of, private enterprise development in Russia today. They are rather abstract or intangible elements, which are likely to respond only very slowly to policy influences.

Formal institutions at the local level, on the other hand, follow from active engagement of different groups of socio-economic actors. They include the co-ordination of various formal influences on the mobilisation of local resources towards the creation of value added. They also include basic services and business support systems. They include actions by local co-ordinating bodies, like clustering of enterprises with links to each other and to supporting public institutions, the development of networks, improving access to knowledge, the evolution of a learning region and, in general, developing social capital. These initiatives in achieving indigenous development presuppose the local ability to co-ordinate the inputs of different ministries and agencies toward effective local development, as well as identifying the specific local requirements and deficiencies, and addressing them. These local formal institutions are extremely weak in Russia and it will take much time and effort to reach the levels already achieved in most western industrialised societies. However, a start must be made in understanding the processes involved, the political will to engage in developing these processes, the administrative and technical competence, and the financial means to systematically put theses processes and structures in place.

Planning for Economic Development

The term economic planning in Russia recalls the failed central planning system of the communist period. There is a misunderstanding and a resistance to regional planning. Indeed, everything in the Putin development "plan" avoids the idea of planning economic activity for the private sector. Consequently, the preparation of regional development plans is slow to emerge. However, experience tells us that it is highly unlikely that the various complementary elements in a market system (output level and mix in final production, intermediate production, service sector output, financial and capital markets in various forms, labour markets, including education and training, housing, infrastructure and social services) will evolve in a balanced fashion, without the intervention of the state. Economic planning, of an indicative nature, is an essential part of the development process, which must be undertaken at the regional and local levels. It must provide, as a minimum, an information base on the general direction of the economy and its component parts over a given period of time (or planning horizon), with indications of approximate magnitudes in order to inform the various private and public actors in their respective decision making.

The indicative plan must consist of a set of objectives, targets to be achieved across the economic sectors, a framework of economic development within which various measures indicated by economic theory are implemented, and set of incentives and disincentives to nudge investment and development along the desired path. The supporting institutional structures must be clearly articulated and established; the implementation mechanisms must be clearly elaborated; the roles of the public and private sectors must be clearly signalled and the sources of financial means - identified.

Establishing co-ordinating implementing bodies, which can take the form of a regional development agencies, which can carry planning, policy implementation and other regional development responsibilities, should be considered by regional governments.

Conclusions

The theory underlying regional economic growth suggests the use of intervention measures, which have evolved to quite a sophisticated level. These measures are being implemented with apparent success in industrialised market economies. However, the long-term sustainability of the enhanced growth rates is still contested by the subscribers to the neo-classical theory. Nevertheless, positive results, in the short to medium term, are achieved. Theory suggests that economic and monetary integration work against the policy initiatives directed at regional convergence.

The reality that will unfold (and indeed is unfolding right now) in Russia is that the stronger regions will be able to respond more quickly and take advantage of the newly emerging positive environment, which the Putin policies are currently addressing. They will, over time, be able to put in place the institutional structures and support systems at the regional and local levels to further exploit the new business and economic environment. The poorer regions will have to contain the downward spiral and stabilise economic growth at levels in keeping with the natural local conditions. These are the regions that will shed labour to the more dynamic regions. These are also the regions where the Federal Government must be able to provide a safety net for those who cannot move or who are unlikely to obtain future gainful employment.

Russia and its regions are clearly challenged by the market process, with varying degrees of success, based on the inherent advantages of the actual regions and the progressiveness of local leaders. Regional analysis, policy measures and their implementation put heavy demands on regional government in establishing the necessary institutional structures, providing the technical expertise for each stage of the process and, above all, finding the financial means to support the various measures undertaken.

All regional development policy measures are directed toward cost reduction and competitiveness of enterprise. These policies and their impact are predicated on the existence of the basic institutional and environmental conditions for the working and interplay of markets within which enterprise operates. These pre-conditions do not yet exist in Russia today. Consequently, regional policy measures can only have very limited impact until such time as these basic pre-conditions are established. This does not preclude the regional and local authorities from addressing the economic development of their own territories and looking to the future opportunities and initiatives to be taken. However, financial expediency dictates that they should only embark on the more sophisticated regional policies, which are part of the kit of measures now applied in the more dynamic regions in the industrialised countries, when the basic market pre-conditions are first met.

Notes

[1] The normal formulation is:

Y=Af(K,L)

Where Y=Output, K=Capital stock, L=Labour stock and A represents the "state of technology".

[2] The following critical assumptions underlie the model:

(i)   The total supply of labour available to all regions together is fixed. The only way in which one region can employ more people is through immigration from other regions.

(ii)   A single homogenous output is produced in each region.

(iii)   There are zero transport costs between regions, so that the price of output is uniform.

(iv)   There are zero costs of converting output to capital goods.

(v)   The same production function exists in each region.

(vi)   Technological knowledge, labour and capital are completely mobile between regions.

References

All-Russia Centre for Living Standards (2001), *Monitoring Population Wages and Living Standards*, no.2 (April-June), Moscow.

Armstrong, H. (1995), *Trends and Disparities in Regional GDP per Capita in the European Union, United States and Australia*, European Commission Report 94/00/74/017, Commission of the European Communities, Brussels.

Blanchard and Katz, (1992), 'Regional Evolution,' Brookings Paper, Economic Activity 2.

Bristow, J. (1996), 'The Economic Rationale of Regional Policy' in *Regional Policy: A Report by the Regional Policy Advisory Group to Forfás*, Shannon Development, Shannon.

Chisolm, M. (1990), *Regions in Recession and Resurgence*, Unwin Hyman, London.

Coulumbe, S. (2000), 'New Evidence of Convergence across Canadian Provinces: the Role of Urbanisation', *Regional Studies*, vol. 34, no. 8.

Glasson, J. (1974), *An Introduction to Regional Planning*, Hutchinson Education, London.

Hart, M. (1998), 'Convergence and Regionalism: Contradictory Trends in the New Europe', in B. Graham (ed), *Modern Europe: Place, Culture and Identity*, Arnold, London.

Higgins, B.H. and Savoie, D.J. (1995), *Regional Development Theories and Their Application*, Transaction Publishers, New Brunswick and London.

Krugman, P. (1991), 'Increasing Returns and Economic Geography', *Journal of Political Economy*, vol. 99, pp. 483-99.

Krugman, P. (1993), 'On the Number and Location of Cities', *European Economic Review*, vol. 37 (April).

Krugman, P. (1996), 'Urban Concentration: the Role of Increasing Returns and Transport Costs', *International Regional Science Review*, vol.19, no. 1& 2.

Krugman, P. (1999), 'The Role of Geography in Development', *International Regional Science Review*, vol. 22, no. 2.

Maillat, D. (1993), 'The Innovatince Process and the Role of the Milieu', in E. Bergman, G. Maier and F. Todtling (eds) (1991), *Regions Reconsidered*, Mansell, London and New York.

Markusen, A. (1996), 'Interaction between Regional and Industrial Policies: Evidence from Four Countries', *International Regional Science Review*, vol. 19, no. 1 & 2.

Marshall, A. (1890), *Principles of Economics*, vol. 1, Macmillan, London.

Martin, R. and Tyler, P. (2000), 'Regional Employment Evolutions in the European Union: a Preliminary Analysis', *Regional Studies*, vol. 34, no. 7.

Maurseth, P.B. (2001), 'Convergence, Geography and Technology', *Structural Change and Economic Dynamics*, vol. 12, no. 3, pp. 247-76.

Mundell, R.A. (1968), *International Economics*, Macmillan, New York.

Myrdal, G. (1944), *An American Dilemma: The Negro Problem and Modern Democracy*, Harper, New York.

Myrdal, G. (1957), *Economic Theory and Underdeveloped Regions*,Gerald Duckworth & Co., London.

Porter, M.E. (1998), *On Competition*, HBS Press, Boston.

Putnam, R. (1993), *Making Democracy Work*, Princeton University Press, Princeton.

Romer, P.M. (1990), 'Endogenous Technological Change', *Journal of Political Economy*, vol. 98, pp. 71-102.

Sweeney, G. (1996), 'Central or Local: Economic Growth or Economic Development', paper presented at the Regional Studies Association (Irish Branch) National Conference: *Shaping our Regions: Subsidiarity, Innovation and Economic Development*, Dublin, Ireland.

Index

accountability 48, 50
accrual accounting xxi–xxii, 131–2
advertising expenditure 123
Afanasiev, M. 138–9, 141
agglomeration factors theory
    xxvi–xxvii, 202–3, 207,
    217–18
Aginsky-Buryatskiy 181
Agrarian Party 102
Ahmad, E. 180
Alexeev, M. 130
All-Russian Centre for Living
    Standards 213
AlRosa 8
Anderson, P. 22, 26
Armstrong, H. 210
Åslund, A. 21, 73, 128–30
Avtovaz 139

Baltic states 55–6, 60
banking system 16–17, 215
barter 82–5, 92, 131, 139
Bashkiria 102–3
Bashkortostan 194
basins of attraction 88–9
Belarus 60, 64, 156
Berezovsky, Boris 50
Berglof, E. 137
"big bang" reform 4
Boex, J. 191
Brainard, S. 143
Brazil 130
Brezhnev, Leonid 41
bribery 156–7

budget constraints 77–8, 81–2,
    140–41; *see also* hard budget
    constraints; soft budget
    constraints
Burgess, R. 146
Business Environment and
    Enterprise Perform-
    ance Survey (BEEPS)
    156–7

Canada 209
capital flight 75
capital markets 17, 205
central planning 7, 38, 199
China 44, 55–64 *passim*
civil society 213
Commander, S. 92, 131, 139
Communist Party 40, 45, 82, 102,
    139
corporate governance 91
corporate income tax 147, 151, 156
corruption 35–50, 156–8
    costs and benefits of 43–6, 50
    responses to 48–9
    in tax administration 127–30
Corruption Perceptions Index
    157–8
Council of Europe 35–6
Craig, J. 180
credit 215
crime, perceptions of 41;
    see also organized crime
Croatia 59
crowding-out of investment 91

customs regulation 109–10
Czech Republic 59, 129

Delors, J. xxiv
democracies, "illiberal" 65, 69
democratization 65–9
deregulation 107, 111, 117
Dewatripont, M. 137–8
distortions in industrial structure
and trade patterns 58–60
Duma, the 21, 100–102, 128, 132

effective tax yields 145–8
elites 8–9
endogenous growth models 198–9,
202
enterprise directors 76, 81–2, 89
entrepreneurship 203
equalisation of factor prices 201,
212
Ericson, Rick 73
Estonia 61, 64
etatist model of the economy
105–6
European Bank for Reconstruction
and Development 156–7,
159
European Investment Bank 210
European Union 35–6, 199,
210–12
evolution by cultural transmission
90
exchange rates 114
external economies 206–7, 212
externalities 82–3

Falconer J. 37
feudal system 10–12; *see also*
industrial feudalism
foreign direct investment 205, 215
Fund for Financial Support of
Subjects of the Regions
(FFSR) 190–93

Gaddy, C. 19
Gaidar, E. 105, 139, 141
Gambetta, D. 36
"gateways" concept 207
Gazprom 8
Georgia 155, 157
glasnost 41
Gorbachev, Mikhail 4, 41, 65, 82
Gosplan 73, 139
Gossnab 73, 82
government expenditure
as a proportion of GDP 62–4,
106
reform of 110–11, 117
gradualism in reform 55–6, 69
Gref program xix, 105–8
Grossman, G. 40, 76, 122
growth poles and *growth corridors*
207
Guriev, S. 92

hard budget constraints 39, 77,
83–4, 90–92, 147
"harm reduction" 48
Hart, M. 210
Higgins, B.H. 203
historical cost accounting 156
Hong Kong 65
Hungary 59, 129, 138

Ickes, B.W. 19, 92
increasing returns 82–3
industrial feudalism xiii, 10–12,
20–25
inflation 38, 60, 63, 69
informal constraints and rules 76,
93–4
initial conditions for economic
development 56, 59–60, 69,
73, 79
integration, economic and monetary
199, 210–12
International Monetary Fund 36

Japan 24, 44
Johnson, S. 122

KamAz 139
Klitgaard, Robert 36, 40, 48–9
Kornai, J. xx, 137–8
Krugman, P. 204, 212
Kuchma, Leonid 156

La Houerou, P. 191
labour markets 17, 205, 214–15
Laffer curve 108–9
Latvia 61
Lavrov, A. 191
Le Breton, M. 180
liberalization
    economic 7, 41, 44, 47, 50,
        55–60, 63–9, 75
    of the media 41
Lithuania 61
location theory xxvi–xxvii, 202,
        206–7, 216
Lukashenka, Alexandr 156

Macedonia 59
macroeconomic stabilization 49,
        55–60, 69
mafia, the 36–7
Magnitka 8
market economy, characteristics of
        5–6, 11–12
market failure 201, 214
marketization 4–5, 8
Marshall, Alfred 202, 212
Martin, R. 210, 212
Martinez-Vazquez, J. 191
Maskin, E. 137–8
Maurseth, P.B. 210
Mayshar, J. 122–3
Mexico 130
monetary policy 91–2
monetization 6–7, 10
monopolies 39, 108
    natural 112–13
monotonicity of reform 78, 81, 84
Moscow 14, 42, 181

multi-drug resistant (MDR)
    tuberculosis 85
Mumssen, C. 92, 131, 139
Mundell, R.A. 211
murders 43
mutation of enterprise behaviour
        83–4, 89–92, 95
Myrdal, G. 202–4

Nagin, D. 123
neo-classical growth model
        xxv–xxvii, 198–204, 208,
        211–14, 219
new institutional economics xii
Newbery, David 146
Nigeria 130
nomenklatura 45
non-monetary means of payment
        (NMMP) xxi–xxii, 130–33;
        see also barter
Norilsk Nikel 8
normalised tax yield xxii–xxiii,
        148–9, 154–5
North, D.C. xii, 76
Novolipetsk Metallurgical 8

obkom officials 81–2
"oligarchs" 104
opportunity cost 73–4
Organization for Economic
    Cooperation and
    Development 35–6, 47
organized crime 35–50, 130, 214
    costs and benefits of 43–5, 50
    responses to 48–9

partial equalization principle
        179–80, 186, 193–5
paternalism 137–42
payment arrears (PA) xxi–xxii,
        130–33
payoff matrix xvii–xviii, 86–8,
        140–42
perestroika xviii, 76, 81
Pirttila, J. 143
Poland 63, 129

politicization
  of economic decision-making
    13–14
  of the tax system 146
Porter, M.E. 203
pricing systems 73–5
Primakov, Yevgeny 100
privatization 7, 16, 47, 104–5
  of relational capital 81–2
property rights 6, 9, 11, 14, 107,
    140
protection payments 40–44
public goods 9, 62, 206
public opinion polls 116
Putin, Vladimir xiv–xv, xviii, xx, 5,
    13–14, 23–5, 35, 100, 105,
    107, 218–19
Putnam, Robert 44

Radian, Alex 145–6
raikom officials 81–2
R-D space 79–80, 89
reform, costs of 39
regional development
  plans and agencies for 208–9,
    218
  theories of xxv–xxvii, 198,
    200–205
regional economic policies 199,
    204–5
  in Russia 212–18
  Western experience of 209–12
regulation of economic activity 9
relational capital 78–85, 90–94,
    142
  and increasing returns 82–3
  privatization of 81–2
  and reform 81–2
rent-seeking behaviour 42, 45, 47,
    83, 158, 214
representative tax system (RTS)
    model 147
Roland, G. 137
Roscoal 140
Roskhleb 8

Roskontrakt 8
rule of law 23, 49, 65–9
Russia
  bilateral treaties 194
  budget expenditure reform
    110–11, 117
  business climate and deregulation
    111
  Central Bank 113
  conflation of politics and
    economics 12–14
  Constitutions 102, 116, 194
  customs regulation 109–10
  destabilizing factors 113–16
  disintegration of state
    institutions
  Federation Council 21, 102–3
  Federation Treaty 194
  financial markets 113
  fragmentary market structure
    16–17
  future path of systemic
    development 22–6
  industrial decay 60–65
  "industrial feudalism"
    10–12, 20–25
  non-viability of markets 18–20
  Nuclear Energy Ministry 113
  political and economic instability
    100–105
  priorities for sustainable growth
    116–17
  progress towards a market
    economy 3–10, 25
  Railway Ministry 112–13
  reform of natural monopolies
    112–13
  regional disparities 179–95
  regional policy 212–18
  State Council 103
  strategic program of development
    105–8
  Supreme Court 25
  tax collection 155
  tax evasion 122–6

tax reform 108–9
Russian Union of Industrialists
    and Entrepreneurs 105
Rutkowski, M. 191

Savoie, D.J. 203
Schaffer, M. 137–8, 141
Schumpeter, Joseph 202
seniorage xiii
Severostal 8
shareholders 112
Shlapentokh, V. 15
"shock therapy" 55, 64–5, 69, 75,
    84–5, 91
single-currency areas 200, 211
Single European Act 211
Slemrod, J. 122–3
Slovak Republic 59
Slovenia 59
social capital 203, 209, 217
social democracy 109
social security tax 147, 149–51,
    155–6
soft budget constraints xx, 137–9,
    143
"soft goods" 9, 19, 142
South Korea 24, 44
Soviet Union, collapse of 4–5
Sperbank 215
stabilization policies *see*
    macroeconomic stabilization
statistics, economic 38
Stepashin, S. 100
Stern, N. 146
Stiglitz, J.E. 73
structural adjustment 58
sunk costs 138
supply-side phenomena 58
sustainability 199

Tanzi, Vito 146
Tatarstan 25. 102–3, 194
tax
    arrears of 137–43
    corruption in administration of
        127–30

collection systems 16–17,
    145–58
evasion of 122–6
reform of 108–9
revenue from 102–3
telecommunications 216
Tennessee Valley project 211
Thailand 44
thick-market externality 82–3, 85
tight money policy 91–2
trade barriers 216
transfer policies (for Russian
    regions) 179–80, 185–95
Transneft 8
Transparency International 36,
    157–8
transparency of transactions 83–4,
    90–91, 113
transport infrastructure and transport
    costs 206, 216
Treisman, D. 193
Treml, V.G. 40
trust in institutions 61
Tuva Republic 181
Tyler, P. 210, 212

UES 8
Ukraine 60, 130, 155–6
United Kingdom xix
United Nations 35–6
United States xix, 200, 209–12
Uralmash 8
Uzbekistan 56, 60, 64

value added tax (VAT) 147–51,
    155
value destruction 73–5, 93
veksel system 131
Verdier, T. 143
Vietnam 56–61 *passim*, 64
"virtual economy" 18–20, 72–3,
    83–94
voluntary exchange and participation
    in the market economy 6
Weber, S. 180, 202
World Bank 36, 157

World Development Report 1996
55–6
World Trade Organization 47, 216

Yeltsin, Boris 4, 21, 41, 65, 100
Yitzhaki, S. 122